CONTENTIOUS
CITY

CONTENTIOUS CITY

The Politics of Recovery in New York City

John Mollenkopf, Editor

Russell Sage Foundation, New York

The Russell Sage Foundation

The Russell Sage Foundation, one of the oldest of America's general purpose foundations, was established in 1907 by Mrs. Margaret Olivia Sage for "the improvement of social and living conditions in the United States." The Foundation seeks to fulfill this mandate by fostering the development and dissemination of knowledge about the country's political, social, and economic problems. While the Foundation endeavors to assure the accuracy and objectivity of each book it publishes, the conclusions and interpretations in Russell Sage Foundation publications are those of the authors and not of the Foundation, its Trustees, or its staff. Publication by Russell Sage, therefore, does not imply Foundation endorsement.

Library of Congress Cataloging-in-Publication Data
Contentious city : the politics of recovery in New York City / edited by John Mollenkopf.
    p.   cm.
  Includes bibliographical references and index.
  ISBN 0-87154-629-9 (cloth)   ISBN 0-87154-630-2 (paperback)
   1. Urban renewal—New York (State)—New York.   2. City planning—Political aspects—New York (State)—New York.   3. World Trade Center Site (New York, N.Y.)
4. New York (N.Y.)—Politics and government—1951–   I. Mollenkopf, John H., 1946–
II. Russell Sage Foundation.
HT177.N5N463   2005
307.3′416′097471—dc22   2005042685

Text design by Genna Patacsil.

RUSSELL SAGE FOUNDATION
112 East 64th Street, New York, New York 10021
10 9 8 7 6 5 4 3 2 1

CONTENTS

CONTRIBUTORS

JOHN MOLLENKOPF is Distinguished Professor of Political Science and Sociology and director of the Center for Urban Research at the City University of New York Graduate Center.

SUSAN S. FAINSTEIN is professor of urban planning at Columbia University.

ARIELLE GOLDBERG is research associate at the Center for Urban Research at the City University of New York Graduate Center.

LORRAINE C. MINNITE is assistant professor of political science at Barnard College.

MITCHELL L. MOSS is Henry Hart Rice Professor of Urban Policy and Planning at New York University.

LYNNE B. SAGALYN is professor of real estate development and planning at the University of Pennsylvania.

JAMES E. YOUNG is professor and chair of Judaic and Near Eastern Studies at University of Massachusetts, Amherst.

FOREWORD

IN THE GRIM WEEKS after the terrorist attack on the World Trade Center on September 11, 2001, many New Yorkers asked themselves how they could contribute their talents and abilities to help their fellow citizens and assist in the effort to restore and revitalize the city. As a research organization with a long history of studying social and economic conditions in the city, the Russell Sage Foundation naturally turned toward the idea of using the analytic capacities of social science to assess the shocking blow New York had suffered and analyze the underlying dimensions of what we fervently hoped would be its full recovery. In the following months, the foundation assembled a working group of nineteen experts on New York and supported their coordinated research on the economic, social, and political implications of the terrorist attack on the city. Now, four years later, we are pleased to present the results of their efforts in three volumes.

Resilient City, edited by economist Howard Chernick, assesses the impact of September 11 on the city's economy. By and large, the book tells a remarkable story of recovery. Fears that New York's competitive position in the world economy would deteriorate as firms fled the city proved to be unfounded. The attractions that New York has always offered—high density and a large, skilled labor force—kept most businesses in the city, despite the perceived threat of another attack. Manhattan's enormous commercial real estate market managed to absorb the loss of 10 percent of its available inventory and still accommodate 80 percent of the firms forced to relocate from downtown. While demand for space in tall buildings suffered a temporary slump, occupancy rates for buildings of more than fifty stories returned to near normal levels over the three-year period following the attack. The job market fared less well, suffering a net loss of over 125,000 jobs by September 2004. By some estimates, it may take another five years for the city's job base to return to its pre-attack peak. The attack has also increased New York City taxes by about 8 percent and caused commercial insurance costs to soar. To the extent that these increased costs raise the price of doing business in New York, the city's long run competitiveness could suffer. While no one can predict the eventual consequences of the attack, the price signals in the real estate and financial markets remain positive. Housing prices and rents have risen more steeply than in the rest of the country, and the shares of firms headquartered in New York City are not selling at a discount. Remarkably, four years after the attack, confidence in the city seems fully restored.

Wounded City, edited by anthropologist Nancy Foner, is a book that digs below the aggregate outcomes revealed by economic statistics to look at especially vulnerable neighborhoods and groups of workers. Here the stories are about lasting scars and painful dislocations. The garment industry in Chinatown nearly collapsed due to security restrictions near Ground Zero that prevented the movement of merchandise, leaving thousands of immigrant workers jobless. Cabdrivers in the city, most of them Muslim, suffered from the increased hostility of their customers and the loss of business as tourism declined, leaving many of them in debt to pay the leases for their taxi medallions. The precipitous drop in air travel after September 11 eliminated thousands of New York jobs in the airline industry, stranding many workers with little prospect of regaining their jobs despite massive federal subsidies for the airlines. Communities as disparate as the Muslims in Jersey City and the white ethnic neighborhoods of Belle Harbor in the Rockaways suffered lasting trauma. Belle Harbor endured the double disaster of its many firefighters lost on September 11, followed eight weeks later by the crash of American Flight 587. The Muslim community in Jersey City experienced both an increase in hate crimes and assaults from their neighbors, and the impact of detentions, investigations, and raids by law enforcement agencies in the wake of the attack. *Wounded City* shows how New York communities and workers have struggled to cope with these problems, some more successfully than others. New York is healing, but the process remains uneven and incomplete.

Contentious City, edited by political scientist John Mollenkopf, offers valuable insights into the bewildering contest among the political actors who have grappled with decisions about how to rebuild the World Trade Center site and memorialize those who lost their lives in the attack. Stories of this ongoing political battle have filled the New York press almost daily for the past four years. As *Contentious City* is published, the outcome remains in doubt, but the political experts who contributed to the book do an excellent job of exploring the underlying logic that continues to drive the process. After the veneer of public participation in discussions about the redesign of the site wore off, the decision process revealed itself as a strikingly undemocratic contest among the governor, the mayor, the Port Authority, and the lease holder. In this game, the city and its citizens held very few cards. As a result, the narrow goal of restoring the commercial revenues from the site has generally trumped broader efforts to establish mixed residential and commercial use for the downtown area and to improve its transportation links to the rest of the city. This, despite the fact that commercial vacancies downtown are at a historic peak and demand for commercial space remains distinctly weaker in downtown than midtown. As our books go to press, it appears likely that some version of the Freedom Tower will be built. It is much less certain that tenants will be ready to occupy this space at viable prices, or that the predominantly commercial redevelopment of the site will be best for the city in the long run.

The brutal shock of September 11 caused profound human suffering for the thousands of New Yorkers who lost loved ones, and a new sense of vulnerability still experienced by everyone in the city. It is commonplace to say that nothing will ever be the same after September 11, and in many ways this is true. But the reaction to the attack also revealed much about the persistent character of the city—the enormous strength and flexibility of its economy, the vitality as well as the fragility of its communities, and the byzantine complexities of its power politics. The tools of social science, deftly wielded in these volumes, bring all these underlying constancies of New York life into sharp relief in an effort to probe the deeper dimensions of what has happened in the wake of September 11. As citizens of New York, we would like to contribute these volumes as a small part of the city's ongoing effort to understand and improve itself—and to recover from its darkest hour.

Eric Wanner
President
Russell Sage Foundation

ACKNOWLEDGMENTS

A COLLABORATIVE EFFORT like this book can succeed only with support from all quarters. The authors all thank the many informants who shared their insights about the rebuilding process over the last several years, often on the condition of anonymity. We hope that the results justify the confidence they placed in us by speaking frankly. We also gratefully acknowledge the financial and organizational support of the Russell Sage Foundation. Its president, Eric Wanner, set forth the vision for this and the two companion volumes and encouraged us to think clearly about and probe deeply the issues raised by the rebuilding process. Bindu Chadaga was a tireless and effective coordinator of our activities. As always, Suzanne Nichols was highly skilled at getting sometimes distracted academics to work cohesively and finish their work on time. Nancy Foner and Howard Chernick, leaders of the other two clusters of researchers, participated in many of our deliberations, offered much helpful advice, and proved to be ideal teammates in moving the enterprise forward. Finally, a group of distinguished thinkers and doers gave the chapter authors valuable criticisms as they moved toward completion. They included Alan Altshuler of Harvard's Kennedy School of Government, Alex Frangos of the *Wall Street Journal*, Herbert J. Gans, the Robert S. Lynd Professor of Sociology at Columbia University, Jack Krauskopf of the 9/11 United Services Group, former MTA chairman Richard Ravitch, Association for Downtown New York president Carl Weisbrod, and Regional Plan Association president Robert Yaro. The authors provided a great deal of support and help to each other as well. Naturally, all conclusions and interpretations are those of the authors alone.

We would like to dedicate this volume to two groups of New Yorkers: those who paid the ultimate price on September 11, 2001, and those young people either growing up in New York or destined to move to it. The first group helped make New York an amazing place, while the second will make it even better in the years to come.

PART I

Introduction

CHAPTER 1

Introduction: Repairing the Hole in the Heart of the City

John Mollenkopf

TUESDAY, SEPTEMBER 11, 2001, dawned as one of the most beautiful days of the year in New York City. The air was crystal clear, the early sun was bright, and the temperature was warming up to a perfect level. It was an exciting day for those interested in city politics because the people going to polls that had opened at 6:00 A.M. for the Democratic and Republican primary elections would determine the choices for the next mayor of New York City and begin to define the post-Giuliani era in New York City politics. In the Democratic primary, Bronx borough president Fernando Ferrer was the first Latino candidate with a real shot at the mayoralty since Herman Badillo's narrow losses in the 1969 and 1973 primaries, while public advocate Mark Green, a white progressive consumer advocate, also enjoyed wide support. (Two other prominent Democrats, city council speaker Peter Vallone and comptroller Alan Hevesi, had failed to gain traction in the public opinion polls.) The Republican side featured two former Democrats. Michael Bloomberg, a political neophyte who had built an extremely successful financial information and news business, was favored over Herman Badillo, who had gravitated to a Republican view on many issues. A distinguished former borough president and member of the U.S. Congress, Badillo had been the first Puerto Rican elected to either position.

No matter who won, the received wisdom went, the primary election would begin to end the polarizing period of Republican Rudolph W. Giuliani's administration. Many observers thought that the Democratic nominee would be-come mayor, since the Republicans were unlikely to support Badillo and Bloomberg was judged to be still on the first, steep part of his political learning curve. Attention therefore focused on the battle between Green, the early front-runner who had historically drawn strong electoral support from blacks as well as white liberals, and Ferrer, whose support from the Rev. Al Sharpton and Harlem's Congressman Charles Rangel had enabled him to fuse a Latino-black coalition and gain ground on Green. The contest was keen and the out-come closely watched and eagerly awaited. Those insiders sufficiently in the know learned that the first early morning wave of the exit poll reported that Green had received 31.5 percent, Ferrer 27 percent, and the others lesser amounts.

As everyone now knows, September 11 did indeed change the political dy-namics of the city and the rest of the world, but in completely different ways than anticipated. Sitting at my breakfast table that morning, drinking coffee and reading the *New York Times*, the first report that a plane had hit the World Trade Center came across the radio shortly after 8:45 A.M. A few minutes later it became clear that the culprit was no wandering Cessna. The television revealed voluminous smoke rising from the North Tower and provided a real-time view of the second plane smashing into the South Tower at 9:03 A.M. My home in Park Slope, Brooklyn, was soon enveloped by the vortex of smoke cascading from both towers and blowing downwind directly toward us. The televised view showed the buildings shedding debris, ephemera, and, horribly, human beings. This was most palpably not going to be a normal day, nor were any of the following ones. The South Tower collapsed at 10:05 A.M., the North Tower at 10:28 A.M. Soon the subways were shut down, then all air traffic was grounded in the United States, and word came that a plane had hit the Pentagon too, while another had gone down in Pennsylvania. Meanwhile, bits and pieces of singed paper began to fall like a light winter snow on our yard.

With swelling tears, I tried to absorb the fact that 10,000 people might have just perished before my eyes. It took time to learn that the number was, blessedly, much lower: 2,749 in and around the World Trade Center, with 189 more at the Pentagon and 44 in the Pennsylvania field, not counting the 19 hijackers who sent themselves to death. It took some time to learn that this total included 13 members of our local firehouse in Park Slope (343 firemen lost their lives in all), the father of a family living around the corner, and the son of the woman who owned a favorite clothing store down the block. It was a real relief to learn that this total did not include a neighbor who worked for the Port Authority on the 67th floor of the North Tower, though that friend was traumatized by the loss of so many colleagues.

After calling my daughter at college to let her know that her parents were safe, the site of the catastrophe beckoned me closer. For hours after the collapse, soot-drenched office workers, shocked and often crying, streamed past me on foot over the Manhattan and Brooklyn Bridges. (For days and months, acrid smoke continued to hang over lower Manhattan, drifting slowly over Brooklyn or up the island, depending on the prevailing wind.) Neighborhood parents searched frantically for their children who were students at Stuyvesant High School, located virtually across the street from the WTC—they had been sent fleeing northward into the streets after watching bodies fall, and then buildings. In succeeding days an intrepid observer could approach the site on foot to see the mangled and smoking wreckage and the stark, burned skeletal remains of the U.S. Customs House, 6 World Trade Center.

These experiences remind us that, no matter how detached we must become to analyze the political implications of 9/11 for the residents of New York City, we must first acknowledge all those who perished, the deep loss to their families, friends, and neighbors, and the gash inflicted by the attack on the social fabric of greater New York. It sent many New Yorkers, especially those whose lives were connected to lower Manhattan, into a collective depression that took a year or more to dissipate. But it also elicited a magnificent response from New Yorkers. The firefighters and police officers who gave their lives seeking to save others showed surpassing heroism, while those who worked feverishly from September to May to clear the site displayed stoic determination. New Yorkers from many other walks of life sought to contribute their particular talents to rebuilding the city and restoring its vitality, optimism, and ability to realize its best hopes and values.

UNDERSTANDING THE POLITICAL CONSEQUENCES OF 9/11

This book is one small part of that effort. The authors assembled here have sought to apply their scholarly skills and insights to clarifying the choices that government made about how to rebuild the city and respond to the attack, explaining how and why these choices were made, and considering the larger political consequences of the attack. All of the contributors to this volume are people who live in, work in, or study the city, who have been closely involved in its affairs, and who were deeply affected by the attack. We gratefully accepted the invitation of the Russell Sage Foundation to participate in this study as our small contribution to the city's recovery process. Along with two companion volumes, *Wounded City: The Social Impact of 9/11* (Foner 2005) and *Resilient City: The Economic Impact of 9/11* (Chernick 2005), this volume seeks to go behind the popular accounts of the rebuilding process, which tend to focus on the many intense and colorful personalities involved rather than the logic that guides their actions, and to go wider than those accounts and consider the larger and longer implications.

The political consequences of the attack were immediate, enormous, and grave. Locally, the mayoral primary election was postponed; nationally, the country went into a political shock from which it has not yet recovered. When the delayed primaries and then the final mayoral general election were held in the months after the attack, they yielded a result quite different from what many had anticipated. Far from ending Mayor Giuliani's career on a down and rather sour note, September 11 made him a national hero and led to discussion about whether his term should have an emergency extension. In the 2002 Democratic gubernatorial primary campaign, Andrew Cuomo suffered a political meltdown after he belittled Governor George E. Pataki's role in responding to the attack, which in fact helped Pataki triumph in the November 2002 general election. The terrorist attack also gave purpose to the presidency of George W. Bush, culminating in his reelection in November 2004, which conferred on him a political legitimacy that the 2000 election had not. More broadly, the attack and its aftermath shifted public opinion and electoral choices—not only in New York City but across the nation—away from jobs and the economy, which might have been expected to be priorities during a recession, toward a concern for physical security, national security, and patriotism in the face of foreign enemies. If we do not yet know if September 11 has changed the course of American history forever, we certainly do know that it had an enormous short-run impact.

In this volume, we consider the local dimensions of this political impact. In the wake of the destruction of the twin towers, the citizens and elected officials of New York City faced many fundamental questions about the future of the city. As the companion volume edited by Howard Chernick (2005) shows, New York City demonstrated great resilience in achieving a fairly full economic recovery four years after the attack, but the attack sharply worsened local economic and fiscal conditions in 2001 and 2002. It destroyed or severely damaged tens of millions of square feet of prime office space, ended or displaced hundreds of thousands of jobs, and cost billions of dollars in economic activity in the historic heart of the city. These impacts posed many questions: How would local officials mobilize to clean up the site? How would the city balance its budget in the face of falling revenues and rising security costs? What help would the federal government provide to the recovery effort? How would government plan for rebuilding the site and creating a suitable memorial? And more broadly, what could be done to maintain lower Manhattan as the nation's third-largest office district—and indeed, Manhattan's role as the engine of the regional economy?

The companion volume edited by Nancy Foner (2005) details the sharp and disproportionately negative impact of the attacks and the attendant economic trends on nearby communities such as Battery Park City, Tribeca, and Jersey City, as well as more distant communities that were home to workers in the most severely affected industries, such as the airlines, hotels, restaurants, and retail. The attacks mobilized these and other constituencies, most notably the families of the victims, who became a powerful voice advocating, among other things, that nothing be built on the footprints of the former twin towers. No politician wanted to be seen as disrespectful of their wishes, and some, like former mayor Giuliani, became powerful advocates for their views. Beyond the specific steps to be taken to help the city recover, the response to 9/11 evoked a complex swirl of advocacy groups. A central question arose: How could the city's political leaders navigate these groups to achieve a modicum of public satisfaction with what they decided to do?

The attack and its economic aftermath led intelligent observers to question whether New York City had a viable future, just as others had done during New York's fiscal crisis in the mid-1970s. A few even proclaimed the end of the tall office building. Particularly in doubt was the role of lower Manhattan in the larger economic geography of the city. The city's historic point of origin in the seventeenth century, this area housed its first business and governmental institutions, its port and shipping and processing activities, as well as places of residence and recreation. It was home to the New York Stock Exchange, founded in 1827, as well as the city's growing complex of commercial and investment banks, insurance companies, and law firms. When the "greater city" was formed by combining Manhattan with Brooklyn, Queens, the Bronx, and Staten Island in 1898, its corporate, commercial, and industrial activities were still largely to be found below Houston Street.

These activities began to gravitate uptown, however, as the highly congested terrain of lower Manhattan was built out and Pennsylvania Station and Grand Central Terminal were opened in 1910 and 1913 (Lockwood 1976). With the construction of the initial buildings of Rockefeller Center in 1939 and continuing with the construction of Lever House as the first glass-walled skyscraper on Park Avenue in 1952, the city's banking, investment banking, corporate headquarters, and corporate service activities were reconcentrated in midtown, and "Wall Street" became a metaphor more than a place, although the stock exchanges, the Federal Reserve Bank, and important banks and law firms remained downtown, as did the city's government office complex. Despite initiatives to reinforce the lower Manhattan office economy, including the construction of the World Trade Center and the adjacent World Financial Center, midtown nevertheless grew more rapidly from the 1950s onward. Indeed, lower Manhattan's legacy of pre–World War II office buildings, which were difficult, if not impossible, to transform into the large, open floors demanded by modern corporate uses, constituted a drag on the lower Manhattan office market, and they became candidates for residential conversion.

The 9/11 attack had potentially devastating consequences for lower Manhattan's office economy. In addition to destroying the sixteen-acre, ten-million-square-foot World Trade Center complex, the attack severely damaged an adjacent skyscraper, the Deutsche Bank headquarters, and temporarily impaired many others, including the World Financial Center in Battery Park City. Much of lower Manhattan, including the southern portion of Chinatown, was closed to nonresident traffic, and mass transit service from New Jersey to downtown Manhattan was suspended. Elected officials and business leaders had good reason to fear that these constraints, along with added costs for security and insurance, might be the straws that broke the back of lower Manhattan, or even Manhattan as a whole. In the face of such doubts, decisionmakers felt a huge imperative to restore confidence in the city and rekindle its economic growth.

The local, state, and federal governments, joined by philanthropies, insurance firms, the private sector, civic organizations, and concerned citizens, responded with an unprecedented flow of funds and professional talent to help lower Manhattan and the rest of the city cope and, ultimately, rebound. The federal government promised some $21.5 billion to clean up the site, repair the infrastructure, provide incentives for businesses and residents to stay in Manhattan, and rebuild the site. The state government deployed the power of eminent domain, its exemption from local regulation, and the borrowing power enjoyed by its Empire State Development Corporation to create a subsidiary, the Lower Manhattan Development Corporation (LMDC), to work with the bistate Port Authority of New York and New Jersey (PANYNJ, or PA), which also was not subject to local regulation. The City of New York's Department of Design and Construction oversaw the initial cleanup and repaired the streets around the site, while the Police Department provided heightened security.

Taken together, the financial scale of the response has been impressive. A recent RAND study estimated that compensation to the victims of the attack (including residents and businesses in lower Manhattan as well as the victims and their families) would amount to $38 billion, including $2.7 billion donated to charities and almost $20 billion in insurance proceeds (Dixon and Stern 2004, 132). Many billions more will clearly be invested in redeveloping the site and other parts of lower Manhattan. The cost of building the proposed structures and supporting transportation improvements (not counting a proposed new direct transit link with Kennedy Airport) is estimated to be around $12 billion.

Rebuilding Ground Zero and the surrounding area may well be the largest, biggest-budget, and highest-visibility urban renewal program ever launched in New York City. (Past projects on a similar scale include the $110 million Lincoln Center urban renewal project built on fourteen acres between 1956 and 1969; the eleven-acre Rockefeller Center office complex built between the late 1930s and the 1960s in midtown Manhattan; and the fifteen-story apartment buildings of Stuyvesant Town and Peter Cooper Village built by the Metropolitan Life Insurance Company on eighty acres between Fourteenth and Twenty-third Streets on the East River in the late 1940s.)

Rebuilding this area of lower Manhattan poses the same questions raised during many previous conflicts over urban renewal: Who will benefit, and who will bear the burdens? What urban functions will it promote, and what will it destroy or displace? The rebuilding process also poses a larger set of questions: What kind of city will New Yorkers use the resources to seek to build? What values will their choices reflect? How well or poorly will the city's leaders do in engaging the complicated array of interests activated by the 9/11 attack—as well as the citizenry at large—in the dialogue over how to rebuild? What problems or conflicts will this dialogue reveal, and how will the city's leaders overcome them? In the final analysis, what will their actions (or inactions), as opposed to their rhetoric, reveal about the kind of city they really hope New York will become?

Lynne Sagalyn and Susan Fainstein address the most immediate question in their analyses of the planning for rebuilding Ground Zero and the neighboring parts of lower Manhattan. Sagalyn opens the volume with a detailed and incisive analysis of the "inner politics" of the rebuilding process. She describes the struggle of the Lower Manhattan Development Corporation, established to manage the planning process for the site and oversee efforts for the surrounding area, to achieve influence in an environment constrained by the Port Authority of New York and New Jersey's ownership of the site and its lease with Silverstein Properties, whose insurance proceeds would provide much of the funding for the redevelopment. Sagalyn provides a detailed master narrative of how these key players interacted with each other and a host of interests with ringside seats, including the city of New York, downtown property owners and business interests, nearby residents, the families of the victims, and a variety of architects and planners. Susan Fainstein inspects the same story from the point of view of the Port Authority. This agency was struggling to survive a near-mortal blow and to reassert itself as the historic engine of the region's transportation system in a political environment where the two governors to whom it reports had tended to treat it like a piggy bank. Moreover, as Fainstein details, the Port Authority was locked in an intimate financial and political relationship with Silverstein Properties and sharply constrained in what it could or would envision for the site.

A key aspect of this process was deciding what trajectory lower Manhattan's development should take. Sagalyn and Fainstein explain why the LMDC and the Port Authority were closely focused on restoring the office and retail space that had been destroyed, whether or not larger perspectives on lower Manhattan recommended such restoration. Mitchell Moss addresses this question from the point of view of city government. In a variety of ways, city policy had sought to diversify both the types of economic activities located downtown and the types of land uses characteristics of the area. It had encouraged owners of older, outmoded class B office space to convert it to residential use and made efforts to attract nonprofit organizations into spaces formerly used by Wall Street or insurance firms. Battery Park City, immediately to the west of Ground Zero and noted for the World Financial Center, was also hailed as a superbly designed setting for upper-middle-income professionals, with some of the most compelling new waterside public spaces in the city. Tribeca, just to the north, had become a trendy area of loft living, fine restaurants, and refined retail opportunities. Further north, SoHo had evolved from a district of declining garment industry activity into a zone of art galleries and loft living and ultimately into an expensive home furnishings and design center. China-town, a few blocks east of Ground Zero, was similarly evolving from a center of garment production and crowded housing for recent immigrants into a more regional center of services and entertainment for a more broadly distributed Chinese community (for discussions of these communities, see Kasinitz, Smith-simon, and Pok 2005). In the city's view, the activities in these neighborhoods were the prime ingredients for transforming lower Manhattan from a 9-to-5 business district that closed with the markets into a 24/7 environment mixing living, playing, and working. In Moss's account, the city expressed its view that lower Manhattan should evolve toward a mixed-use community, but key decisionmakers did not adopt this perspective.

The rebuilding of the World Trade Center site has been an exercise in articulating public values within a deeply traumatized civic realm and drawing diverse constituencies into a meaningful debate about the city's future. In addi-tion to the immediate interests activated by the rebuilding process, described by Sagalyn, Fainstein, and Moss, the challenge of rebuilding the site evoked a huge outpouring of public interest and a broad public desire for involvement in the decisionmaking process. Arielle Goldberg explores the fascinating interplay between the five major civic organizations that evolved to address the rebuild-ing issue and the key decisionmakers, as well as how LMDC in particular used these decisionmakers to strengthen its own position. She shows how these players articulated their positions, how they sought to have influence, and what they ultimately accomplished. Although they did not alter the decisions made by LMDC and the Port Authority in any fundamental way, they did put before the public basic questions about the values that the decisionmaking process should advance.

James Young focuses on a particularly intense value question: what kind of memorial should be placed at the site? This seemingly simple question has many complicated ramifications. On the one hand, those who lost loved ones on September 11 are a symbolically potent constituency—or rather constituen-cies, since they are internally differentiated about whom they want to remem-ber and how. On the other hand, the decisionmaking institutions and important stakeholders like downtown business interests and residents of Battery Park City have not wanted the memorial to compromise the commercial success of the redevelopment project or "turn the area into a cemetery." Moreover, as Young shows, the memorial selection process also became a vehicle through which the LMDC could reshape parts of the site design. His is a fascinating case study of how highly accomplished members of the jury sought to resolve such difficulties as: How should these individual constituencies be recognized? Which broad categories of people should the memorial serve, and in what ways? What values should it embody? And how should the imperative to remember those who suffered losses be weighed against the imperative to restore the commercial functions of the site?

The articulation of values and the political consequences of the attack, of course, flow far beyond the site itself, and beyond lower Manhattan. What were the larger political consequences of the attack? How were they felt by New Yorkers, and what political responses did they make? Lorraine Minnite explores a critical dimension of these questions by examining the adverse impact of the Patriot Act and other domestic security measures on the Muslim immigrant communities in New York City, their responses and those of their advocates, and what this interaction says about an important trend in New York City politics. Her chapter shows how the anti-immigrant trend in national politics diverges from the basically pro-immigrant orientation in local politics. Even Mayor Giuliani, often criticized as being insensitive to minority New Yorkers, consistently took a pro-immigrant position. Despite the significant personal trauma suffered by the mayor on September 11, he asked all New Yorkers to show fairness and compassion to Muslim residents of the city and not to take out their anger and bitterness in any misdirected acts against them. As Minnite shows, the same cannot be said about the ways in which the federal security and immigration agencies treated South Asian residents in places like Coney Island Avenue in Brooklyn.

The volume concludes with my own discussion of how the attack created disequilibria in city, state, and national politics, driving them all in new directions. The attack played a central role in electing Michael Bloomberg mayor of New York, altered the issues dominating city, state, and national politics, and shifted voters' priorities in the 2001, 2002, and 2004 elections. Before 9/11, the New York City mayoral election had been dominated by debates among the Democrats about how to temper the racial polarization that had marked the Giuliani and Dinkins administrations and how to address the Giuliani administration's unfinished business. Afterwards, reestablishing security, coping with the immediate physical and economic consequences of the attack, and rebuilding the city's economic confidence came to the fore. This chapter details the restoration of Mayor Giuliani's reputation and the political glow acquired through close association with 9/11 by Governor Pataki, whose second term had evolved in a lackluster direction. The governor's leadership in that period and his embrace of the rebuilding process served him well politically in 2002. Finally, the September 11 attacks enabled George W. Bush to assert the strongest and most unhindered power of the presidency—namely, being commander in chief—to establish a legitimacy for his office that he was not able to achieve in the election of November 2000.

ASSESSING THE OUTCOMES

How do we evaluate what our decisionmakers have done? What do their decisions and actions tell us about what they want the city to be or become? The scholars contributing to this volume show that participants in the process have put forward three broad alternatives. Lynne Sagalyn and Susan Fainstein detail the first approach, which is to make whole the economic value of Ground Zero. Owing to the Port Authority's charter restriction against building residential housing, the terms of its lease with Silverstein Properties, its dependence on the revenue from that lease, and its reliance on Silverstein's insurance settlement to finance the construction, the Port Authority was committed to ensuring that Silverstein Properties could build 10 million square feet of office space and 450,000 square feet or more of retail space on or near the site, along with restoring PATH service to it. This primary objective, which was embraced by the LMDC and other actors in the inner circle, such as Governor Pataki, would also provide economic and political benefits to Brookfield Properties (owner of the World Financial Center) and the residents of Battery Park City, the tax collectors of New York City and State, and elected officials, who could reap electoral support and campaign contributions from its success. If the matter were left up to the most interested parties, this would be the approach taken, albeit dressed up with a memorial and cultural facilities.

The second broad of course of action would be to use the rebuilding of the WTC site and the area around it to change the economic and social relationships of lower Manhattan to the rest of the city and region. As Mitchell Moss points out, the city has made a good case that lower Manhattan would make a greater addition to the overall economic vitality of the city if it were to place greater emphasis on residential housing (especially housing for corporate service professionals), attract economic activities that are being priced out of midtown Manhattan office space, and generate new kinds of cultural and recreational activities. (Governmental activities will continue to be vital to lower Manhattan's economy.) In this view, lower Manhattan should continue to house major financial service activities, like the stock exchanges and Goldman Sachs, and government should encourage these activities, but the area should diversify.

The Bloomberg administration and the civic organizations described by Arielle Goldberg, particularly the Civic Alliance, have both argued against replacing what previously stood on Ground Zero and in favor of taking new directions in lower Manhattan. Moving in these directions would require much more attention to building housing and creating new amenities in lower Manhattan, as the mayor's plan for lower Manhattan urges. It might call for long-sought transportation improvements that have no direct bearing on the WTC site, such as building the Second Avenue subway. Mayor Bloomberg made his policy clear by refusing to provide public subsidies for constructing a new facility for the New York Stock Exchange, pushing for construction of new class A office space in far west midtown, and advocating construction of housing for all income ranges, including for the middle-class professionals who would work downtown or in midtown Manhattan. In the long term, the real estate and job markets in New York may judge this second alternative to be a more rational course than the first.

A third course of action would be even more radical. As Goldberg has shown, the Labor Community Advocacy Network (LCAN) and the Civic Alliance have called for shifting the focus of public development away from promoting office construction in Manhattan's business districts toward other parts of the city. This perspective, advanced by mayoral candidate Fernando Ferrer during the runoff campaign in September 2001, and again in the 2005 mayoral race, rests on the idea that the attack was against the whole city, not just downtown property owners, and that the resulting suffering was experienced by janitors, restaurant workers, firefighters, and secretaries, who live all across New York, not just by high-income financial services professionals. From this point of view, the resources made available for rebuilding should be used to help people living outside lower Manhattan to find better jobs, live in more affordable housing, and enjoy better public amenities, not just to promote new office buildings in existing business districts. The fate of Chinatown exemplifies what those who hold this view would see as the misallocation of resources in the first and even the second courses of action. Because much of Chinatown was in the "frozen zone" established after September 11, trucks were unable to reach garment firms or supply neighborhood restaurants. Employment and foot traffic fell sharply as a result, yet the rebuilding authorities paid little attention to the difficulties being experienced by Chinatown's residents and firms (Asian American Federation of New York 2002a, 2002b; Chin 2005). Although this course of action received support from many quarters, the key decisionmakers gave it lip service at best.

A fourth alternative might have been inaction. As Sagalyn notes, this danger always faces ambitious development schemes in New York City. For example, the Forty-second Street Development Project, which began to be discussed in the Lindsay administration in 1969, was not realized until a third of a century later (Sagalyn 2001). In a political environment as complex as New York City, almost any proposal will be subject to a Newton's Third Law of Political Dynamics: any action produces an equal and opposite reaction. The emotional force of 9/11 and the large scale of the resources made available for the response might have made it difficult for political actors to act in a concerted manner in such an environment. As one commentator told us, "For many groups, September 11 represented the opportunity to strike out the first line of their pet proposals and insert 'in light of September 11' to pursue their long-standing agendas." Political actors seeking to please everyone in the face of such conflicting interests might have taken the rebuilding process as an opportunity to delay or temporize. The announcement in May 2005 that the Freedom Tower would have to be redesigned owing to security concerns reflects these cross-cutting currents.

In the final analysis, it seems that they did not. Although it may be too soon to say definitively what will happen in and around Ground Zero, the initial outlines of this critical period in the city's history have become clear. This volume suggests that the legal structure of the site's ownership by the Port Authority, its lease to a private developer, and the reliance on state development unencumbered by accountability to the people or government of New York City have strongly shaped the outcome to date to favor the first course of action over the two other alternatives.

This has not been a particularly democratic process. Although Sagalyn and Goldberg describe how the "Listening to the City" event brought 4,500 concerned citizens together to evaluate the first set of plans issued by the PA and the LMDC, they also suggest that this and other public forums had only marginal impacts on the final outcome. This happened because all the key agencies concerned with the rebuilding process report to the governor, not the mayor. Governor Pataki, not Mayor Bloomberg, has made, and will continue to make, the critical decisions. Indeed, the procedures for rebuilding were apparently designed that way to ensure that a potential Democratic victor in the 2001 mayoral election would not be able to influence the outcome. As a result, the city of New York and its citizens have had little influence over the response to its most traumatic experience in decades, if not a century.

The September 11 attack created openings for all sorts of people to do all sorts of things. It certainly provided many people with an opportunity to display heroism and generosity. As Goldberg shows, the attack generated a strong if perhaps transitory sense of community among New Yorkers, prompting many to offer their help in rebuilding the city. The attack also provided many opportunities for self-interested behavior. A former pornographer used silver stored in the Bank of Nova Scotia's vault in the basement of the WTC to put a thin plating on base metal coins commemorating the event, which he sold for $19.95 apiece until New York State attorney general Eliot Spitzer put a stop to the sales (Barry 2004). The FBI agent in charge of screening WTC debris permitted thirteen other agents to take mementos, including a Tiffany globe, for their own use (Fried 2004). New York City police chief Bernard Kerik used an apartment donated as a resting place for workers cleaning Ground Zero as a place to conduct affairs with both a Corrections Department officer and his publisher (Seelye 2004). A police official commandeered vehicles removed from the site for his own use, while several people falsely asserted that they had lost family members in order to receive compensation. Some people took advantage of the Environmental Protection Agency's (EPA) cleanup program to get free air conditioners even when their old ones were not contaminated. Some of the businesses that have benefited from state aid have also been large contributors to the governor's campaigns (Saltonstall 2004). Such is human nature.

How do we evaluate the choices that have resulted from taking the first course of action? According to the RAND Corporation study, $10.6 billion of the total $38 billion in compensation, mostly from the federal Victims Compensation Fund, will flow to the families of those killed or severely harmed by the attacks, especially the first responders (Dixon and Stern 2004, 25–27). The other two-thirds of this money, including most of the $21 billion in federal funds, will flow to cleaning up the site, making emergency repairs, providing business incentives, building new infrastructure, and erecting new structures on Ground Zero (Hecker 2003, 9–13).

As Sagalyn reports, Larry Silverstein of Silverstein Properties plans to use his insurance proceeds, which may be as much as $4.5 billion, to build the Freedom Tower and four other office buildings on the project site. He has already nearly completed a fifty-two-story, $700 million building just to the north of the WTC where the former 7 World Trade Center was located. To facilitate that plan, the LMDC will tear down the former Deutsche Bank building south of Ground Zero and plans to create the memorial, a museum, cultural facilities, and two transit centers, a new PATH station for the PA and the Fulton Street Transit Center for the subway system. (It is not clear whether the $6 billion or more needed to build a proposed new direct transit link with JFK Airport will be found.)

What are we to make of this emerging new complex? From a design and planning point of view, many would agree that the new site plan will accomplish some important goals, such as restoring part of the city's street grid, thus integrating the site into the surrounding urban fabric. The plan also calls for providing a better link with Battery Park City. The area will enjoy much better links with the PATH train and the subway lines, and its public spaces will certainly be far more attractive and draw far more users than the windswept plaza between the twin towers.

Despite squabbling between the site planner, Daniel Libeskind, and the architect retained by Silverstein Properties, David Childs, which resulted in a hybrid and perhaps questionable design for the Freedom Tower, many leading architects have been engaged to design buildings in the complex, including Frank Gehry for the performing arts center and Santiago Calatrava for the PATH station. The resulting buildings are likely to be far bolder and more interesting than the modernist facades of the twin towers. Even if economic uncertainties prevent the realization of all aspects of the plan, it seems likely that New York will have an attractive and compelling replacement for the twin towers. Moreover, by New York standards, it may be built with far less community opposition than has sometimes been the case.

Although the site plan may represent a significant accomplishment in its own terms, we nevertheless have every right to expect, and should have gotten far more, in the response of our elected officials to such a grave crisis. By allowing the Port Authority's institutional needs and the lease privatizing the twin towers to define the core nature of the problem as a matter of commercial real estate development, public officials—in particular Governor George Pataki—greatly narrowed the scope of the issue. As a result, consideration of important, arguably superior courses of action was precluded.

Even considered within its own narrow boundaries, however, the plan for Ground Zero faces a number of persistent concerns. First, it is far from clear whether the first buildings to be erected, 7 World Trade Center and the Freedom Tower, will find tenants and become economically viable. Neither is being built on the basis of loans from a financial institution backed by leases signed with prospective tenants. Indeed, no major tenant has been identified for either building. (Governor Pataki has made a possibly empty promise to move his New York office into the Freedom Tower, assuming that he will still be in office when the building is ready; the Port Authority, at his urging, has also signed up for some of the space.) Whether Silverstein can find a market for these buildings and go on to construct and market the others has been the subject of considerable debate (Frangos 2004). The obvious unstated problem is that few commercial tenants would want to move into a building that takes over from the twin towers as "the world's tallest target." In May 2005, concerns expressed by the police department forced a reconsideration of the building's design. Similar concerns caused Goldman Sachs to put on hold its plan to construct a new headquarters across the street from Ground Zero. It is also possible that 7 World Trade Center and the Freedom Tower—containing about as much space as one former twin tower—will constitute a drag on the office market in lower Manhattan, where vacancies have already been at a historic peak.

A second concern involves opportunity costs. New York City has never before seen, and will never again see, $21 billion in federal aid over a few short years. To the extent that government can most effectively hone the city's competitive advantage by enhancing underlying factors of productivity, such as increasing skill levels, lowering general costs of doing business, or improving physical and electronic access, the plans adopted for Ground Zero may not be a logical course of action. It might well have been far wiser to invest the federal aid in the region's many unfunded transportation infrastructure needs, in the integration of the existing transit system, in lower Manhattan's shift toward housing and entertainment, or even in the city's research universities.

Despite considerable agitation from civic organizations and the New York City government, Governor Pataki and the agencies he commands did not choose to alter the constraints facing the agencies responsible for making decisions about how to respond to 9/11. The governor designed the LMDC so as to deny influence to the state legislature and the incoming mayor. He named many close associates to manage it for him. At points of conflict, he stepped in to make key decisions. Clearly, he made rebuilding the World Trade Center his principal legacy and main purpose as governor. This decision served him well in his 2002 reelection campaign, just as holding the Republican National Convention in New York City on the eve of the third anniversary of the attack helped to underscore President Bush's role in responding to terrorism and bolstered his reelection chances.

As a direct consequence, the people of New York City and their mayor have had little impact on the decisionmaking process, though they cleaned up the site, cared for those who were harmed, and administered various sources of assistance. Perhaps making a virtue of necessity, the mayor apparently struck a deal for a political division of labor in which he ceded rebuilding lower Manhattan to the governor but received the governor's support for his plans for the far West Side, including $300 million in state capital funds to build a $1.2 billion facility to provide a new stadium for the New York Jets and expansion space for the Jacob K. Javits Convention Center. In the process, each official has quieted his staff's concerns about aspects of the other's pet project (Steinhauer 2004).

It is worth noting that New York City residents have taken a different attitude toward the war on terror than the country at large. Mayor Giuliani, Governor Pataki, and President Bush wrapped themselves in the political symbolism of Ground Zero to build support for a forward-leaning policy of armed intervention in Afghanistan and Iraq. As Lorraine Minnite points out, the federal government defined members of Muslim, Middle Eastern, and South Asian communities as potential threats and deported a great many improperly documented but otherwise law-abiding immigrants. In New York City, by contrast, even Mayor Giuliani, the local politician most strongly identified with the heroism of the first responders to 9/11, urged New Yorkers "not to engage in any form of group blame or group hatred" (Giuliani 2001).

New Yorkers responded to the attack with grief more than with anger. City residents continue to worry deeply that they may bear the brunt of another terrorist attack, and they are much less likely than other Americans to support the war in Iraq. The depths of these feelings were evident in the differences between a *New York Times* poll of city residents undertaken on the eve of the Republican National Convention and a national poll taken just after the November election (*New York Times* 2004a, 2004b). City residents gave George Bush a 24-to-71 approval-disapproval rating, compared to the 51–44 rating nationally. Most (48 percent) felt that life in New York City had gotten worse over the preceding two years (16 percent felt that it had gotten better, while 34 percent said things were the same). Although national sentiment had turned against the war in Iraq by November 2004 (46 percent saying it was the right thing to do, 48 percent saying we should have stayed out, and 5 percent being uncertain), New Yorkers predominantly opposed it (25 percent saying it was the right thing to do, 65 percent saying we should have stayed out, and 11 percent being uncertain). Two-thirds of New Yorkers worried that terrorists would attack the city again, and half thought such an attack might well happen during the convention. More than three-quarters of all New Yorkers thought that the war in Iraq was not worth the cost in American lives, 60 percent thought that Washington was not doing enough to help New York recover, and 47 percent felt Washington was not doing enough to protect the city from another attack. More than one-quarter felt that they were still dealing with the fallout of the 9/11 attack and that their lives had not returned to normal (*New York Times* 2004a).

Hidden behind the overwhelming "blueness" of New York City, President Bush increased his share of the vote from 18 to 24 percent between 2000 and 2004. His share of the vote in 2004 ran well ahead of the Republican share of the voter registration in the ultra-orthodox Jewish neighborhoods of Williamsburg, Crown Heights, and Borough Park, Brooklyn, and the Italian American neighborhoods of Dyker Heights and Bensonhurst. Such neighborhoods have been the traditional bedrock of the vote for candidates like Rudolph Giuliani and Michael Bloomberg. John Kerry also ran ahead of Democratic registration in neighborhoods with many well-educated professionals, which provided critical swing votes in recent mayoral elections, for example, helping Michael Bloomberg win office in November 2001. Opinion polls from the end of 2004 suggest that Mayor Bloomberg paid a price for being associated with the president, the war, and the perceived inadequate federal response to the risks facing the city (*New York Times* 2004a).

What, then, can we conclude about the political implications of 9/11 for New York City? The chapters in this volume offer evidence that the economic, political, and legal imperatives surrounding the site pushed the officials charged with responding to the attack to focus on real estate development and transportation infrastructure at the site to the exclusion of other ways of understanding and responding to the crisis caused by the attack. They did not ignore other interested parties, whether the families of the victims, neighbors living in Battery Park City or Chinatown, or even the mayor of New York, but they paid attention to them mainly only to the extent necessary to achieve their primary objectives. The governor, the authorities under his control, and the leaseholder, Silverstein Properties, succeeded in defining the process their way.

On the positive side, residents of the city did not react to its Muslim, Middle Eastern, and South Asian immigrant communities in the angry, punitive manner that might have been expected. Despite the federal registration program and the incarceration and even deportation of many men of these communities, most New Yorkers expressed no ill will toward them. Given the family experiences of some New Yorkers with the Holocaust, their historically strong support for civil liberties, and the negative example of the internment of Japanese Americans during World War II, many city residents instead showed concern for these vulnerable immigrants.

Of the rebuilding process the Regional Plan Association (2004, 5–6) observed that its aspirations for civic engagement "have yet to be realized," that the authorities had "neglected many...recommended strategies," and that their receptiveness to public input was "uneven over time and across subject areas." Most pointedly, it stated that the plans "have not supported the diversification of Lower Manhattan's economy nor do they promote a range of housing options that would encourage a socially, economically, and racially diverse residential community."

The vigor of the civic coalitions, the evident concern for immigrant rights, the unease with the war on terror, and the lack of support for President Bush in the 2004 election suggest that New York does not lack critics of the response to September 11. With the economic uncertainty about whether it is possible to realize the plans for the site and the looming 2005 mayoral election and 2006 gubernatorial election, it may still be possible for these critics to push public policy toward measures that would better integrate Ground Zero into a more diverse lower Manhattan economy. If so, the city would achieve something closer to the best aspirations of its citizens.

REFERENCES

Asian American Federation of New York. 2002a. *Chinatown After September 11: An Economic Impact Study*. New York: AAFNY (April).

———. 2002b. *Chinatown One Year After September 11: An Economic Impact Study*. New York: AAFNY (November).

Barry, Dan. 2004. "A Silver Coin, Wrapped in Plain Brown." *New York Times*, October 2.

Chernick, Howard, ed. 2005. *Resilient City: The Economic Impact of 9/11*. New York: Russell Sage Foundation.

Chin, Margaret M. 2005. "Moving on: Chinese Garment Workers After 9/11." In *Wounded*

City: The Social Impact of 9/11, edited by Nancy Foner. New York: Russell Sage Foundation.

Dixon, Lloyd, and Rachel Kaganoff Stern. 2004. *Compensation for Losses from the 9/11 Attacks*. Santa Monica, Calif.: RAND Corporation, Institute for Civil Justice.

Foner, Nancy, ed. 2005. *Wounded City: The Social Impact of 9/11*. New York: Russell Sage Foundation.

Frangos, Alex. 2004. "Uncertainties Soar at Ground Zero." *Wall Street Journal*, October 20.

Fried, Joseph P. 2004. "Following Up." *New York Times*, October 24.

Giuliani, Rudolph W. 2001. "Muslim Communities Respected in New York." Statement to United Nations (October 1). Available at: http://usinfo.org/usia/usinfo.state.gov/usa/islam/s100101.htm.

Hecker, JayEtta Z. 2003. *Disaster Assistance: Federal Aid to the New York City Area Following the Attacks of September 11 and Challenges Confronting FEMA*. GAO-03-1174T. Washington: U.S. General Accounting Office (September 24).

Kasinitz, Philip, Gregory Smithsimon, and Binh Pok. 2005. "Disaster at the Doorstep: Battery Park City and Tribeca Respond to the Events of 9/11." In *Wounded City: The Social Impact of 9/11*, edited by Nancy Foner. New York: Russell Sage Foundation.

Lockwood, Charles. 1976. *Manhattan Moves Uptown*. Boston: Houghton Mifflin.

New York Times. 2004a. New York City poll, August 20–25. Available through the New York Times poll archives.

———. 2004b. National poll, November 18–21. Available through the New York Times poll archives.

Regional Plan Association. 2004. *A Civic Assessment of the Lower Manhattan Planning Process*. New York: RPA (October).

Sagalyn, Lynne. 2001. *Times Square Roulette: Remaking the City Icon*. Cambridge, Mass.: MIT Press.

Saltonstall, David. 2004. "GOP Donor's Liberty Haul." *Daily News*, February 14.

Seelye, Katharine Q. 2004. "One Scandal Tells the Tale of Two Cities." *New York Times*, December 19.

Steinhauer, Jennifer. 2004. "The West Side's Yours, Ground Zero Mine." *New York Times*, March 27.

PART II

The Politics of Rebuilding

CHAPTER 2

The Politics of Planning the World's Most Visible Urban Redevelopment Project

Lynne B. Sagalyn

THREE YEARS after the terrorist attack of September 11, 2001, plans for four key elements in rebuilding the World Trade Center (WTC) site had been adopted: restoring the historic streetscape, creating a new public transportation gateway, building an iconic skyscraper, and fashioning the 9/11 memorial. Despite this progress, however, what ultimately emerges from this heavily argued decisionmaking process will depend on numerous design decisions, financial calls, and technical executions of conceptual plans—or indeed, the rebuilding plan may be redefined without regard to plans adopted through 2004. These implementation decisions will determine whether new cultural attractions revitalize lower Manhattan and whether costly new transportation investments link it more directly with Long Island's commuters. These decisions will determine whether planned open spaces come about, and market forces will determine how many office towers rise on the site. In other words, a vision has been stated, but it will take at least a decade to weave its fabric.

It has been a formidable challenge for a city known for its intense and fractious development politics to get this far. This chapter reviews the emotionally charged planning for the redevelopment of the WTC site between September 2001 and the end of 2004. Though we do not yet know how these plans will be realized, we can nonetheless examine how the initial plans emerged—or were extracted—from competing ambitions, contentious turf battles, intense architectural fights, and seemingly unresolvable design conflicts.

New York Governor George E. Pataki launched this process by creating the Lower Manhattan Development Corporation (LMDC) in November 2001. It picked up pace when LMDC designated Studio Daniel Libeskind's master plan, "Memory Foundations," for the site in February 2003. The process took on further weight when designs were unveiled in December 2003 and January 2004 for the 1,776-foot-high Freedom Tower, Santiago Calatrava's expansive, multitiered transportation portal, and Michael Arad and Peter Walker's memorial design, "Reflecting Absence." The initial planning period ended in December 2004, when a federal trial jury ruled in favor of Silverstein Properties on the insurance-recovery question and set the likely financial parameters for the rebuilding process.

During this period deliberations about what to do on the site were intense and closely watched. While the decisionmaking environment was fluid, it also seemed marked by extemporized decisions, perhaps deliberately so. Three conditions exacerbated this most visible of urban redevelopment projects: a lack of clarity from public officials (despite public pronouncements otherwise) about whether they gave priority to remembrance or rebuilding; institutional and jurisdictional competition between the state of New York, the city of New York, and the Port Authority of New York and New Jersey (PANYNJ, or PA); and the inability of any principal stakeholder to submerge its interests to the greater civic good.

Competing institutional claims were central to this ambiguity, although Governor Pataki partly resolved them by exercising the authority and institutional resources at his command. Though the city of New York had a tremendous interest in what happened on the WTC site and the surrounding area of lower Manhattan, the site itself was owned by the Port Authority. The PA was ultimately accountable to the governor, who appoints half the PA board, designates its executive director, and shapes its actions in New York in a division of labor with the governor of New Jersey, who does the same for his state. (Susan Fainstein elaborates on the Port Authority's role in the next chapter.)

Rather than put his political capital on the line at the outset, Governor Pataki remained cautious and uncommitted during the first part of the debate, husbanding his political resources and exercising his powers "in a spirit of political opportunism rather than broad commitment to the public interest" (Alan Altshuler, private communication, October 1, 2004). Pataki's actions and those of people around him were shaped by his desire to be reelected in November 2002, his aspirations in national politics, his relations with President Bush (who faced reelection in November 2004), and the swirl of political loyalties around both men.

Absent concerted leadership from the governor, no other single agent could assert primary authority over the dual tasks of assuring remembrance while rebuilding the site. Instead, the confusion and conflict in the planning process were compounded in the leadership vacuum, and many decisions about Ground Zero's redevelopment seemed to reflect an ad hoc interplay of commanding personalities, fervent loyalties, powerful emotions, and strong interests, particularly downtown business interests. Roland W. Betts, chair of the LMDC's site-planning subcommittee, kept the process moving along through the glare of high-profile coverage by the print media. But even when key decisions were made, they often seemed to presage staff conflict over how to resolve the technical issues.

When the public dramatically rejected the first set of plans issued by the LMDC and Port Authority in July 2002, LMDC officials initiated a second design process, the "Innovative Design Study." (Arielle Goldberg's chapter in this volume describes this episode in detail.) Run like an architectural competition from September 2002 to February 2003, it became the focal point of worldwide coverage, extensive debate among design professionals, and intense lobbying on all sides. Architectural interests were thrust into the spotlight of an unprecedented level of popular attention. On the day he chose Libeskind Studio's "Memory Foundations" as the winning design, Governor Pataki became the arbiter of a highly politicized process. His key role in the planning process lifted it above the level of a typical "old-fashioned New York brawl." Had the mayor's agenda or conventional interest-group politics been predominant instead, the outcomes might have been different.

Selection of the memorial design took place on a completely separate and quite different institutional track from master planning for the site, perhaps deliberately so. (Further exploration of this matter is offered by James Young in this volume.) In the process, the independent jury's selection challenged the Libeskind master plan and firmly resolved how the tension between remembrance and commercial reconstruction would be managed on the site. Meanwhile, efforts by Mayor Michael R. Bloomberg and his senior officials to insert the city into the decisionmaking arena were largely unsuccessful (a topic explored by Mitchell Moss in this volume).

COMPETING CLAIMS

That the process of planning the rebuilding of the WTC site would be complicated and contentious was not unexpected. Not only were the objectives of repairing an emotionally traumatized neighborhood, physically rebuilding a devastated site, and memorializing the losses experienced there likely to run counter to each other, but all of the figures involved in the decisionmaking had big ambitions, strong emotions, and conflicting goals. Three imperatives shaped the planning process: first, the hallowed site must memorialize the 2,749 persons who died there; second, the site represents a long-term public commitment to city building; and third, whatever is built on the site must recognize the ownership claims flowing from a business transaction completed only weeks before the disaster and sustain the income it provides to the Port Authority.

How would public officials reconcile these competing claims? How would the interests and forces swirling around each of these claims shape the decisionmaking process? How could any master plan survive the political fray, move through multiple regulatory reviews, and still meet the test of market feasibility? Put concretely, would Studio Daniel Libeskind's designated master plan survive as a blueprint for rebuilding the WTC site? Or would it fall victim to irreconcilable claims, weak political commitments, and ever-shifting practical considerations?

The high density of the island makes all large-scale projects in Manhattan targets for opposition. The unprecedented emotional context and worldwide interest in the World Trade Center site raised the ante even higher, requiring an especially deft planning response. The institutional environment complicated matters. The Port Authority had built and owned the sixteen-acre site, but six weeks prior to 9/11, after a long and exacting process, the PA had successfully privatized the twin towers complex for $3.2 billion through a ninety-nine-year lease with a group of investors led by Larry A. Silverstein. Barely freed from its status as landlord, the Port Authority faced decisions about the WTC site with interest both as a landowner exempt from local regulations and as an operator of a regional transportation system. The main financial resource for rebuilding—private insurance proceeds—was subject to lengthy litigation. That process would determine how much money Silverstein could recover from the destruction of the WTC, and therefore how much would be available to rebuild the site. Silverstein argued that the attack was two separate events, allowing recovery of as much as $7 billion, while the insurers considered it to be one, worth $3.55 billion. (In the end, split decisions will award a figure somewhere in between.) The relatively weak position of New York State and outstanding commitments of the Port Authority's capital budget made other sources of financing, apart from federal aid, highly uncertain. Yet it was clear that the memorial would be costly and that priority transportation improvements would far exceed the funds committed by the president and Congress in the wake of the attack.

As a matter of political wisdom, if not statutory requirement, government officials must seek public input on major development decisions whether they like it or not. Early in the rebuilding dialogue, some advocated for a powerful rebuilding czar, a modern-day Robert Moses, who could overcome the conflicting imperatives and incessant pressures to show quick progress in the effort. Others decried command-and-control strategies carried out by a small set of power players. As Arielle Goldberg's chapter details, a group of civic coalitions quickly arose to assert the public's interest in how the planning would be carried out and what its substance should be.

THE SITE

Ground Zero is a 16-acre superblock layered with significant political legacies. The PA used a hotly contested condemnation action to assemble the site in the early 1960s, erasing the historic grid of five city streets and eliminating 12 blocks of Radio Row.[1] Demolition cleared 164 buildings within a 21-sided polygon of 14.634 acres (Dunlap 2004e). When fully tenanted, the WTC was a city within the city, with its own zip code (10048). More than 42,000 people worked in a vertical commercial landscape of 10.5 million square feet of office space, 450,000 square feet of retail space (the nation's third-largest-grossing mall), an 820-room hotel with conference facilities, and a vast underground of 2,000 parking spaces, storage vaults, mechanical and loading facilities, and other supporting infrastructure, including the PATH station and subway complex. In creating this complex, the PA took the unusual step of acting as the developer, a risky position typically left to the private sector. This policy intervention was unprecedented in scale and went far beyond numerous earlier high-profile plans seeking to revitalize lower Manhattan.[2]

Half of the site, the so-called bathtub foundation, covers areas that used to be the Hudson River. A three-foot-thick concrete wall, 70 feet deep, tied to bedrock with steel cables running 3,100 feet around the rectangular perimeter, kept the river at bay. The excavated fill created 23.5 acres of new land immediately west of the site for the creation of Battery Park City (BPC), yet another extension of lower Manhattan's western boundary.[3] This technical feat would become an important constraint on the practical reality of rebuilding, particularly as it affected the design of the 9/11 memorial (Wyatt 2002i). Other encumbrances included the PATH tracks and the need for security, truck access, and underground bus and car parking facilities, all of which bedeviled the design process by triggering conflict among the stakeholders. As one of the last of the massive urban renewal efforts, the WTC was widely regarded as evidence of urban renewal's brutal disregard for the urban fabric. It wore this legacy boldly, just the way its domineering developer, Austin Tobin, the executive director of the Port Authority had intended (Glanz and Lipton 2003, 60–61, 145–75). Tobin deliberately sought to fashion a symbol of concentrated power and financial resources.

The towers gradually became an icon. As a city-within-a-city that physically dominated the surrounding low-density neighborhood, they remained iconic even after other cities around the world built even taller skyscrapers. The twin towers contained 12.5 percent of lower Manhattan's office inventory and 20 percent of its post-1960s office buildings.[4]

Rebuilding the site presented city planners with the opportunity to correct past mistakes and remedy the deficits in the area's quality of life.[5] Reinserting part of the historic street grid emerged as a rare point of consensus among city planners, downtown business interests, and residents of Battery Park City, the adjacent mixed-use development that had become a prized part of lower Manhattan. As Moss (this volume) elaborates, city policy and area residents both placed a priority on building more housing and cultural facilities to reinforce the nascent trend toward downtown living. By statute as well as proclivity, however, the PA was forbidden to build housing on the WTC site or elsewhere, and it would require legislation from New York and New Jersey to amend the agency's bylaws.

As Goldberg (this volume) reports in greater detail, New York New Visions (NYNV), a group representing "an unprecedented coalition of 21 architecture, planning, and design organizations committed to honoring the victims of the September 11 tragedy by rebuilding a vital New York," issued the first blueprint for rebuilding the site in January 2002. The result of a three-month voluntary collaboration of 350 professionals and civic leaders, *Principles for the Rebuilding of Lower Manhattan* (2002a, 5) set out "to inform the large-scale urban, economic and real estate decisions to be made in the coming months." The professional design community assumed that the governor had given the LMDC the authority to manage the rebuilding process; through this and subsequent reports and actions, NYNV sought to influence the planning taking place in the LMDC's offices.[6]

The report was ambitious, substantive, and wise in the ways of city building. It set the task of rebuilding the site within the broader context of regional growth, transportation, and planning issues, reflecting an early and well-debated decision by NYNV professionals to focus on general principles, not site design.[7] While acknowledging that "these principles and recommendations do not replace the broader public discourse about the future of our city that must and will take place among policy and decision makers," the NYNV report recommended an open memorial process, a flexible, mixed-use future for lower Manhattan, a more interconnected downtown, renewing lower Manhattan's relation to the region, design excellence and sustainability, an effective and inclusive planning process, and immediate action as a foundation for decision-making. In short order, the LMDC embraced these goals. After a public outreach campaign involving the creation of nine advisory councils for various stakeholders, the LMDC issued its first planning statement, *Principles and Preliminary Blueprint for the Future of Lower Manhattan* (2002a), in April 2002.[8] The NYNV leadership noted that it "closely parallels and echoes" the NYNV *Principles* document (Choa 2002).

The LMDC's blueprint set forth fourteen broad but specific public goals: reserving an area of the WTC site for one or more permanent memorials; facilitating the immediate revitalization of lower Manhattan to ensure its viability; restoring a portion of the street grid to reintegrate the site into downtown; eliminating West Street as a barrier for Battery Park City; better integrating mass transit services with the rest of the city and region; creating a distinctive transit gateway to lower Manhattan; creating facilities to accommodate the anticipated surge in charter and tour buses; expanding the residential population; promoting retail opportunities to serve the residential community; providing new cultural and civic institutions; creating more parks and open space; using sustainable design and "green building" technologies; preserving outstanding historic structures; and diversifying the area's economy beyond financial services. The LMDC addressed the revival of lower Manhattan, not just rebuilding the WTC site. "These plans represent the best possible consensus we can find at the moment," said Alexander Garvin, the corporation's vice president for planning, design, and development. "Now we need to put meat on these bones" (Wyatt 2002b). The metaphor might have been a bit inappropriate, but his optimism was critical for the complicated task ahead. After public hearings and outreach, a revised blueprint was issued in June.

The principles seemed "benign," the architectural critic Paul Goldberger (2002) wrote in his review of how the future of Ground Zero was being resolved:

> But is it possible to create an appropriate memorial and also increase the area's strength as a financial center? Is improving the neighborhood going to get in the way of developing lower Manhattan as a tourist and cultural magnet? And if you create a "comprehensive, coherent plan for transit access to lower Manhattan"—in other words, a new station for the mess of disconnected subway and other transit lines downtown—will it cost so much that it will put other transit plans, like the Second Avenue subway, at risk?

The LMDC was ambiguous about how it would reconcile competing priorities. It would push simultaneously for the "preservation of the site as a place of remembrance and memorial" and for new development that would "enhance and revive Lower Manhattan as a center of new financial, cultural, and community activity" (LMDC 2004a, S6–7). These goals would also have to take a backseat to the Port Authority's non-negotiable demand to replace the ten-million-plus square feet of office space that generated $120 million annual ground-lease payments stemming from the ninety-nine-year lease encumbering the site to Silverstein (for the two towers) and Westfield America (for the retail mall). Absent buying out these claims, PA officials intended to honor the lease, which gave Silverstein and Westfield the right as well as obligation to rebuild exactly what was in place prior to the attack. As Fainstein (this volume) outlines, the lease payments were essential to supporting the PA capital program and enabling it to meet its paramount commitment to its bondholders.

The sixteen-acre site is large by New York standards, equal to all of Rockefeller Center or the entire Grand Central Terminal district. Still, it was not large enough to accommodate all the ambitions for Ground Zero voiced by different interests. There would not be much room to maneuver or to explore notions of city building that might not address the PA's financial concerns. This created the constant refrain in public discourse that planners were loading the site with densely packed commercial towers that threatened to crowd out a meaningful memorial space. In time, the principal decisionmakers came to realize that the only way out of this dilemma was to expand the site beyond Ground Zero.

The first report that "rebuilding may expand beyond the site" appeared in June 2002, before any visual plans had been presented to the public. The LMDC's planners, the *New York Times* reported, "had begun studying the use of up to 16 adjacent blocks to accommodate some of the 10 million square feet of office space and 450,000 square feet of retail space that had been at the center" (Wyatt 2002c). Speaking to the New York Building Congress, LMDC president Louis R. Tomson, a longtime Pataki associate, pointed out that additional land could be needed because a memorial might take up half the site while new office towers would probably be no taller than 60 stories (in contrast to the original 110-story towers). With an expanded site, "we can plan to accommodate the needs of the Port Authority, the wishes of the community and the mayor, the memorial, cultural institutions, residences and retail space" (Haberman 2002b, 2002c). Since nearly all adjacent property was privately owned, the implication was that the LMDC would have to exercise eminent domain. Other possibilities included swapping land with the city or transferring development rights off the site.

Whatever their merits, each option promised to trigger complicated negotiations between the city, the state, and the Port Authority. For city officials, expanding the site would give them new leverage over the LMDC and PA. With the Republicans in control of the governor's mansion and city hall, political power was more closely aligned than usual, but the city controlled only streets and sidewalks, and the Port Authority, the site owner, was exempt from city regulations. The city's hamstrung position after 9/11 recalled the Port Authority's aggressive push in first developing the WTC in the 1960s (Glanz and Lipton 2003, 145–54). By a legal fluke, the city retained title to approximately two and a half acres of former streets within the sixteen-acre superblock. This nearly forgotten detail was the city's only legal point of leverage in the matter. It became relevant when the LMDC's *Amended General Project Plan* (2003a) released in September 2003, proposed to expand the site to include two city blocks south of the WTC site (see figure 2.1). This action brought the severely damaged Deutsche Bank property at 130 Liberty Street into the project area as the site of a fifth office tower.[9] That the city made a point of this issue reflected its lack of influence. "I don't want to overemphasize the need to stake a claim to property rights. That's not what we're trying to do,"

FIGURE 2.1   WORLD TRADE CENTER MEMORIAL AND REDEVELOPMENT PLAN: PROPOSED SITE PLAN AS OF DECEMBER, 2002 (EXHIBIT A)

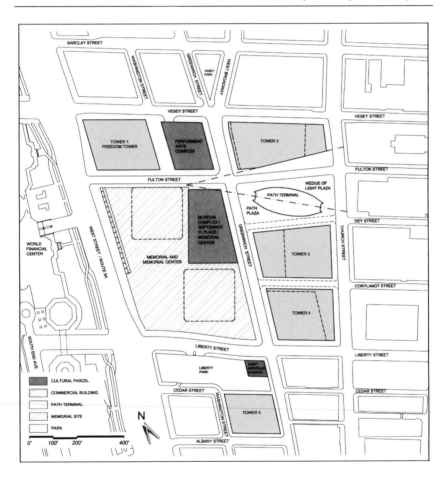

Source: Lower Manhattan Development Corporation. Reprinted with permission.

remarked deputy mayor Daniel E. Doctoroff. "We're merely saying that's one of the issues that needs to be resolved" (Dunlap 2004d).[10]

Although Port Authority executive director Joseph J. Seymour, a former chairman of the New York Power Authority, had been a longtime loyal aide and friend of Governor Pataki, the PA is a bistate agency. As such, its decisions had to be approved by the governors of both New York and New Jersey. Since the governor of New Jersey could in theory veto anything proposed for the site, he ironically had more power over it than the mayor of New York, a fact that would make any mayor unhappy. After Governor Pataki rejected in June 2003 the city's proposal to swap the land under Kennedy and LaGuardia Airports to the PA in exchange for the WTC site, the mayor said:

> In the end, I think it should be up to the City of New York. It is part of our city. The [PA] was there for the WTC, but now tragically, it is no longer there.... While I understand New Jersey has an interest in what goes on in the region, I don't think the governor of New Jersey should have a big say, or the New Jersey Legislature, in what developed there.

Bloomberg believed the city should control its own destiny (Lombardi and Haberman 2003; Seifman 2003; Neuman 2003).

The Port Authority's legal and financial constraints posed an obvious problem for the LMDC. Like the city, the LMDC had no authority over the PA, a state of affairs that was bound to create tensions with it. The LMDC's key representatives, first Alex Garvin and then Roland Betts, did not challenge the PA's commercial program for the site:

> "It's the Port's site from an ownership standpoint and what's the point of developing a whole plan and getting into a pissing contest with the Port because they don't like it?" Betts said. Both he and Garvin started out believing that if the Port Authority had the right to determine the program for the site—that is, what functions would occupy the land and how much space would be devoted to each—while the LMDC would have the right to figure out what the whole thing would look like. (Goldberger 2004b, 87)

Betts recalled continuous fighting over the issue of how much commercial space would be built on the site. A working group met regularly to review many different plans that covered the walls in a PA conference room in lower Manhattan. The room was large because all the entities wanted to bring their own architects, lawyers, and staff. At the high count, the number of attendees reached seventy. The large size of the meetings made them a circus, Betts said. Reporters were supposed to be excluded, but sometimes they sneaked in, disguised in the crowd. To manage the process and plug the press leaks, Betts set up a smaller steering group that included John C. Whitehead, LMDC chairman; Louis R. Tomson, LMDC president; PA commissioners Charles Kushner and Anthony J. Sartor; PA executive director Joseph J. Seymour; Diana Taylor, deputy secretary to Governor Pataki; and Daniel E. Doctoroff, New York City deputy mayor for economic development and rebuilding.

Although it may have seemed obvious to this group that they needed to reduce the square footage built on the site, figuring out how to find money to make the Port Authority whole for the rent lost was not so obvious. The Port Authority kept asking where the money would come from and why it should have "to take a haircut." According to Betts, the option of expanding the site was always on the table but not yet part of the solution. He could recall Doctoroff making the only serious bid to buy out Silverstein through the land swap, but that negotiation fell apart after many rounds. In time, Betts wore down the PA and brought it into an agreement about the square footage; in time, Seymour recognized that the issue would not go away, that the site was too cluttered, and that the market might not support the planned volume of commercial space. To get to this point, however, Betts noted, Seymour had to go against his whole board—his commissioners saw the rebuilding as just another real estate deal. A man on a mission and not one to let a hard-won concession slip away, Betts quickly grabbed a scrap of paper when the moment arrived, scrawled an outline of the terms reducing the square footage on the site, and had everyone in the room sign it. He still has the paper (Betts 2004).

THE GOVERNOR'S POLITICS

Because the early planning process coincided with the 2002 gubernatorial election, even seemingly technical site issues became high-profile political decisions. Seeking a third term, Governor Pataki faced two Democratic hopefuls: former secretary of the Department of Housing and Urban Development (HUD) Andrew Cuomo and New York State's comptroller, H. Carl McCall. Often reticent on thorny political issues in normal times, Pataki seemed unusually quiet about what should happen at Ground Zero, how much government should intervene, and how fast the process should go. Since his loyal aides Seymour and Tomson held the key positions at the Port Authority and the LMDC, Pataki controlled the downtown site, yet the press kept reporting dissension among his staff over whether the governor should support a slow and deliberate pace or push for immediate action (Rice 2002; Nagourney 2002; Haberman 2002a; Bagli 2002a).

The influential *Times* editorial page regularly criticized the project's snail-like pace throughout 2002. In early April, it found that the LMDC seemed "to be taking its time in devising a master plan. . . . If this year passes without concrete public proposals, critics may begin to ask whether Governor Pataki, who powerfully influences the redevelopment process, was delaying hard choices until after the November election."

A couple of weeks after the LMDC and PA had issued the first request for proposals (RFP) for design services, the *Times* credited Pataki for sending a message to the various governing boards that "it is time to set up a workable process for reimagining and rebuilding downtown." After the unveiling of six "dismal" plans, though, it told the governor that "the buck stops at his desk, that he needs to listen. . . . That means he must take the lead in negotiating with companies that hold leases to the World Trade Center, while also pushing planners for more inspired visions of how to use the space." The *Times* found his performance dismal: so far, there had been "very little to indicate that the governor is exercising the kind of leadership that adds luster to the Pataki name." When Pataki told the Port Authority to look beyond the site to build the ten million square feet of office space, *Times* editors continued their goading:

> Governor Pataki's recent remarks are a sign that he understands how central the rebuilding of Lower Manhattan will be to his own political legacy. Now he needs to follow through with action, to keep demonstrating that his core concern is coming up with the best possible plan, not simply keeping the issue on hold until after this fall election.

After Pataki was reelected, the *Times* opined that rebuilding had been "deadened by the benign neglect provided by election-year politics"; now the governor needed to "prove he could get things going for the people and businesses of Lower Manhattan" (*New York Times* 2002a, 2002b, 2002d, 2002f, 2002g). Although the *Times* was the most insistent voice calling for more assertive leadership, the business weekly *Crain's* also editorialized after the election that "unless Pataki displays the leadership he had avoided, little progress would be made. He needs to make it clear that he will make the final decisions, or he should cede control of the World Trade Center site to the city" (*Crain's* 2002).

The governor had made only one decision about the WTC site before his reelection. To an audience of six hundred attending a memorial ceremony at the Jacob K. Javits Convention Center, he unexpectedly announced that "we will never build where the towers stood. They will always be a lasting memorial for those that we lost" (Santos 2002). By sealing an informal decision among rebuilding officials that the memorial would be placed on the southwest quadrant where the twin towers had stood (see figure 2.1), Pataki's "footprints statement" preempted design plans soon to be unveiled. This was an instance in which rebuilding officials tipped their hand that a decision, while subject to change, had been made but not made (Wyatt 2002b, 2002d).

Meanwhile, downtown business interests had also grown impatient with the governor's lack of leadership. Worried that political paralysis was jeopardizing downtown's prospects for recovery, the CEOs of three of downtown's biggest commercial tenants, American Express, Merrill Lynch, and the Bank of New York, threw down the gauntlet. In a strongly worded confidential memo addressed to Henry Kravis and Jerry Speyer, influential co-chairs of the Partnership for New York City, they called for clear government leadership and more rapid decisionmaking. They noted that debris removal around the WTC site had made lower Manhattan a very difficult place to work. "If redevelopment tracks the kind of three-decade timetable that eventually produced the New Times Square," they wrote, corporate departures were likely. "A 20- or 30-year schedule is unacceptable," they wrote. "It is time for a clear definition of accountability and responsibility for Ground Zero and the rest of downtown" (Cuozzo 2003a, 2003b). Several of their recommendations found their way into a well-publicized speech the governor made three weeks later, on April 24, 2003, to downtown business leaders at a luncheon of the Association for a Better New York (ABNY). In this talk, Pataki laid out an ambitious plan and comprehensive timetable for the revitalization of lower Manhattan.

The governor's response to this wake-up call detailed something for every constituency. For business interests focused on transportation, he suggested initiatives for the subway, PATH, and ferry service, and a study of how to provide new rail access from Long Island and JFK Airport. For downtown residents, he proposed a new high school, streetscape amenities on Broadway, and community parks throughout lower Manhattan; for Battery Park City residents, he offered pedestrian bridges and improvements to West Street to link that neighborhood with the rest of lower Manhattan. For Wall Street, he suggested security improvements for the New York Stock Exchange; and for the citywide civic groups, he proposed that a start be made on parts of Libeskind's master plan, including the 1,776-foot-tall "Freedom Tower." Finally, for the 9/11 families and the world at large, he proposed a memorial design. Governor Pataki slated sixteen initiatives for completion in 2003 and 2004, with another six in the pipeline for 2005, another for the year after, and still another five by 2009. He pledged $50 million for short-term capital projects and spoke of multiple billions in long-term investments. This "aggressive timetable" became Pataki's true rebuilding agenda (Pataki 2003). He reiterated its pledges and gave a progress report in similar speeches before the ABNY later that fall (see his press release of October 30, 2003) and on May 5, 2004.

Having secured reelection, Pataki was less concerned about angering constituencies vital to his campaign by taking forceful positions; moreover, completing this agenda provided plentiful opportunities for ribbon-cuttings, press conferences, photo ops, and other forms of credit-taking. Although the governor may not have had a vision for rebuilding, he was keenly attentive to how his actions could bolster his political legacy. With his aggressive timetable, he tied that legacy to rebuilding Ground Zero, and Ground Zero in turn became a potent platform for his future political ambitions.

The governor's ambitions became more apparent when he announced that the groundbreaking for the Freedom Tower would take place July 4, 2004. A remark by Larry Silverstein to reporters and editors of the *Daily News* the previous year had pegged that event to coincide with the GOP convention in Manhattan at the end of the summer, near the third anniversary of the terrorist attacks. The governor's office denied this report, which Silverstein's spokesman immediately disavowed, but the rumor persisted in the press (Haberman and Gittich 2003; Bagli 2003d; Cockfield 2004a). Though the new date skirted the charge of rank opportunism, critics quickly pointed out that the "groundbreaking" had more to do with Pataki's ambitions than any business considerations. The emblematic cornerstone ceremony took place before anyone knew how high the tower would actually rise in relation to its symbolic 1,776 feet, what the building would look like, how much it would cost, who would finance it, and what tenants might be willing to lease a significant amount of its 2.6 million square feet of space.

As long as determined optimism about rebuilding prevailed, these details were not likely to matter much. Unattached to a permanent in-place foundation, the cornerstone was ready to be moved wherever a fully designed building went into construction. The real question lurking behind the ceremony was the same one that prevailed in the earliest days of the master plan process: what would really be built? Reporting on the ceremony, veteran *Times* reporter David W. Dunlap (2004f) succinctly captured the spirit of this event: "Guessing the future of long-term megaprojects is a fool's game. Their momentum depends on an alignment of political will, popular support, market demand and economic conditions that shift constantly, beyond the ability of anyone to control or predict."

INSTITUTIONAL STRUGGLES

According to Roland Betts, Governor Pataki created the LMDC a month before the city's mayoral election to minimize the influence of the Democratic candidate, Mark Green, who seemed to have a chance of winning the close race (Betts 2004). With term limits preventing Republican mayor Rudolph W. Giuliani from standing for reelection, Republicans could ensure their political control over the WTC by declining to give the city equal representation on the LMDC and giving the state a majority of its eleven board seats. (As Moss [this volume] relates, the governor gave the city additional seats after Republican Michael Bloomberg won office; the city and the state now have equal representation on a sixteen-member board.) The LMDC's trusted and respected lawyer, Ira M. Millstein, told the board that its mandate, at least on paper, was total control over the WTC site. But given that the Port Authority owned the site, Betts asked himself how the LMDC could actually exercise this control (Betts 2004).

The struggle over who would control site decisions came into public view in early April 2002, when the LMDC, on its own, put out a request for proposals for urban planning consulting services for the site and surrounding areas. The LMDC quickly pulled the RFP after angered Port Authority officials vehemently objected that they had not been asked for advice. Shortly afterwards, they issued a nearly identical joint RFP, but with the Port Authority listed as the lead agency on the cover page. Said PA chairman Jack Sinagra, "We can't lose sight of the fact that it's the Port Authority's property and the Port Authority's responsibility for what is eventually recreated on the site" (Lentz 2002; McGeveran 2002a). The Port Authority funded the $3 million comprehensive consulting contract, though the LMDC ultimately paid part of it.

The Port Authority and the LMDC announced at the same time that they had negotiated a memorandum of understanding spelling out their respective roles in the rebuilding process. "They [LMDC] are managing the public input, the citizen-participation process. We will be managing the development of the plan on the site and the plan on the periphery," said PA executive director Seymour (Neuman 2002b). The next day LMDC chairman John C. Whitehead, who had a reputation for being independent, stated that "both boards" would approve the plans for the WTC site. "I think [PA chairman Jack Sinagra] would agree that we must agree, too, with the final plan" (Neuman and Haberman 2002). The memorandum provided that the LMDC would control the memorial design process and reportedly contained concessions from the Port Authority releasing some land for a memorial, allowing cultural facilities as well as commercial buildings on the site, and considering reopening the street grid, all of which might reduce the land available for the original program of ten million square feet of office space.

Five weeks later the agencies jointly selected Beyer Blinder Belle Architects & Planners (BBB), in association with Parsons Brinckerhoff, to provide consulting services to the agencies; the full team included eleven other specialty and engineering firms.[11] Both New York–based firms had strong credentials for creating an urban design and planning study for the WTC site. Phase 1, scheduled to be completed in July 2002, promised up to six concepts for land use on the site; phase 2 was "to further develop and define these options based on the public input received"; and phase 3 would lead to a "preferred land-use and transportation plan." The work never got beyond phase 1, after a highly publicized meeting of some 4,500 people in July 2002 left no doubt that they rejected all six plans presented.

The Civic Alliance to Rebuild Downtown New York, a coalition of more than eighty-five civic, business, environmental, community, university, and labor groups convened by the Regional Plan Association (RPA), organized this "Listening to the City" event in cooperation with the LMDC and the Port Authority. These eighty-five groups, along with private foundations and corporate donors, provided $2 million for the event, which was designed to develop consensus strategies for redeveloping lower Manhattan. The meeting used a technological format developed by America Speaks, a nonprofit organization specializing in facilitating consensus-building events, to project the alternative plans and gauge face-to-face responses to them. As Arielle Goldberg details in her chapter, this event altered the trajectory of the debate and was hailed by some as setting a new standard for public participation. Hundreds of round tables seating ten were placed in the cavernous Javits Center exhibition space. In the center of that vast field of tables was a raised stage for the proceedings. No one attending the meeting on that blistering hot summer Saturday would forget the overwhelmingly negative comments that participants offered about the six plans, which were variously described in the press as "strikingly similar," "dismal," "disappointing," "uninspiring," "mediocre," "no soul," "lacking vision," and "not broad enough, bold enough, or big enough." Nor would participants forget the orderly but intense group dynamic that produced the clear consensus that the six plans were simply inadequate.

The excessive amount of office space was a chief complaint. New Yorkers are used to density, but however configured, a dense cluster of office towers seemed an inappropriate setting for remembering those who tragically perished on September 11. Participants recommended making every effort to cancel the Silverstein lease so that the Port Authority's commercial requirements would not govern planning decisions. "Listening to the City" attendees put forth rebuilding proposals that were more clearly articulated, if not completely different, from those in the LMDC's revised blueprint. They called for a suitable memorial as the centerpiece, restoring lower Manhattan's skyline, eliminating West Street as a barrier to the waterfront, restoring the street grid, emphasizing street-level activity, reducing the amount of office space on the site, and providing memorable architecture (Civic Alliance 2002).

The press savaged the alternatives in ways no elected official could ignore. In "The Downtown We Don't Want," the *Times* editorial page called the plans "dreary, laden proposals that fall far short of what New York City—and the world—expect to see rise at ground zero." The editorial put the onus squarely on the requirement that the site "be packed with a full 11 million square feet of office space, 600,000 square feet of retail space and another 600,000 square feet for a hotel." It also noted that "some of the overcrowded designs may be posturing, with the aim of resolving complicated legal disputes involving" the leaseholders of the complex. And the *Times* put officials on notice that they would be held accountable for something visionary: "What these pro-posals demonstrate most conclusively is that nothing memorable can be done in Lower Manhattan if the Port Authority insists on reclaiming every inch of commercial space that it controlled before Sept. 11" (*New York Times* 2002c). A couple of days later the *Times* made a more direct call to hold Governor George Pataki accountable in "Talk to the Man in Charge" (*New York Times* 2002d).

Editors at the *Daily News* penned a sharper critique of the Port Authority, which they said was "flawed by design." "The LMDC, though filled with tal-ented people, had been handcuffed by its boss, the Port Authority. It had to follow orders.... As the design concepts prove, the PA still places its own needs first.... It is accountable to no one. And that's the real problem." Over the next ten days, the *Daily News* followed up with two more editorials, upping its criticism of the Port Authority's "severe limitation on the land use," which made "a visionary plan impossible." The problem was structural: "This insulated agency is simply too self-centered, unimaginative and bureaucratic to handle such a sensitive project" (*New York Daily News* 2002a, 2002b, 2002c, 2002d).

Newsday told its readers: "None of the WTC Proposals Is Good Enough." Its editors similarly laid the blame squarely on the broad shoulders of the Port Authority and the requirement for putting the leaseholders first. They argued several positions: "forget about legalisms," "slow down," "creativity is key," and "hold Pataki responsible" (*Newsday* 2002). Among the city's dailies, only the *Post* seemed to like what had been produced: remarkably, considering the near universal sentiment otherwise, its editors said, "So far, so good" (*New York Post* 2002).

The LMDC and the Port Authority had both upheld a public rhetoric of working collaboratively, but each agency set an independent course after this public relations disaster. Silverstein and the owner of the World Financial Center in Battery Park City, Brookfield Properties, had their own architects and planners working on rebuilding. All four were preparing a master plan for the site, and planning exercise meant something different to each owner.

PARALLEL PLANNING

Striving for Legitimacy

After bungling phase 1, the LMDC obviously needed to get it right the second time. Betts believed that lack of specific enabling legislation made the LMDC's ad hoc planning process susceptible to legal challenge, but he considered it critically important to move the process forward. To "organize" would have taken a year of precious time. Called the "most visionary member of the LMDC board" by the architectural critic Paul Goldberger (2004b, 111), Betts took charge of the site-planning committee formed shortly after the hiring of Beyer Blinder Belle. This committee was "comfortable enough, but not very enthusiastic" about the design 1 schemes, Betts recalled. After "Listening to the City," it took to heart the lessons that the historic street grid should be reinserted, a transit hub created, a first-rate memorial built, West Street broadened and landscaped, and the skyline of lower Manhattan remade with an iconic tower (Betts 2004).

Although design 1 was an embarrassment, LMDC was called to task for failing to articulate clear priorities and manage the consensus-building process. News stories reported that "no one's home over there" and that the memorial design process was moving too slowly while the overall site planning was moving too quickly for so momentous a decision. Other reports charged that LMDC officials were meeting with private interests behind closed doors while keeping their own board in the dark over the planning process and the selection of a design firm. One reporter charged that the agency's secret meetings contravened New York State's open-meeting law (Haberman and Neuman 2002a; Neuman 2002a, 2002b, 2002c, 2002d; Wyatt 2002e). One insider who asked to remain anonymous put it this way: "Everyone thinks they are missing something going on in another room, even the governor."

The decision to make a master plan for the entire site *before* designing the memorial struck many citizens and professionals alike as proceeding in reverse gear. Shouldn't the memorial design come first and constrain the master plan? Starting with a master plan focused decisionmaking on how much territory would be reserved for a memorial, whereas the critical planning question might logically have been how best to integrate an appropriate memorial design into the redevelopment of the site and the fabric of lower Manhattan. The LMDC's strategic decision to proceed first with a master plan put it on the defensive when its handpicked memorial jury selected Michael Arad and Peter Walker's "Reflecting Absence," an unapologetic and dramatic violation of Daniel Libeskind's "Memory Foundations" master plan. In short, the LMDC appeared opportunistic, uncoordinated, and confused. Even its president, Louis Tomson, acknowledged in a January 2003 breakfast speech at New York University Law School that "we've screwed up lots of times along the way." One of the biggest mistakes, Tomson said, was releasing the first set of rebuilding plans. "We did not convey to the public what we were trying to do with the plans we released in July" (Rogers 2003).

To recover momentum, Betts decided to throw out the BBB plans and start all over. The "mistake" in the first round, he said, was to present the plans as massing models showing a layout without defining what the buildings would look like, when the public "thinks you're designing a building." Betts felt that the BBB architects had not been invested in their plans; he now wanted to involve the world's best architects in the process. With support from his committee, which included the architect Billie Tsien, LMDC vice president Alex Garvin, who would manage the process, was also keen on the idea. To sell this course of action to the Port Authority and the city, LMDC executive director Tomson, who had a good relationship with Seymour, would work the Port Authority, while Betts, who had a long and close relationship with Doctoroff, would work the city. They would mention that the design 1 website had received 50 million hits, that the eyes of the world were watching what they were doing, that such a big project demanded world-class talent, and that they had to do it right. Before they could launch their campaign, however, someone leaked their plans to the *Times*; as Betts recalled later, the task then became "very difficult" (Betts 2004).

Garvin understood the strategic value of playing "the architectural card" to make the LMDC, "at least for a few months at the end of 2002, into the most conspicuous architectural patron in the world," as Paul Goldberger (2003a) explained in his well-informed account of the inside maneuvering. "It was a shrewd decision, because it moved the planning process to an area that the Port Authority had traditionally shown little interest in." Within the month the LMDC had launched a worldwide "Innovative Design Study" (design 2) with a request for qualifications (RFQ) to select as many as five architecture and planning firms to offer new ideas for the WTC site. The LMDC emphasized the word "innovative" to signal how different this process (and presumably the product) would be.

Design 2 ran from August 2002 to February 2003, ending in the selection of Studio Daniel Libeskind's master plan for the site. As with design 1, this process was fraught with controversy and reflected an ongoing struggle between the Port Authority and the LMDC. It left the conflicts between the site's competing claims unresolved. During this time the governor was getting more comfortable with doing something great, Betts recalled, but Pataki did not weigh in until the final selection process. Design 2 implicitly challenged the designers to resolve competing claims—in effect, to accomplish the political task that politicians were reluctant to do.

Design 2 unveiled nine design schemes in December 2002, yielding praise for the LMDC (if not for the actual designs) for calling for a big vision and a standard of world-class design.[12] Yet the bold ideas and visual clues of a new future for the WTC site could not paper over the continuing confusion among civic groups, design professionals, and the public about how these critical decisions would be made. Nor did they mute the persistent call for less commercial space. As they redrafted their message to the public and the design participants, the LMDC and PA made two telling revisions.

The first revision seemed to suggest some softening of the Port Authority's position on commercial space. A few weeks after the seven teams were chosen from a field of 407, the LMDC announced a revision of the office space component from 10 million square feet to 6.5 million. (This was the signed scrap-paper agreement Betts had secured from the four principal entities.) The Port Authority had not changed its position ("You can't assume the Port Authority is going to give up its real estate interests," a PA source was quoted as saying), but rather suggested that some of the space would be accommodated outside the WTC site. Since the city and the Port Authority were still at loggerheads about where this might occur, "it was left purposely amorphous" (Wyatt 2002g). The new revision also allowed for as much as 2 million additional square feet each of hotel and retail space. These revisions reflected the fluidity of the ongoing negotiations between the city and the Port Authority over "a raft of issues," including the airport-WTC land swap put on the table by Doc-toroff ten weeks earlier (Neuman 2002e).

Second, despite what the RFQ stated (in boldface: "This is NOT a design competition and will not result in the selection of a final plan"), the Innovative Design Study had morphed into a design competition among world-class architects that would produce one winner. "Once the designs began to emerge," Goldberger (2003a) wrote, Garvin "decided to give up on his notion of treating the architects' work like a smorgasbord, picking and choosing what was best." As Betts said, "It will be one central idea. Whatever plan survives is going to be subject to modifications, but it's far less likely that two plans would be combined. It's like combining two different artists whose style is completely different" (Thrush 2003). Given the high-profile talent brought to bear on the task and the worldwide attention, it could hardly have been different. Port Authority officials, however, were reportedly holding out for the possibility of combining aspects of several designs (Wyatt 2003f).

The LMDC was not in a good position to manage this process. It had planning expertise, but no design capability. To fill this gap, LMDC met regularly with New York New Visions members to provide a "kitchen cabinet of sorts" for Garvin, who asked them for advice on how to run a competition, input on the criteria to include in the Innovative Design Study RFQ, and a list of architects and planners to review the RFQ responses. Garvin initially asked NYNV to run the competition, but the group said no. Marcie Kesner, an experienced planner who had worked in the Queens borough president's office and who co-chaired the group's executive committee, firmly believed that the LMDC should run the process. She was not sure why NYNV was being asked to manage it. Like other "on-call advisers," she was concerned that the LMDC might just want them to provide cover. The extent to which Garvin relied on the group was "flattering," but always caused NYNV committee members to ask, "What is our role?"

The group kept up a near-vigil on the LMDC's actions. It regularly voiced distress about the corporation's lack of coordination, kept a sharp eye on procedural details, and pushed for openness and full participation in the planning exercise. It was constantly concerned about the integrity of the planning process and put forth a formal design critique at each stage on the way to a final master plan. After the Libeskind selection, NYNV saw itself as protecting the "immutable" planning principles put forth in its *Principles for Rebuilding Lower Manhattan*, as these were reflected in the selected master plan. The group believed its role was to keep the pressure on the LMDC; "retiring" from the field would send the wrong message to decisionmakers. Ironically, NYNV was playing the role of the Department of City Planning (DCP); just why this was so remained the unspoken open question among planning professionals.[13] NYNV's advice offered the LMDC a needed source of legitimacy. That ability to have input in turn held great meaning for those who took part (New York New Visions 2002b, 2002c, 2003a; see also minutes of the NYNV Steering Committee: 5/1/02, 11/22/02, Executive Committee: 5/22/02, 10/16/02, 10/30/02, 11/13/02, 3/12/03, 5/28/03, 6/25/03,3/24/04,5/12/04,and Coalition: 8/27/02, 11/6/02).

Restoring the Revenue Stream

As described by Susan Fainstein (this volume), the Port Authority took on the process of planning for Ground Zero wounded and shaken by the losses it suffered on 9/11, including its executive director, seventy-four other employees, and its signature headquarters. Yet its distinctive and insular institutional culture buffered the PA from some of these wounds. Used to operating without legislative oversight, the engineering-dominated authority was not accustomed to sharing its institutional turf. It had earned a reputation as a strong-willed institution over decades of activity that reshaped the landscape of the New York–New Jersey region. Although its halo of power had dimmed since the rule of its autocratic first director, Austin Tobin, his larger-than-life legacy could not be ignored.

When the Port Authority developed the WTC in the 1960s, this move into the realm of commercial real estate signaled aggressive risk-taking, an unusual position for a public transportation agency. It took two attempts at privatization (Governor Hugh L. Carey initiated the first review of a potential sale in 1980, and Governor Pataki initiated the second in 1997) before the Port Authority succeeded in capturing the $3.2 billion value of this gamble in bricks-and-mortar by selling a ninety-nine-year leasehold to Silverstein and his investors. In exchange, the PA relinquished day-to-day control over the twin towers and retail mall, while the land parcel remained a part of its $15.6 billion portfolio.

Much as the $120 million in annual WTC lease revenues (4 percent of the authority's 2001 total revenue intake of $2.7 billion) motivated the PA to re-build on the original commercial scale, the Port Authority had other compel-ling aspirations that would influence its actions. Fueled by criticism that the big real estate projects had distracted it from its core mission of easing the region's transportation bottlenecks, the PA made a strategic policy shift back to transportation-based projects in 1995. For regional transportation groups and downtown business interests, the PA faced two pieces of unfinished busi-ness that were central to the future of lower Manhattan: addressing its long-standing failure to build a rail-freight tunnel between New York and New Jersey and providing a commuter-rail link to the suburbs of Long Island.

After 9/11, "straitened times" for the PA budget, increased security costs, and related capital improvements caused the agency to scale back its recently approved five-year capital program. Port Authority officials saw demands to place open spaces and cultural facilities alongside the memorial space as a threat to the revenue-producing potential of the site. "However that property is ultimately planned, the important thing from the PA's point of view is that we address the need to have a comparable revenue stream," one commissioner said (McGeveran 2002a). By rebuilding the WTC site, the Port Authority also hoped to evoke its institutional legacy in a way that would give meaning to its emotional losses and enhance its diminished reputation. "It was going to be a great opportunity for the Port Authority to reestablish itself as a great and majestic builder," said Christopher Ward, the organization's former chief of strategic planning. "It was what I thought we would do for the next ten years" (Machalaba 2002).

Port Authority officials appeared indecisive during the earliest stage of plan-ning, but the public debacle over the BBB designs and the LMDC's architec-tural competition triggered the PA into an even more intense struggle for con-trol over site decisions. It felt that determining the configuration of the memorial, the commercial space, and the cultural facilities was equivalent to programming the financial equation. If the LMDC maintained the lion's share of responsibility for planning the sixteen-acre site, the LMDC would be deter-mining how much revenue the Port Authority would get. PA executives were tellingly absent when the LMDC launched the Innovative Design Study. LMDC's Lou Tomson remarked that the two agencies "have different points of view on how to proceed" (Wyatt 2002f). Within the month, just days before the LMDC was set to announce the seven new design teams, the PA hired Ehrenkrantz Eckstut & Kuhn (EEK) to do in-house transportation planning and design coordination. This further confused observers about how key decisions would be made and who would really lead the effort (Hetter and Janison 2002).

In this period, a dark cloud hung over both the current and long-term pros-pects of the real estate market in lower Manhattan. The attack had destroyed 12.5 million square feet of office space and damaged an additional 13.8 million

square feet, taking out nearly one-quarter of the downtown office inventory—
and even more, 44 percent, of its recently constructed class A space. (The total
represented only 6.5 percent of the Manhattan inventory and even less for
the region.) It was valuable space in Manhattan's dueling office hierarchy and
important to its ongoing battle to retain office jobs that were otherwise being
lost to New Jersey waterfront cities (Jersey City, Hoboken, and Newark) and
the northern suburbs of New York (White Plains, New York, and Stamford,
Connecticut). In the short term, lower Manhattan managed to retain 49 percent of the displaced office tenancy, yet the landscape of future demand grew
weaker with each month of planning confusion and political indecisiveness.

Downtown real estate executives thought the viability of downtown as an
employment center was at risk. Hugh Kelly (2002a, 69), a well-known real
estate economist with a deep understanding of the city's office market, concluded that it would be "difficult to envision employers committing to a district where more than 30 percent of its most modern space had been destroyed
and not replaced." He cautioned that "the absence of an adequate office stock
to accommodate job growth will retard or even reverse downtown's resurgence
as a residential community, along with development of the attractive recreational and entertainment amenities that will flow from such a mixed live/
work environment." Just how much new space would be deemed "adequate,"
however, was less clear. Did 10 million square feet need to be replaced, or
would a lesser though still critical mass of 5 to 7 million square feet be enough?
Building 10 million square feet of new space when 17 million square feet already stood empty downtown (a vacancy rate of around 19 percent) made
many business executives, especially landlords, extremely nervous.

The city's three downtown business groups—the Alliance for Downtown,
the Association for a Better New York, and the Partnership for New York
City—and the Real Estate Board of New York were united behind the firm
belief that transportation improvements were their highest priority. Without
improved access to the region, downtown business leaders thought the WTC
site would be unmarketable (Alliance for Downtown 2002, 2003; Partnership
for New York City 2003). They wanted the two regional transportation agencies—the Port Authority and the Metropolitan Transportation Authority
(MTA)—to move their agenda. Having long time horizons and steady sources
of funds, these agencies have a far different institutional profile than the
LMDC. Because they are engineering bureaucracies focused on serving current
customers, they are not development-oriented (Weisbrod 2002). But to achieve
its goals as a landowner, the Port Authority would have to promote the transportation agenda in a big way.

The Port Authority initially focused on rebuilding the towers and associated
infrastructure demands. Its institutional authority over infrastructure was unchallenged. Indeed, the May 2002 memorandum of understanding with the

LMDC gave the PA full responsibility for everything but managing the memorial design process and organizing public input, which, in turn, were the unchallenged mandate of the LMDC. Few observers could be convinced that the efforts of the two agencies would converge in joint decisionmaking at some fuzzy point in the future, however, and signs of what was happening behind closed doors did nothing to diminish their skepticism.

To the Port Authority's way of thinking, the LMDC would supply the "vision" thing, which would be inserted into the PA site plan like a Lego toy. In other words, the LMDC's role in the decisionmaking for the master plan would be limited to "pretty building designs," as EEK partner Stanton Eckstut reportedly said, adding that he alone was developing substantive plans for the site's streets, transportation facilities, and underground infrastructure (Neuman 2002f; Wyatt 2002i). This infuriated Garvin, who had broader ambitions in mind when the LMDC commissioned the seven high-profile design teams.[14]

Skeptics and veterans could not help wondering aloud whether the LMDC's Innovative Design Study was really just a sideshow while the PA made the real decisions. "It's a beauty contest and a distraction," said Robert D. Yaro, leader of the Civic Alliance (Flint 2002; Bagli 2003a; McGeveran 2003). "Fundamentally it's a sideshow because none of these things will be built," said one LMDC director about the December 2002 unveiling of the nine conceptual visions produced by the design 2 competition. "But they did show a variety of ways the site could have commercial development and a memorial without looking like a mess" (Bagli 2002b). Shortly after the design 2 visions were presented, the *Daily News* (2002f) let go with force: "What a healthy, open process. And what a monumental waste of time," the editors complained. "One suspects the PA will dismiss the LMDC plans outright and selfishly plow ahead with what it wants. If that is not the intention, why does Eckstut's work continue in secret?" the editors asked. "Both sides have promised to work together, but it's not easy to trust the PA promises."

When Roland Betts invited the PA to exhibit its master plan alongside those commissioned by the LMDC, the answer was no. He was told that their work would not be ready to show the public until February. "It's a work in progress and doesn't lend itself to that kind of presentation," a PA spokesman said (Haberman 2002d). When it came to its transportation agenda, however, the PA did not seem to have any problem revealing its work in progress. The PA's chief architect, Robert I. Davidson, showed early designs for a transportation hub (which included many elements of the temporary PATH station already under construction) at the annual "Build Boston" architectural conference just a month before the LMDC's seven teams of architects were scheduled to show their conceptual master plans for the WTC site. The PA released a second well-timed set of visuals for the new transportation center just days prior to the press conference announcing the LMDC's final selection of a master-plan design. The Port Authority had not selected an architect for the $2 billion downtown terminal it envisioned on the scale of Grand Central Terminal, but it laid out the underground engineering requirements for commuter and subway connections (Wyatt 2003b).

The behavior was disingenuous. The Port Authority was planning behind closed doors in a manner befitting its legacy of independence and its bureaucratic capacity. Eckstut had developed a full-scale model of the site, above and below ground, which the Port Authority insisted would yield far more specific and detailed engineering plans than those of the LMDC teams, even though those teams were also working with extensive models of the underground to plan for the retail shops, bus depots, and commuter train terminals required by the Port Authority. Those who saw Eckstut's plans reported that they resembled the rejected Beyer Blinder Belle schemes (Haberman 2002d; Kesner 2002).

Reports that intense interagency sparring was slowing the pace of the rebuilding efforts led LMDC president Lou Tomson to acknowledge previous disagreements. It also led to a second effort by the PA and the LMDC to clarify the messy and confused decisionmaking process. Signed in early December as "a process to lead to a single master plan for the WTC site," including transportation circulation and infrastructure, land/parcel distribution, land-use controls, and phased implementation, the goal was to present a common plan to the Port Authority and LMDC boards by January 31, 2003 (Wyatt 2002i, Port Authority 2003, 1–10). This would require Eckstut and Garvin to work together—a difficult undertaking considering their well-known and long-standing rivalry (Goldberger 2003a).

Planning professionals working with the Civic Alliance and New York New Visions had reasons to be wary of the Port Authority. Key decisions about the underground electrical substation, the footings for future office buildings, bus parking, vent tunnels, and security screening would forever foreclose possibilities for changing what happened on the surface of the site. It would be a challenge to get timely information from PA staff before advanced technical and engineering work precluded alternatives.[15] Work that had already begun on an electrical substation near Liberty Street would compromise the implementation of Libeskind's conceptual master plan. Likewise, the PA had approved and was carrying out a $544 million program to design and construct a temporary PATH station at the WTC site. "The LMDC is not ahead of the agenda," remarked one design insider who requested anonymity.

The PA felt that restoration of its revenue stream trumped the interests of any other stakeholder. In one plan, it placed five structures within the foundation walls of the WTC bathtub that encroached upon the footprints where the twin towers stood, considered "hallowed ground" by family members and placed off limits by Governor Pataki. An earlier design scheme had a temporary PATH transit concourse cutting through the North Tower footprint (Wyatt

2003e). (It was a bit figurative to say that the footprints should be kept inviolate down to bedrock because PATH trains had always run through this area.) The families of the victims killed were incensed that the Port Authority was insensitive to their concerns.

The agency also evoked the ire of its office leaseholder, Larry Silverstein, who continually sought a free hand to do what he deemed necessary to meet his commercial interests. The Port Authority laid out an underground plan for the southwest quadrant of the site that detailed a pedestrian through-pass at multiple levels, a design calculated to enhance the revenue-generating potential of an underground four-story interior mall, which WTC retail leaseholder Westfield America was insisting upon. Silverstein, who wanted to maximize the marketability of his office space, did not like this arrangement because it would require him to put office-tower lobbies on the third floor. He insisted that they must instead be on the ground floor. An earlier Eckstut design had angered Silverstein by putting a truck access ramp and loading dock on Greenwich Street, preventing the roadway from being fully restored through the former site of 7 World Trade Center, for which Silverstein had already given up 300,000 square feet of commercial space to permit reinstatement of the street grid (Haberman 2002e; Shin and Haberman 2002).[16]

For the most part, press coverage during this period focused on the "superbowl of design" and how the dramatic architectural visions produced by the seven design teams were whittled down to the semifinalist runoff between Daniel Libeskind and Rafael Viñoly. Despite their visually arresting models, however, their designs were merely conceptual. The competition's fundamental goal was to produce a master site plan—the unglamorous but essential blueprint for juxtaposing the memorial, transit center, and various commercial, retail, and cultural buildings in a way that could actually be built and then function well.

The final selection of the Libeskind plan did not resolve the key master plan issues—whether there would be four or five office towers, how the cultural facilities would be integrated into the plan, how much of the historic street grid would be reinstated, where to place underground security screening and bus parking facilities, and how deep to expose the slurry wall. To the contrary, the two agencies and their respective teams of designers, planners, engineers, and associated professionals debated these issues for weeks on end. Silverstein's architects and planners, Skidmore, Owings & Merrill (SOM), also put plans on the table.[17] At one point, his team proposed three towers on the southeast quadrant and located the entrance to one tower in the middle of Libeskind's high-profile symbolic space, the "Wedge of Light." Eventually, even Silverstein concluded that the site could not hold ten million square feet and backed off, as had top Port Authority officials.

In addition to its commercial agenda, the Port Authority's chief goal was to design and build a great transit terminal. At the end of July 2003, PA officials announced that they had selected Santiago Calatrava, a world-renowned architect and engineering poet of soaring stations and bridges, to design the transportation hub. Widely praised, the selection reframed the Port Authority's reputation for being indifferent to aesthetics. This inspired strategic choice simultaneously signaled the agency's unyielding position in the decisionmaking process. When unveiled six months later, Calatrava's soaring vision for the PATH terminal positioned the Port Authority with an elegant and permanent rebuilding signature superior to the designed-by-committee Freedom Tower extruded from the LMDC's politicized planning process.

THE GOVERNOR'S POWER

The appearance that no one would accept any designated master plan, even a broadly conceptual one, reflected an underlying reality. No major stakeholder was ready to relinquish its desired objective, despite the history of conflict over earlier proposals. This reflected a history in New York of actors being able to revive their proposals through persistence. The possibility that the LMDC might not be able to take the accepted plan through the technical blocking and tackling of environmental impact review and other procedural hurdles is another plausible explanation. The possibility that no plan might succeed kept each stakeholder enmeshed in parallel planning, opportunism, mistakes and false steps, fractiousness and interagency tensions, and public retreats and delays. Any forward advances remained mired in conflict and political disarray.

Roland Betts's steering committee of principals from the LMDC, the Port Authority, the city, and the state met regularly to resolve the broad-based policy issues of site planning. Unless invited in for specific input, staff members were not included. Resolving all the technical details and problems of a site plan is always a staff function, however. Because of the multiple demands on the WTC site, its complex underground infrastructure, and high demands for security, the technical problems were especially complicated. Typically, contentious issues bounced back and forth for weeks, even months, between these two levels before a higher authority made a decision.

The pattern of decisionmaking was also confused and contentious, even in disarray at times, because the governor typically demonstrated leadership only in response to some pressing political constituency—the families of the 9/11 victims or business constituencies in lower Manhattan—or in preparation for a ribbon-cutting event. The governor seemed to let the principals work through the issues on their own, however noisy and conflicted this might get. His loyal aides headed both the Port Authority and the LMDC, and they would watch out for his political interests. Governor Pataki directly weighed in only when absolutely necessary to break deadlocks on critical planning decisions, when the public reaction promised to be favorable, or when symbolic gestures would afford him good publicity. His behavior, in other words, was consistent with the rational calculus of American politicians.[18]

The power of the governor was never more apparent than when he decided to award the master plan to Daniel Libeskind's "Memory Foundations." He made this decision against the recommendation of the LMDC site-planning committee, which had taken a consensus vote for the other semifinalist, Rafael Viñoly's THINK team and its latticework scheme "Towers of Culture." The morning before the mayor and governor were to be briefed on the two final plans, the *Times* ran an exclusive story that the site committee favored the "Two Tall Towers" (Wyatt 2003d). In bold print, midcolumn standoff space, the article reported that "rebuilding officials challenge the politicians who appointed them." The article quoted one LMDC director as saying, "It's going to be a close one; it could simply come down to how the governor and the mayor feel." A site committee member, speaking on condition of anonymity, said that the committee expected the governor and mayor to follow its recommendation: "We don't expect anyone to overrule us." If this was a bold tactic by those who wanted the THINK team to win, it backfired. Betts, who saw himself as the steward of the design process, was left standing alone, out on a limb, exposed to the governor's anger.

Betts had spent the previous three weeks in daily meetings with both architectural teams. He had given both a short time frame in which to refine the physical plans and engineering details so that their visions could be rendered feasible. Betts wanted to keep the design process moving forward. He had the THINK team focus hard on the tremendously challenging details of making the towers lighter and less expensive. They would be built in eighty-foot modules off-site, then assembled like an erector set on-site; that way, he explained, no scaffolding would be needed. Betts talked to corporate tenants who saw Libeskind's design as more like a memorial, a graveyard. They wanted something more uplifting. As these meetings progressed, Betts became more involved with the THINK team plan and less with Libeskind's vision. He constantly updated Dan Doctoroff, who turned from skeptic to strong supporter of the twin latticework towers. In retrospect, Betts (2004) said, "I made a mistake by not involving many people in the process; if so, they too would have gotten excited."

Up to this point, the governor and the mayor had not been involved with the design process. When the nine designs were on display in mid-December, the governor had walked around the Winter Garden with Betts, Charles Gargano (chairman of the Empire State Development Corporation, LMDC's parent organization), and LMDC's Alex Garvin for about an hour asking questions. He wanted to see the Viñoly and Libeskind plans again. Now, just before the decision day, Tomson told Betts that the governor was okay with both plans. Doctoroff told Betts that the mayor was okay with both plans. Betts did not foresee a problem with either selection.

The full site committee heard the worked-through revisions to both master plans only the day before the vote. The committee, said Betts, liked both plans; his job was to persuade them to go with the Viñoly plan. He did not want the LMDC to dissent on the final vote, so if something went awry, it would support the Libeskind plan. The site committee voted unanimously for the Viñoly plan, though Tomson abstained. "This should have told me something," Betts later remarked, but "I missed this, because Tomson did not care about the aesthetics of the decision," just the power and politics of the situation. At 5:30 A.M. the next day, Doctoroff called Betts to tell him that the report in the *Wall Street Journal* that they worried would highlight Viñoly's association with the Argentine junta prior to his immigration to the United States was buried and harmless. Something else, however, was brewing: the *Times* piece. The phones started ringing incessantly, and the governor's press agent was yelling, who do you think you are? "This introduced a new factor—pride and who calls the shots" (Betts 2004).

The governor and the mayor met in a tiny room for a final review of the two plans. Betts still recalls the "steam" coming from Pataki. The architects had not been scheduled to make presentations, but they were called in early that morning. By several accounts, Libeskind was said to have done a great job; not so Viñoly. The governor made a series of emotional statements and, according to one person speaking on condition of anonymity, said, "I hate these towers, skeletons of death. I will never build them." The meeting fell apart soon after the governor left. Later, when Betts called Pataki, the governor repeated his preference for the Libeskind plan. Maybe he decided the twin towers were too risky, Betts (2004) said. Yet as one participant noted, with regret, "Pataki is too much of a politician to say, 'I taught you a lesson,' but he had."

The governor continued to play the arbiter for the rest of 2003, supporting Libeskind's vision through a bitter struggle with Silverstein's architect, David Childs, over the design of the Freedom Tower. The governor's support did, however, have a limit: he would not compromise his "aggressive timetable." During the summer his aides had brokered a "forced marriage" in which Childs would be "design architect and project manager" while Studio Daniel Libeskind would be "collaborating architects during the concept and schematic design phases." When this ever-frail "collaboration" collapsed in a series of blowups three weeks before Pataki's deadline in December, the governor insisted on a consensus design, which produced an uncomfortable merger of Childs and Libeskind's ideas that finally debuted with further intervention by the governor.[19]

MEMORIAL ASSERTION

The memorial design process followed an entirely different pattern of decision-making, as detailed by James Young in this volume. It proceeded in a straight-forward way because this task floated above the institutional turf fights and political gray areas besetting the commercially sensitive decisions over density, land use, street patterns, pedestrian ways, and vehicular traffic. That is not to say that it was not subject to delays or criticism. The salient element for the overall story, however, was the way in which the LMDC carefully structured this process and protected it from political interference. This presents a sharp contrast to the intense politicization that plagued the site-plan selection.

LMDC officials did not structure the memorial design competition as an "open, inclusive process," but rather as a series of controlled forums where members of the jury could hear the views of different constituent groups. Confidentiality governed the jury's activities. Its thirteen members all signed agreements barring them from speaking to the press about the memorial selection process until the winner was announced. The eight finalists and their model makers, illustrators, and computer animators also signed confidentiality agreements. To head off the public relations battles that had poisoned the site-plan competition, these agreements included a clause prohibiting negative comments about peer designs that extended through December 31, 2005. The jurors' notebooks never left the office where they reviewed the 5,201 entries, mounted on 30-by-40-inch boards and propped up on easels in rooms protected by a double-key system. As Young explains, the eight finalists were selected anonymously.

The hard-learned lessons of the site-plan competition led LMDC officials to decide to keep politics at bay. They succeeded in part because Governor Pataki, Mayor Bloomberg, and former mayor Giuliani (who was not far removed from commenting in public on 9/11 events) all agreed that the memorial decision should be the jury's alone. The remembrance element was too hot for them to touch. "We want to be very clear," Kevin M. Rampe, LMDC's interim president, said at the outset of the memorial process. "We will entrust the jury with the ultimate responsibility to select a design and once entrusted we must respect the jury's role in making the selection" (Wyatt 2003d).

Governor Pataki's voice was heard only at the final press conference, not before. The Port Authority was nowhere in the conversation, let alone the deliberations, on this sensitive element of the WTC site. It was not represented on the memorial jury. The political calculus of this model was likely to work for the governor, regardless of the outcome. If it went well, the governor could take credit; if not, he was distanced from the result. "You can't have a memorial designed by politicians," Pataki remarked after the winning design had been unveiled (Collins and Dunlap 2004). Ironically, the LMDC's ability to shelter the memorial process from the Port Authority and the city enabled it to negate important parts of the master plan designed by Studio Daniel Libeskind.

The rules set forth by the LMDC "Memorial Competition Guidelines"—which is to say, no rules—gave the jurors complete flexibility to alter the parameters of the Libeskind plan. The "rules" specified that competitors could create a memorial "of any type, shape, height or concept" so long as it included five specifically enumerated physical elements essential for a fitting 9/11 memorial.[20] Design concepts needed only to be "sensitive to the spirit and vision of Studio Daniel Libeskind's master plan for the entire site." And the jury was not restricted in reviewing design concepts that "exceed the illustrated memorial site boundaries" (LMDC 2003b). Rampe reiterated this point at the press conference launching the international design competition, saying that, if competitors were to express their creativity, "it may take going outside those guidelines." By professional inclination, the jurors were intent on considering all proposals. To attract high-caliber jurors, LMDC officials undoubtedly assured them that they would be the sole authority in this matter. Well-known juror Maya Lin was often mentioned as someone who "broke some of the rules" to produce the spectacularly successful Vietnam Veterans Memorial in Washington, D.C. (Wyatt 2003f; Graves and Neuman 2003).[21] In short, jury members could disregard Libeskind's site plan if it created problems in selecting what they considered to be the most creative proposal.

The unique surviving element of Libeskind's vision was the slurry wall of the bathtub, which he deliberately left exposed as an ever-present reminder that the foundation held even as the seemingly invincible buildings crumbled. Libeskind's site plan defined a memorial area of 4.7 acres depressed 30 feet below the level of the street—called "the pit," "the commemorative pit," "the sunken pit," or "the desolate pit" by the news media. The site plan articulated place-holding museum and cultural buildings at the edges of the memorial area to shelter it from adjacent commercial activities. These conceptual elements created a specific physical template for the memorial, in effect predesigning aspects of the memorial.

The LMDC's memorial program drafting committee did not want to sequester the memorial in isolation: "Designs should consider the neighborhood context, including the connectivity of the surrounding residential and business communities" (LMDC 2003c, 10). Reading between the lines, this could be understood as giving applicants permission to violate the approved master plan. The committee wanted "the memorial and site-planning processes to influence and be coordinated with one another for mutual benefit." The memorial program would be "used as one of the criteria for the site plan selection. Once the memorial designer is selected, both the memorial designer and the site planner will work together to integrate their efforts." The words sounded right, but the site plan had already been selected when the memorial competition was launched; the premise of the jury's actual charge signaled permission to reject the LMDC's own approved master plan. "The jury was always thinking it is smarter than the others and removed some placeholders," one juror said at an academic meeting. "All memorials are negotiated. Nothing is set in stone."

The logic of the master plan was to define a blank space that the memorial design competition would fill in, but the competition rules unambiguously defined the memorial selection as *the* planning priority to which the site plan would have to respond. "It was the memorial *site* competition," one juror said to the press. "How many artists are given four and a half acres?" (Collins and Dunlap 2004). The jury objected to the way the master plan called for the memorial to be depressed thirty feet below street level; many jurors preferred a grade-level solution. (This feature also bothered downtown business interests and Battery Park City residents, who considered the pit an obstacle to passage through the WTC site.) Regardless of the logic or merit of the Libeskind vision, the jury wanted the memorial design to knit the Trade Center site back into the neighborhood. "We also had to face the stark reality of reintegrating into the urban fabric a site that had been violently torn from it," the jury emphasized in its statement on the winning design. Its recommendations were made contingent on achieving that end (LMDC 2004b).

It seems obvious that the jury would not want to cede even a small degree of its prerogative over the selection. Yet the jury was resolving an ambiguity that had bedeviled the entire planning process—how to balance remembrance with rebuilding. It used the moral authority of the memorial mission and its prerogatives as an independent jury to assert remembrance as *the* centerpiece of the endeavor. And it chose to do so in a way that would reunify the WTC site with the urban fabric of lower Manhattan, healing the planning wounds of the past.

All eight final designs ignored the idea that the entire memorial should be depressed below street level, and the three top proposals all violated Libeskind's master plan. "Libeskind's big-hole-in-the-ground-as-memorial was a particularly cruel joke to perpetrate on the future of the city. It was uncivic and strangely inappropriate as a long-term urban element," recounted one juror. "All of the schemes that were serious contenders brought the memorial back into relationship to the everyday life of the city" (Campbell 2004). The final choice also repudiated the master plan in the latest and perhaps most serious of steps weakening its integrity. The executive editor of *Metropolis*, a widely read design magazine, remarked on the "near-erasure" of "Memory Foundations" (Pedersen 2004). All the signature elements of the plan—the "Wedge of Light," the "Park of Heroes," the exposed slurry wall, and the companion sunken memorial site—had been "altered, reduced or eliminated," wrote Robin Pogrebin (2004b) from the *Times* cultural desk. Further revisions to designer Michael Arad's initial memorial scheme, completed jointly with one of the country's celebrated landscape architects, Peter Walker, may have recaptured bits of the Libeskind plan, but it failed to capture any of its emotional significance, especially viewed against slides detailing the plan's vision.

Op-ed commentators and architectural critics were lukewarm to hostile about Arad and Walker's "Reflecting Absence" and its twin "voids" of remembrance. A few defended the Libeskind plan by chronicling the erosions, while others bemoaned Libeskind's willingness to compromise so completely. The jury's decision also put LMDC's Rampe in a bind. "Kevin Rampe couldn't reverse the independent jury, nor could he afford to alienate Libeskind, whose ideas for Ground Zero had been enthusiastically endorsed by Pataki, Rampe's boss," Paul Goldberger (2004a) wrote in *The New Yorker*. "The solution to this dilemma was, like everything else at Ground Zero, a delicately stitched-together web of politics, policy, and disingenuous public statements."

A less frequently stated but perhaps more accurate interpretation, however, lay the blame on the original planning effort's unchallenged program for maximum commercial space. Martin C. Pedersen (2004) of *Metropolis* explained:

> This long, torturous route to rebuilding has led us practically full circle; back to July 2002 and the universally reviled site plans originally credited to Beyer Blinder Belle. If you look at those schemes on the LMDC web site and then mentally Photoshop in the new memorial design, you arrive in most cases at something close to what we have today—which shouldn't come as a shock, since the original program of 10 million square feet of office space was *never* seriously challenged.

Could that original program ever have been seriously challenged—without cash or equivalent currency to buy out the leasehold interests of Silverstein and his investors? Who could have mounted such a challenge? The Port Authority? The governor? The city? When would a buyout have been initiated? In the weeks and months after 9/11? Before the court ruled on the insurance litigation that possibly included a negotiated settlement with the insurers? After the jury trials on the insurance cases?

When viewed through the lens of interests competing for primacy on this contested ground, the LMDC's memorial contest allowed its independent jury to make the first controlling claim on the remembrance-versus-rebuilding conflict separate from the factors that inevitably put the LMDC at a disadvantage relative to the Port Authority or the leaseholders. Soon after the winning announcement, LMDC president Rampe announced, "We said from the beginning—and I think the selection by the jury shows that we didn't just say it, we meant it—that the memorial is the centerpiece" (Dunlap 2004a).

WHERE ART THOU, O CITY?

In *Leaves of Grass*, New York's Walt Whitman wrote a prophetic ode to his

> Proud and passionate city! mettlesome, mad, extravagant city!
> Spring up, O city! not for peace alone, but be indeed yourself, warlike!
> Fear not! submit to no models but your own, O city!

More than 150 years later, Whitman's words evoked the city government's poignant position in the three-way political struggle to rebuild at Ground Zero. To the city's elected officials, it seemed logical that they should shoulder the mandate to rebuild Ground Zero. Yet they were left at a severe disadvantage in influencing decisions that would shape the physical and economic landscape of lower Manhattan for decades to come. The Port Authority had owned the site for nearly forty years, was statutorily free of the city's regulatory and land-use powers, and reported to higher levels of government. City officials maneuvered opportunistically, tactically, and repeatedly to gain influence, to no real avail.

Their first thrust was the bold proposal in August 2002 to swap the land under LaGuardia and Kennedy Airports, owned by the city but operated by the PA under a lease due to expire in 2015, for the land under the WTC. The politics of any swap would require offering something to New Jersey. It also required a complicated fiscal calculation (weighing future airport lease revenues against future commercial rents from a rebuilt WTC) that did not look promising for the city, but the land swap enjoyed support from many quarters because it would return control of the site to the city. Even if the PA, the city, and New Jersey could all be satisfied, however, the land swap would diminish the governor's control of the site and the political benefits he derived from that; after months of fitful negotiation, Pataki suspended the talks in June 2003 (Wyatt 2002e; McGeveran 2002c; Lueck 2002; Smothers 2003; Neuman 2003a, 2003b; Bagli 2003c; *Crain's* 2003).

The city made a second thrust four months after the first, and a week before the LMDC released its second round of designs, when Mayor Bloomberg outlined a broad, expansive, and graphic "Vision for the Twenty-first Century for Lower Manhattan" (Bloomberg 2002). Described in further detail by Mitchell Moss (this volume), this multifaceted $10.6 billion agenda advanced by the mayor covered all of lower Manhattan below Canal Street from the East River to the Hudson River. To "reinforce Lower Manhattan's position as a premier financial district," it proposed three types of public investments: transportation to connect lower Manhattan to the areas around it, street improvements and open spaces to build new neighborhoods, and public places to create new amenities throughout the district. Once floated, the plan was not pushed by city hall, which focused its attention instead on the Hudson Yards Project on the far West Side of midtown Manhattan.

The city made a third thrust after the planned departure of Lou Tomson, who had been living alone, away from his family, in a downtown hotel and had finally served as president of the LMDC long enough to do what his friend, Governor Pataki, expected of him. In a confidential letter to John P. Cahill, the governor's chief of staff, Mayor Bloomberg proposed to revamp the LMDC to give the city more authority over reconstruction of the WTC site (subject to the approval of an advisory board of state, city, LMDC, and Port Authority officials). The proposal laid out shared decisionmaking over the LMDC's remaining $1.25 billion of federal recovery money consonant with the mayor's "Vision for Lower Manhattan" (Doctoroff 2003). "The effect of having such an advisory board giving approval," the *Times* reported, "would be much the same as in the city's proposed land swap with the Port Authority, giving the city control of the trade center site while keeping the development process exempt from the complicated review process the city would experience, a process from which the Port Authority is exempt" (Wyatt 2003d).[22]

Still pushing for an expanded role, city officials next attempted to refuse to approve the governor's choice to lead the LMDC, then operating with an interim president, until it received greater clarity on a wide variety of downtown building issues (Levy 2003). The city had been pressing the LMDC for months on site planning details concerning retail frontage and through streets. These details were key to the city's agenda for reintegrating the WTC site with lower Manhattan and creating pedestrian-friendly neighborhoods. Confident in its position, the city could be persistent in demanding a role in how the WTC redevelopment plan would reshape *its* cityscape. "Currently, the most important unresolved issue," deputy mayor Doctoroff wrote to PA executive director Joe Seymour, "is the plan for the ground level: how retail, streets, open spaces, and sidewalks will work together to ensure that the site is full of people walking the streets, shopping in the stores and spilling over to the rest of Lower Manhattan" (Matthews 2003).

The city's position on streets clashed with those of the Port Authority and its retail leaseholder, Westfield America (subsequently bought out of the project), which both sought revenue from a more extensive underground mall of retail shops. The city could press its position on this point, however, because it retained regulatory power over streets and sidewalks. It could also exercise this power over the LMDC's plan for the Deutsche Bank site south of Ground Zero.

By statute, the *World Trade Center Amended General Project Plan (Amended GPP)* (New York City Department of City Planning 2004) was subject to review by the City Planning Commission. Completed in early March 2004, the commission's fourteen-page review made numerous detailed recommendations in line with the mayor's vision for lower Manhattan (Burden 2004). It asked the LMDC to modify its plan to restore Dey and Cortlandt Streets (which at one time ran through the sixteen-acre site) between Church and Greenwich. Restoring these streets would knit the WTC site back into the street grid (see figure 2.1), but it would also hamper the Port Authority's plans for the site, as well as those of the developer, who, according to Betts, was constantly pushing back on the master plan.[23] The city further sought to insert language into the *Amended GPP* that made the Department of City Planning a player in developing the project's design guidelines.

The review and recommended modifications carried "more than the power of positive persuasion," remarked David Karnovsky, counsel for the Department of City Planning (Dunlap 2004b). If the commission recommended disapproval or modification of the plan, state law required that the LMDC override by a two-thirds vote of its board of directors. Beyond that, however, the city could only get its way through negotiation, since the *Amended GPP* was binding only on the LMDC, not the Port Authority. If the LMDC only had authority over managing the memorial project, overseeing public input, and managing the remaining federal funds, how long could it stay in existence? In other words, the LMDC was an unlikely candidate to exercise long-term public stewardship over the rebuilding of Ground Zero. As a result, city officials wanted the three public bodies governing the redevelopment to forge an agreement not unlike the 1967 compact with the PA (Dunlap 2004c).[24] Anxious to move the rebuilding plan for substantive and political reasons—the cornerstone ceremony was scheduled for July 4—the LMDC agreed to further negotiation on the streets issue. The *Amended GPP* was approved in early June, but a formal agreement on the roles of the Port Authority, the LMDC, and the city had yet to be concluded.

Many observers found Mayor Bloomberg's efforts to exert influence on Ground Zero surprisingly low-key in comparison with his forceful advocacy of the Hudson Yards Project. It was natural for them to ask whether the mayor and the governor had cut a deal for credit for and control over their respective development priorities. At least one journalist noted that the governor and the mayor's staffs had come to agreement on who would do what work on each project (Steinhauer 2004).

It seems unlikely that the city's efforts to date will afford Mayor Bloomberg and his city planning commissioner, Amanda Burden, or the city's future elected officials, any real leverage over decisionmaking about Ground Zero. The Port Authority and the LMDC plan to develop guidelines for the full build-out of the site consistent with "Memory Foundations." These guidelines are supposed to define the framework for future development. Whether these future guidelines draw on those first drafted by Studio Daniel Libeskind is unclear, but the next guidelines are likely to be general and flexible enough to accommodate private interests and the vicissitudes of market demand. Questions about how the *Amended GPP* could be further amended, if necessary, and what would happen if the LMDC no longer existed had no answers in early 2005.

What actually gets built will reflect market demand for new office space and retail investments and the stamina of the players. As noted, many serious encroachments have been made on "Memory Foundations." In the past, New York City has often executed large-scale development projects on the basis of a second plan, not on the first.[25] It will be essential to follow the path of money in this special case of public-private development. In the end, the Port Authority, as landowner, is likely to act in line with its interests and initial intentions.

FOLLOW THE MONEY

To a degree that surprised some, Larry Silverstein managed to maintain his position as presumptive master redeveloper of the planned ten million square feet of commercial space on the WTC site. His power to command development decisionmaking, to win crucial battles with the LMDC, and to gain access to the governor and other key decisionmakers stemmed from his right and obligation to rebuild the commercial space. These contractual rights, however, were inextricably linked to his financial ability to do so—in short, his claims to multiple billions in insurance coverage.

From the beginning, the question, as the court phrased it, was how much was "recoverable for the total destruction of the WTC that occurred after the buildings were struck by two fuel-laden aircraft that had been hijacked by terrorists." Acting for his investor group, related interests, and the Port Authority, Silverstein had obtained property and business-interruption coverage for the complex from twenty-five insurers in the total amount of $3.55 billion "per occurrence."[26] Since only one of the many insurers had issued a final policy, legal uncertainty surrounded the "double indemnity" question: did the events of September 11, 2001, constitute one or two "occurrences"? The answer would determine whether Silverstein could recover only once, to an upper limit of $3.55 billion, or twice, up to a limit of $7 billion. Since the buildings were depreciated assets, insurers would conduct a valuation under either scenario and Silverstein would have to prove actual cash value to an arbitration panel. The outcome of three jury trials would determine Silverstein's long-term financial power in the rebuilding process.

Insurance monies were *the* source of funds for rebuilding the commercial space in a way that was unconstrained by the typical business demands of real estate development—namely, finding tenants willing to commit to large blocks of space at competitive rents and convincing lenders to provide financing on the basis of those commitments. The insurance proceeds would allow Silverstein to build "on spec" on a scale large enough to command a dominant market share of new class A space in lower Manhattan without the cash costs of servicing debt while the space was being leased up. Building the five office towers with the maximum amount of insurance monies would also help the governor meet his aggressive building timetable. As a senior Port Authority official put it: "I don't want to reach the third anniversary of the attack and it's still a big hole" (Bagli 2003d). The governor was reportedly concerned about how much money was being consumed in legal fees. Two years into the costly and contentious insurance battle in state and federal courts, Pataki attempted but failed to forge a settlement between Silverstein and his insurers. If adverse legal findings reduced Silverstein's insurance payout, it would limit his role in rebuilding and diminish what could be accomplished.

In the first phase of the three-part trial, the jury ruled in favor of the insurers, reducing the payout potential to a maximum of $4.6 billion or a minimum of $3.55 billion, down from the maximum $7 billion cap Silverstein had sought. The stakeholders, civic groups, business interests, and other real estate developers immediately started to evaluate the new math. Rebuilding 10 million square feet of office and retail space and four levels of underground infrastructure had been estimated in 2004 to cost $9 billion to $12 billion. (Decisions about who would pay what part of these underground costs had yet to be determined.) The insurance question neither altered the Port Authority's plans for Calatrava's $2 billion transportation center nor jeopardized the remaining $4.55 billion for transportation coming from the federal government. If it appeared questionable whether the total commercial build-out could be financed from the insurance payouts before the jury decision, it seemed impossible afterward.[27]

In response to the insurance-loss verdict, the Port Authority called on the investor group to produce a financial plan showing how it would meet the lease terms requiring them to rebuild ten million square feet of commercial space. Silverstein hired Morgan Stanley for the job. In conventional real estate analysis, the numbers would depend on the critical assumption about how much rental revenue the developer could anticipate getting for the square footage of office space. To attract tenants downtown in a high-vacancy environment, Silverstein would have to offer significantly lower rents than the alternatives, namely midtown, as well as large move-in concessions.[28] One estimate put this discount at $20 to $25 per square foot, to which a Silverstein vice president responded: "We're in a position to capture the market that wants that space but doesn't want to pay the $70 to $80 a foot that midtown might command" (Cockfield 2004b).

The timing made many observers nervous. "An endless delay in commercial development at Ground Zero could thrust this massive project into direct competition with city plans to redevelop downtown Brooklyn and the rail yards of Manhattan west of Pennsylvania Station. There is a limit to how much new commercial office space the city can absorb," wrote the editors of Newsday

(2004). "Why not take this opportunity to scale back office plans? And why not seize the change to make sure the district winds up with more housing?" The editors at the *Daily News* (2004b) shared the sentiment: "The fundamental question now for Pataki, Bloomberg and the Port Authority is whether the demand for office space downtown will be sufficient to justify faith that the Trade Center site will not become frozen as home to the world's tallest building and little else of consequence. The market suggests such an unappealing future while indicating that other uses, such as housing and expanded open space, would be roaring successes. Reconsidering the master plan is in order." Editors at the *Times* (2004) noted the fact that the four office towers scheduled to follow construction of the tallest tower might not be built as rapidly as possible: "Now those towers will have to be developed in a manner that is more responsive to market conditions and we hope to the concerns of the public as well."

The Port Authority had a number of strategic options to consider. If insurance proceeds guaranteed that Silverstein could build the first and tallest tower (2.6 million square feet estimated to cost $1.5 billion), all else remained uncertain, except that his leasehold was likely to be renegotiated. The office development rights he would retain in these negotiations would depend in part on how much financing he would or could raise. Most significantly, it would depend on how much development the Port Authority believed the market could realistically absorb in the decade ahead.

Silverstein's financial position improved dramatically when he won an additional potential $1.1 billion from nine insurers in December 2004 on the basis of the second trial jury's decision that the destruction of the WTC constituted two separate attacks. The total possible payout was now $4.6 billion, substantially less than $7 billion and subject to appeal, but more than what had seemed likely to prevail after the first jury ruling. Silverstein had "extra clout," the *Times* reported. How much extra depended on what Silverstein would have to pay for his share of common underground at the site—the estimated $1.5 billion in roadways, ramps, loading docks, and utilities—which remained a matter of negotiation with the Port Authority (Dunlap 2004g). The ruling seemed to ensure much of the financing for the second tower, though it did not change the long-term question of market feasibility. Silverstein was already well along in building 7 World Trade Center but had not signed up any tenants as of March 2005. The pivotal question remains how much of the lost WTC office space really needs to be replaced to ensure the future economic viability of lower Manhattan.

The Port Authority's strategic option to buy out the various private investment interests, in effect undoing its privatization, existed from the beginning. In 2004 as in 2002, this was a matter of determining the optimal time for a buyout. As Susan Fainstein (this volume) notes, the Port Authority had more to lose than gain by an early buyout as long as the insurance case remained unsettled. By May 2004, the agency had reacquired the leasehold rights to the former 820-room Marriott Hotel (on the southwest edge of the site for redevelopment as a memorial), the U.S. Customs House (site for redevelopment of the tallest tower), and the one million square feet of retail shops held by Westfield America; it also had bought out Silverstein's lender, GMAC, which had extended $563 million to finance the leasehold purchase. The exit of these parties reduced the number of players seeking input into decision-making over the site's commercial redevelopment and resolved some persistent conflicts over the configuration of the retail space. Yet these steps did not diminish the complexity of renegotiating the Silverstein lease agreement. The combination of insurance payouts and leasehold buyouts did shift more attention to the question of market feasibility. This may return the political dynamic to the more familiar (and somewhat predictable) terrain of development politics as opposed to electoral politics.

Larry Silverstein, Governor Pataki, and even Mayor Bloomberg used the power of a huge anticipated insurance payout as a strategic lever over the redevelopment of Ground Zero (Bagli 2003b). With a focus on the specifics of the claims before it, the insurance trial jury, in effect, resolved the contentious issue of how fast and in what configuration the commercial portions of the project would proceed. For the time being, rebuilding will now go forth more slowly and at lower densities, with evolving possibilities for different land uses. It will go forward at a pace dictated by the vicissitudes of the real estate market, undoubtedly with some help from the public sector. The new timetable will also allow more symbolic space for the memorial remembrance, once funds for its construction are raised. In this case, delay has been positive. It is an ironic end at a phase of planning that was so deeply subjected to political pressure to show quick progress.

CONCLUSIONS

Among the many goals for the WTC rebuilding project, four stood out as essential: deciding on a memorial design, selecting a master plan for the site, implementing the public pieces of the rebuilding agenda (the open spaces and the plan's cultural components), and enhancing regional access to lower Manhattan.[29] Existing institutional arrangements put the transportation components in the hands of the Port Authority (the PATH terminal) and the Metropolitan Transportation Authority (the Fulton Street subway station). Only the memorial process was spared political struggle, though the chosen design was not greeted with universal acclaim. In contrast, the selection of Libeskind's "Memory Foundations" master plan and the designation of the cultural facilities have engendered gigantic tussles over who will manage the process and caustic debates over the final decisions.[30]

These controversies have differed from previous development battles among business interests, unions, and civic and citizen groups in New York. They have not just been about a symbolic memorial, or the design of a particular building, or how best to rebuild an entire neighborhood. They have been about all of these and more—a wished-for healing vision. The multifaceted scope of this task fell outside established institutional arrangements. In the highly visible first phase of planning, neither the LMDC as lead agency, nor the Port Authority as landowner, nor even the mayor as democratically elected steward of the body politic, could successfully claim legitimate authority to manage the dual objectives of remembrance and rebuilding. No established procedure existed for this unprecedented task, and ad hoc arrangements struck among the contending principals failed as substitutes. Each public agent brought its own statutory authorities and administrative processes to bear on parts of the process, but none could achieve mastery over the process. The result was fragmentation and confusion. The authorities tried to fill this gap by charging designers with arriving at a plan, but while they could articulate possible alternatives, they too failed to find a way to resolve the competing claims on this contested site. In the end, only Governor Pataki could resolve these conflicts and make final decisions, but he stepped in only when compelled by circumstances to do so.

The conflicts between rebuilding and remembrance were ultimately resolved in ways that were both predictable (expand the site, have the governor step in, assert the primacy of the Port Authority's commercial interests) and unexpected (actions by an independent memorial jury and the verdicts of insurance trial juries). Yet the absence of the political will to pull contending forces together for the greater civic good defeated the early big ambition to achieve an inspired civic vision. Why, in the face of compelling tragedy and irreproachable intentions, did this civic ambition dissolve into disarray and discord? When other megaprojects have suggested that decisionmakers can find creative means to resolve conflicts without sacrificing the overall vision—by making tough trade-offs, by mitigating major impacts, by accommodating key stakeholders—why did state and city officials and private interests flounder in this most profound endeavor?

It may be too early to answer these questions in any definitive manner. Where other cities like Boston have found ways to resolve ongoing conflicts over large-scale projects implemented over long time horizons, New York seems incapable of overcoming its intense political fragmentation. The endless posturing, symbolic rhetoric, and institutional competition over planning for the WTC site produced a political narrative that was at times opaque, at other times transparent, but always complicated. Although it remains uncertain what actually will be built at Ground Zero, the silver lining may be that delay could produce a less dense commercial project in line with evolving market possibilities in lower Manhattan. In particular, it may be possible to satisfy the widely and deeply held desire of many New Yorkers to reintegrate the superblock created in the 1960s into the fabric of lower Manhattan, erasing the traces of the aggressive urban renewal project imposed on the city. However tall towers come to be configured on the site, the template for rebuilding will restore much of the site's former street grid, reinforce the primacy of mass transit to the city's future, and reaffirm a pedestrian orientation within the city's dense domain of skyscrapers. These are not small victories.

NOTES

1. Including 7 World Trade Center, which was developed under the auspices of the PA but is not technically part of Ground Zero, would increase the count to fourteen blocks combined into two superblocks.
2. These included nine major studies: the Regional Plan Association (RPA) of New York's *Regional Plan for New York and Its Environs* (1929); the New York City Planning Commission's preliminary master plan (1940), which was never adopted; two plans by the Downtown Lower Manhattan Association (DLMA, a business group led by David Rockefeller), *Lower Manhattan: Recommended Land Use, Redevelopment Areas, and Traffic Improvements* (1958), and *Major Improvements, Land Use, Transportation, Traffic* (1963); two plans for lower Manhattan from the New York City Planning Commission (1966, 1969); another plan from the RPA, *Second Regional Plan* (1969); a joint public-private effort between the DLMA and the city's Department of City Planning and Economic Development Corporation, *The Plan for Lower Manhattan* (1993); and a third regional plan by the RPA, *Regional at Risk* (1996). See Birch (Forthcoming).
3. This land expansion was nothing new to Manhattan. Century after century since 1660, the island had accommodated its hunger for additional land through landfill projects, adding approximately 3,742 acres of new waterfront by 1972, after which similar moves would be prohibited by the federal Clean Water Act.
4. In 2004 lower Manhattan was still the third-largest central business district in the United States, though as Moss (this volume) points out, its economic fortunes have gradually faded relative to midtown. David Rockefeller and Austin Tobin's efforts to create the WTC were only the most tangible among many initiatives to promote the area dating back to 1929 and were followed by the successful creation of Battery Park City in the early 1980s. Lower Manhattan's traditional employment base is a mix of business, finance, and government offices; it has been a national financial hub with significant corporate headquarters interspersed along the district's dense and complex pattern of streets. But the district has been steadily losing ground as the preferred location for new class A towers to Manhattan's larger and better-connected midtown office district.
5. Before 9/11, as Moss details in his chapter (this volume), downtown had begun to emerge as a residential address, signaling a renewed future. Using tax benefits, zoning changes, and landmark designations, Mayor Rudolph W. Giuliani's 1995 revival plan stimulated conversions of obsolete office buildings into apartments. Aided by a rebound in financial services employment during the 1990s, lower Manhattan was heading toward a live-and-work community supporting residential growth, hotels, restaurants, museums, movie theaters, and shopping. The dis-

trict's residential areas, primarily rental, were the fastest-growing in the city, attracting those with a walk-to-work attitude. This trend was important, but still embryonic. The new residential population was in small pockets, none of which, from a real estate perspective, were "large enough to sustain the kinds of services and high quality retail enjoyed by residents of areas like East Midtown, the Upper West Side, or Greenwich Village" (Dunlap 1995; Popper 1996; Denitto and Feldman 1996; Kelly 2002b; Lower Manhattan Development Corporation 2002a, 8; New York New Visions 2002a, 25).

6. NYNV's growth strategies report (New York New Visions 2002d) won the New York Chapter Project Award from the American Institute of Architects and became, as Goldberg (this volume) shows, one of the most influential civic coalitions.

7. I was a participant observer in this group; see NYNV minutes from the Steering Committee meeting, May 1, 2002, 3.

8. In addition to a General Advisory Council, the advisory councils included the following constituencies: arts, education, and tourism; development; families; financial services firms; professional firms; residents; restaurants, retailers, and small business; and transportation and commuters.

9. The project area also gained the below-grade portions of site 26 in Battery Park City to serve as a potential location for a bus garage serving visitors to the memorial (Lower Manhattan Development Corporation 2003b).

10. Because the site is being expanded to include a parcel not currently owned by the PA, the city has a right to collect taxes on the land, leverage it lacks over other PA-owned properties.

11. The controversy stemmed from Alexander Garvin, the LMDC's chief planner, scoring BBB higher than the other firms, prompting the directors of both agencies to ask for a review of the evaluation criteria. There was dissension over BBB within the LMDC as well. Lou Tomson favored working with BBB, but Roland Betts and Billie Tsien were not as enthusiastic about the firm (Haberman and Neuman 2002b; Goldberger 2003a). Garvin had already hired an in-house urban planning firm, Peterson/Littenberg Architecture and Urban Design, on a $375,000 contract. The task had a large scope, as revealed by the list of specialists: landscape planning and design, economics and programming, civil and subsurface engineering, security planning, bus transit planning, traffic forecasting, traffic database, sustainable design, structural engineering, cost estimating, and 3-D computer database services (LMDC 2002b). BBB had worked in New York for more than thirty years on such notable planning projects as Grand Central Terminal, Governors Island, Ellis Island, and the Queens West Development at Hunters Point. In turn, Parsons Brinckerhoff's work in the city extended back more than one hundred years and included transportation planning for the Access to the Region's Core Project, Farley Post Office Building Redevelopment, and many others.

12. The LMDC site committee chose six teams, not five, and Garvin added his in-house consultants, Peterson/Littenberg, to the list of competing architectural teams. The THINK team led by Rafael Viñoly submitted three designs, making for a total of nine designs from the seven teams.

13. For reasons unknown to this author, neither the commissioner, Amanda Burden, nor the Department of City Planning was brought into the early planning process for Ground Zero, and according to Betts (2004), Doctoroff took the heat for their

exclusion. DCP staff participated in the meetings that worked through the details of the Libeskind master plan after its selection.

14. Paul Goldberger (2004b, 128) reports that Betts and Garvin saw the design study as a way to get inspired designs from architects more creative than BBB: "They had long ago accepted the notion that a truly visionary plan for Ground Zero stood no chance of surviving the political process. They saw their roles as trying to squeeze as much design quality as they could out of that process, not of by-passing it altogether."

15. New York New Visions was unsuccessful in pushing the PA to disclose its plans for transportation and also failed in its constant efforts to establish regular liaison meetings with the PA like those that it had with the LMDC.

16. Silverstein's architects and planners, Skidmore, Owings & Merrill, had a scheme for three towers on the southeast quadrant with the entrance to one tower in Libeskind's master plan "Wedge of Light." "Everyone was operating as if no mas-ter-plan scheme existed," one design player recalled (Hack 2003).

17. Silverstein started planning with his architects soon after September 11. By mid-2001, his team reportedly had had reasonably detailed concepts on the drawing board for several months (McGeveran 2002b).

18. Alan Altshuler made this point to me.

19. The press intently covered these struggles; see Dunlap (2003), and Goldberger (2003b, 2004a).

20. The five physical elements were a recognition of each victim of the attack, an area for quiet contemplation, a separate area for visitation by the families of the victims, a 2,500-square-foot area for the unidentified human remains collected at the Trade Center site, and a way to make visible the footprints of the original twin towers.

21. This point was also made by James Young at our Russell Sage working group meetings.

22. Mayor Bloomberg could register his position at LMDC board meetings through the city's eight appointees and deputy mayor Dan Doctoroff, who attended most LMDC board meetings. The mayor was also in constant communication with Roland Betts about site-planning issues.

23. The city wished to create a pedestrian environment with more than half of the retail space at or above grade with minimum retail frontage required at key streets, continuous retail on Church and Greenwich Streets, and transparency. To meet the requirement for street-level retail activity, office lobbies for towers 2, 3, and 4 would have to be on the third floor, a condition that Silverstein, reacting to the Port Authority's plan for underground retail, demanded be dropped because he believed it would hurt market prospects for his office space (New York City Department of City Planning 2004; Dunlap 2004b).

24. Deputy mayor Doctoroff issued a letter calling for such a formal agreement on April 5, 2004. The Department of City Planning recommended that the agreement cover five areas: the public realm and open space (reintegrating the site with lower Manhattan); commercial and cultural programs (creating a pedestrian envi-ronment); traffic and transportation (lower Manhattan street management); infra-structure (managing user needs); and below-grade concourses and related above-grade infrastructure.

25. Other notable large-scale projects besides the Forty-second Street Development Project that fit the second-time-around pattern include Battery Park City and the Coliseum at Columbus Circle (now the Time Warner Project); see Sagalyn (2001).

26. The investors consisted of one group led by Lloyd Goldman, head of a major New York real estate family, which put up two-thirds of the $125 million equity investment, and another formed by Larry A. Silverstein.

27. A second loss would have left Silverstein with $3.55 billion, but on December 7, 2004, the second trial ruled that the destruction of the WTC did constitute two separate attacks, entitling Silverstein to collect up to $4.6 billion. Of this sum, $1.3 billion had already been spent on the buyout of GMAC, Westfield Properties, and its lender; lease payments to the Port Authority; legal bills to fight the insurance suit and defend private lawsuits; lost profit and management fees; and design and engineering fees. With $1.5 billion committed to the first tower, that left $1.8 billion as equity to fund the four other towers. The second trial verdict is likely to be appealed. Useful for understanding the insurance issues are Frankel (2002), Starkman (2004), and Starkman and Morrissey (2004a, 2004b).

28. Silverstein had to find tenants not only for the Freedom Tower but for 7 World Trade Center, his recently topped-out office tower across the street from Ground Zero.

29. Selection of the cultural components of rebuilding the WTC site is beyond the scope of this chapter.

30. In June 2004, after some delay, state and city officials announced that they had chosen four institutions as cultural anchors for the WTC site: the Signature Theater Company, the Joyce Theater, the Freedom Center, and the Drawing Center (Pogrebin 2004a).

REFERENCES

Alliance for Downtown New York. 2003. *Transportation Priorities for Lower Manhattan: Executive and Users Group Survey on Transportation and Infrastructure*. New York: Alliance for Downtown New York (April).

Alliance for Downtown New York, et al. 2002. *Key Principles in Rebuilding Lower Manhattan*. New York: Alliance for Downtown New York, Association for a Better New York, Partnership for New York City, and Real Estate Board of New York (September).

Bagli, Charles V. 2002a. "Commercial Space Mix Could Affect Revenues and Race for Governor." *New York Times*, July 17.

———. 2002b. "Visions for Ground Zero: The Debate: Architects' Proposals May Inspire but Have Little to Do with Reality." *New York Times*, December 19.

———. 2003a. "Agencies Jockey for Control over Future of Ground Zero Design." *New York Times*, February 7.

———. 2003b. "Trade Center Developer Objects to City's Insurance Talks." *New York Times*, February 16.

———. 2003c. "Queens Politicians Oppose Airport–Trade Center Land Swap." *New York Times*, April 2.

———. 2003d. "Pataki Seeks Insurance Settlement So Work Can Begin on Trade Center." *New York Times*, October 10.

Betts, Roland. 2004. Interview with the author. November 22.

Birch, Eugenie. Forthcoming. "U.S. Planning Culture Under Pressure: Major Elements Endure and Flourish in the Face of Crisis." In *Comparative Planning Cultures*, edited by Bishwapriya Sanyal. New York: Routledge.

Bloomberg, Michael R., Office of the Mayor of New York City, 2002 "New York City's Vision for Lower Manhattan." December.

Burden, Amanda (American Institute of Certified Planners, AICP). 2004. Letter to John Whitehead (LMDC chairman). March 8.

Campbell, Robert. 2004. "Proposed Twin Towers Memorial Makes a Virtue of Simplicity." *Boston Globe*, February 15.

Choa, Christopher. 2002. Letter to John Whitehead (LMDC chairman). April 26.

Civic Alliance. 2002. *Listening to the City: Report of the Proceedings, July 20 and 22, 2002, Jacob K. Javits Convention Center, New York City*. New York: Civic Alliance.

Cockfield Jr., Errol A. 2004a. "Rebuilding the World Trade Center; Despite a Gloomy Forecast for Financing, Groundbreaking for the Freedom Tower Gets Pushed Up." *Newsday*, May 6.

———. 2004b. "Getting Ground Zero Off Ground; Critics Are Saying That Silverstein's Plans for the Area Are the Biggest Gamble of the Developer's Career." *Newsday*, May 24.

Collins, Glenn, and David W. Dunlap. 2004. "The 9/11 Memorial: How Pluribus Became Unum." *New York Times*, January 19.

Crain's New York Business. 2002. "Downtown Needs Pataki" (editorial). November 11.

———. 2003. "Gov's Downtown Vision Dims Land Swap Hopes." May 5.

Cuozzo, Steve. 2003a. "Damage and Delay." *New York Post*, March 31.

———. 2003b. "Downtown Wake-up Call Builds." *New York Post*, April 1.

Denitto, Emily, and Amy Feldman. 1996. "Downtown Is Boomtown." *Crain's New York Business*, June 24.

Doctoroff, Daniel (deputy mayor). 2003. Letter to John P. Cahill (chief of staff for Governor George E. Pataki). March.

Dunlap, David W. 1995. "Bringing Downtown Back Up." *New York Times*, October 15.

———. 2003. "After Year of Push and Pull, Two Visions Met at 1,776 Feet." *New York Times*, December 26.

———. 2004a. "At Ground Zero Memorial, Trying to Make Three Plans Work as One." *New York Times*, January 12.

———. 2004b. "Planners Seek More Streets Through Trade Center Site." *New York Times*, March 2.

———. 2004c. "The Fine Print on the Trade Center Site." *New York Times*, April 22.

———. 2004d. "Redevelopment Pact is Sought for World Trade Centers." *New York Times*, April 21.

———. 2004e. "In a Space This Sacred, Every Square Foot Counts." *New York Times*, April 29.

———. 2004f. "One Cornerstone, but Many Loose Ends." *New York Times*, July 4.

———. 2004g. "Developer at Ground Zero Has Twice the Capital, and Extra Clout." *New York Times*, December 8.

Flint, Anthony. 2002. "WTC Site Designs to Be Unveiled; Second Round of Ideas on Rebuilding Stirs Lively Debate." *Boston Globe*, December 18.

Frankel, Alison. 2002. "Double Indemnity." *The American Lawyer* (September 4).

Glanz, James, and Eric Lipton. 2003. *City in the Sky: The Rise and Fall of the World Trade Center*. New York: New York Times Books.

Goldberger, Paul. 2002. "The Skyline: Groundwork." *The New Yorker* (May 20): 86+.

———. 2003a. "The Skyline: Designing Downtown." *The New Yorker* (January 6): 62+.

———. 2003b. "The Skyline: Urban Warriors; Daniel and Nina Libeskind Thought They Had Figured Out How to Get a Building Built. Then They Came to New York." *The New Yorker* (September 25): 73+.

———. 2004a. "The Skyline: Slings and Arrows: The Architectural Machinations at Ground Zero Can Be Treacherous." *The New Yorker* (February 9): 84+.

———. 2004b. *Up from Zero: Politics, Architecture, and the Rebuilding of New York*. New York: Random House.

Graves, Neil, and William Neuman. 2003. "No-Rules Memorial Contest." *New York Post*, April 29.

Haberman, Maggie. 2002a. "The Heat's on Pataki in Effort to Rebuild." *New York Daily News*, May 31.

———. 2002b. "WTC Land Grab—Gov Mulls 'Eminent Domain' Move to Expand Site." *New York Daily News*, July 31.

———. 2002c. "9/11: The Aftermath PA Plan: Push WTC Offices Off Site." *New York Daily News*, August 11.

———. 2002d. "PA No-Show for WTC Plans; Won't Be Part of Ground Zero Design Display Next Month." *New York Daily News*, November 23.

———. 2002e. "PA Design Enrages Silverstein." *New York Daily News*, December 23.

Haberman, Maggie, and Greg Gittich. 2003. "Gov's WTC Plan for GOP Parley." *New York Daily News*, May 2.

Haberman, Maggie, and William Neuman. 2002a. "Conflicts Plague Planners—War of Words Heating Up over Efforts to Rebuild." *New York Post*, February 18.

———. 2002b. "WTC Designer-Pick Delay—Rebuild Panel Back to the Drawing Board." *New York Post*, May 22.

Hack, Gary. 2003. Interview with the author. October 19.

Hetter, Katia, and Dan Janison. 2002. "Too Many Architects? Some Question Hiring of Another Firm in WTC Rebuilding." *Newsday*, September 20.

Kelly, Hugh F. 2002a. "Raising Lower New York." *Urban Land* (November–December): 62–69.

———. 2002b. *The New York Regional and Downtown Office Market: History and Prospects After 9/11*. New York: Civic Alliance.

Kesner, Marcie. 2002. Interview with the author. April 3.

Lentz, Philip. 2002. "Indecision Roils Port Authority; Patronage Soars at Key Agency." *Crain's New York Business*, April 22.

Levy, Julia. 2003. "Mayor Refuses to Okay Pataki's Choice for LMDC Boss." *New York Sun*, May 5.

Lombardi, Frank, and Maggie Haberman. 2003. "Fixing Ground Zero Is City's Job." *New York Daily News*, June 28.

Lower Manhattan Development Corporation (LMDC). 2002a. *Principles and Preliminary Blueprint for the Future of Lower Manhattan*. New York: LMDC (April).

———. 2002b. "PANYNJ and LMDC Select Consultant to Assist with WTC Site Plan" (press release). May 22.

———. 2003a. *World Trade Center Amended General Project Plan.* New York: LMDC.

———. 2003b. *Final Scope, World Trade Center Memorial and Redevelopment Plan: Generic Environmental Impact Statement.* New York: LMDC (September 16).

———. 2003c. *World Trade Center Site Memorial Competition Guidelines.* New York: LMDC.

———. 2004a. *World Trade Center Memorial and Redevelopment Plan: Draft Generic Environmental Impact Statement.* New York: LMDC (January).

———. 2004b. "WTC Memorial Jury Statement for Winning Design" (press release). January 13.

Lueck, Thomas J. 2002. "McGreevy Calls Trade Center Land Swap Unlikely." *New York Times*, August 22.

Machalaba, Daniel. 2002. "Towering Ambition: Low-Profile Actor Takes Center Stage at Trade Center." *Wall Street Journal*, October 23.

Matthews, Karen. 2003. "City Critique of World Trade Center Plan: Needs More Ground-Level Retail." Associated Press, October 28.

McGeveran, Tom. 2002a. "Port Authority Reasserts Grip on Towers Site." *New York Observer*, May 6.

———. 2002b. "At Tower Site Vast Top Seen as Memorial." *New York Observer*, June 17.

———. 2002c. "WTC-Airports Swap Unsheathes Conflict with Gargano, City." *New York Observer*, August 12.

———. 2003. "Will the Real Architect of the World Trade Center Site Please Stand Up?" *New York Observer*, February 10.

Nagourney, Adam. 2002. "Cuomo Faults Pace of Downtown Recovery." *New York Times*, May 16.

Neuman, William. 2002a. "Rebuild Panel's in the Dark." *New York Post*, February 1.

———. 2002b. "WTC Planners Mend Fences." *New York Post*, April 23.

———. 2002c. "What's the WTC Rush? Downtown Planners Rail Against Short Deadlines." *New York Post*, May 7.

———. 2002d. "State Blasts LMDC Secrecy." *New York Post*, June 13.

———. 2002e. "Building Resentment over PA's Ground Zero Wish List." *New York Post*, October 28.

———. 2002f. "Double Vision for WTC—PA Disses Rebuild Team with Own Master Plan." *New York Post*, November 22.

———. 2003a. "Jersey Barrier to WTC Land Swap." *New York Post*, April 2.

———. 2003b. "Pataki Withdraws Support for WTC Land Swap." *New York Post*, June 27.

Neuman, William, and Maggie Haberman. 2002. "Rebuild Boss: Everybody Has the Final Say." *New York Post*, April 25.

Newsday. 2002. "None of the WTC Proposals Is Good Enough" (editorial). July 21.

———. 2004. "Ground Zero Fund Cut" (editorial). May 5.

New York City Department of City Planning. 2004. *World Trade Center Amended General Project Plan: City Planning Commission Review.* New York: Department of City Planning (March 1). Available at http://www.nyc.gov/html/dcp/html/wtc/wtc1.html.

New York Daily News. 2002a. "Rent Controls Ground Zero" (editorial). July 17.

———. 2002b. "Port Authority Flawed by Design" (editorial). July 20.

————. 2002c. "PA Backs Off, But Not Far Enough" (editorial). July 23.

————. 2002d. "Just Say 'No' to the Port Authority" (editorial). July 31.

————. 2002e. "Port Authority's Downtown Scam" (editorial). December 29.

————. 2004. "Rethinking the Future of WTC Rebuilding" (editorial). May 5.

New York New Visions (NYNV). 2002a. *Principles for the Rebuilding of Lower Manhattan.* New York: NYNV (March 9).

————. 2002b. "NYNV Criteria for Judging the Master Plan" (draft). June 28.

————. 2002c. Letter to Louis Tomson (president of LMDC) and Joseph Seymour (executive director of PA). September 30.

————. 2002d. "Growth Strategies Team Report: Possible Futures." May.

————. 2003. Letter to Kevin Rampe (president of LMDC). May 30.

New York Post. 2002. "A Fair First Draft" (editorial). July 17.

New York Times. 2002a. "Rebuilding Downtown" (editorial). April 3.

————. 2002b. "Foundations for Lower Manhattan" (editorial). April 29.

————. 2002c. "The Downtown We Don't Want" (editorial). July 17.

————. 2002d. "Talk to the Man in Charge" (editorial). July 20.

————. 2002e. "Listening to the City" (editorial). July 23.

————. 2002f. "Governor Pataki Weighs In" (editorial). July 31.

————. 2002g. "Under the Surface of Downtown" (editorial). November 26.

————. 2004. "Rebuilding Lower Manhattan" (editorial). May 6.

Partnerhip for New York City. 2003. *Transportation Choices and the Future of the New York City Economy.* New York: Partnership for New York City.

Pataki, Office of Governor George E. 2003. "Governor's Remarks ABNY Lunch." April 24.

Pedersen, Martin C. 2004. "Goodbye Memory Foundations, Hello Reflecting Absence." *Metropolis* (January 21). Available at: http://www.metropolismag.com/cda/urbanjournal .Php.

Pogrebin, Robin. 2004a. "Four Arts Groups Chosen for Lower Manhattan." *New York Times,* June 11.

————. 2004b. "The Incredible Shrinking Daniel Libeskind." *New York Times,* June 20.

Popper, Ellen Kirschner. 1996. "Developers Are Bullish on Wall Street." *New York Times,* June 30.

Port Authority of New York and New Jersey (PANYNJ). 2003. $250,000,000 *The Port Authority of New York and New Jersey Consolidated Notes, Series UU, Official Statement.* January 22.

Rice, Andrew. 2002. "Pataki's Side Grabs Control of Tower Site." *New York Observer,* February 8.

Rogers, Josh. 2003. "Tomson to Leave LMDC in February." *Downtown Express,* January 21–27.

Sagalyn, Lynne B. 2001. *Times Square Roulette: Remaking the City Icon.* Cambridge, Mass.: MIT Press.

Santos, Feranda. 2002. "Gov Backs Big Memorial 'Will Never Build Where Towers Stood.'" *New York Daily News,* June 30.

Seifman, David. 2003. "9/11: The Road Back; Bloomy Bids for Control." *New York Post,* June 28.

Shin, Paul H. B., and Maggie Haberman. 2002. "Secret PA Plan Cuts Through WTC Footprint." *New York Daily News*, December 27.

Smothers, Ronald. 2003. "Pataki Offer on Airports Has Two Goals, Aide Says." *New York Times*, January 24.

Starkman, Dean. 2004. "Jottings May Cut Insurers' Payouts on Twin Towers." *Wall Street Journal*, February 4.

Starkman, Dean, and Janet Morrissey. 2004a. "'Double Indemnity' with Stakes High, Trade Center Trial Hinges on Two Forms." *Wall Street Journal*, March 26.

———. 2004b. "Jury Rules for Silverstein on Trade Center Insurance." *Wall Street Journal*, December 7.

Steinhauer, Jennifer. 2004. "The West Side's Yours, Ground Zero Mine." *New York Times*, March 27.

Thrush, Glenn. 2003. "World Trade Center Officials to Choose Single Site Design." Bloomberg News Service, January 9.

Weisbrod, Carl. 2002. Interview with the author. July 9.

Wyatt, Edward. 2002a. "New Issues as Hearings Address Rebuilding." *New York Times*, January 13.

———. 2002b. "Blueprint for Ground Zero Begins to Take Shape." *New York Times*, May 4.

———. 2002c. "Rebuilding May Expand Beyond Site." *New York Times*, June 20.

———. 2002d. "Pataki's Surprising Limit on Ground Zero Design." *New York Times*, July 2.

———. 2002e. "For All Sides, a Land Swap Offers Much to Consider." *New York Times*, August 6.

———. 2002f. "Further Designs Are Sought in Rebuilding Downtown." *New York Times*, August 15.

———. 2002g. "Fewer Offices, More Options in Planning for Ground Zero." *New York Times*, October 10.

———. 2002h. "Designs Unveiled for Transit Hub at Ground Zero." *New York Times*, November 13.

———. 2002i. "Trade Center Designs Will Be Shown." *New York Times*, December 1.

———. 2002j. "Rebuilding Below Ground Zero Is at Issue." *New York Times*, December 20.

———. 2003a. New Issues as Hearings Address Rebuilding." *New York Times*, January 13.

———. 2003b. "Designs for Transit Hub Let Travelers See Sky." *New York Times*, February 22.

———. 2003c. "Panel Supports Two Tall Towers at Disaster Site." *New York Times*, February 26.

———. 2003d. "City Is Seeking Bigger Role in Rebuilding." *New York Times*, March 7.

———. 2003e. "Panel, Not Public, Will Pick Final 9/11 Memorial Design." *New York Times*, April 9.

———. 2003f. "In 9/11 Design, Rules Are Set to Be Broken." *New York Times*, April 29.

———. 2003g. "Relatives Say Plans Infringe on Twin Towers' Footprints." *New York Times*, July 9.

CHAPTER 3

Ground Zero's Landlord: The Role of the Port Authority of New York and New Jersey in the Reconstruction of the World Trade Center Site

Susan S. Fainstein

AS THE result of decades of earlier political maneuvering, the Port Authority of New York and New Jersey (PANYNJ, or PA) found itself as the lead govern-ment agency in the rebuilding of downtown Manhattan after the attack of September 11, 2001. This situation was anomalous in that the Authority had been founded as a builder of transportation and port facilities, not office struc-tures, and after its ventures into property development during the 1970s and 1980s it had vowed to return to its core functions. Because it owned the World Trade Center (WTC) site and the PATH facilities lying beneath it, however, the Authority necessarily assumed the responsibility of guiding development in the wake of the attack. At the same time, its capacity to do so was limited by its own personnel and physical losses in the attack, its engineering culture, charter restrictions preventing it from developing property for residential uses, and the recently signed leases and mortgage agreements governing the manage-ment of and revenues from the WTC property.

This chapter examines the role of the Port Authority in relationship to its history, its institutional development as a public agency with private charac-teristics, its rebuilding activities, the constraints of its leasing arrangements, its interactions with other governmental bodies and the public, and some of the transportation issues in which it is involved. I conclude with an assessment of the Authority's achievements and missed opportunities. Because the rebuilding story is still in process, any evaluation is necessarily tentative.[1]

THE PORT AUTHORITY ON SEPTEMBER 10, 2001

The Port of New York Authority came into existence on April 30, 1921, with the mandate of administering the common interests of the states of New York and New Jersey in the port.[2] Modeled on the Port of London Authority, the PANYNJ was the first organization of its kind in the Western Hemisphere.[3] Beginning in 1930, when the Authority gained control of the Holland Tunnel linking New York and New Jersey, it became a massive fund-raising machine that did not depend on the assent of taxpayers and legislatures in order to launch projects.[4] With the power to issue revenue bonds based on its anticipated proceeds, it could engage in huge infrastructure enterprises, subject only to the approval of its board and the governors of the two states. But given its fiduciary responsibility to its bondholders, underpinned by court rulings that contracts with bondholders have primacy over legislative mandates, it chose its projects with an eye to their profitability. As a PA employee put it to me, "The Authority was created to be self-supporting, not to be a public service agency." It is not bound by the usual civil service regulations, and it makes its decisions behind closed doors. Although its board meetings are nominally open to the public, their venue is obscure, and decisions made at open meetings are preordained. While the Authority remains a governmental institution, its orientation and entrepreneurial tradition give it many of the aspects of a private, for-profit entity. In this respect, it conforms to the model depicted in an article by Roger Friedland, Frances Piven, and Robert Alford (1978), who argue that public participation has little effect on agencies concerned with capital accumulation, while social welfare agencies are far more open. The division of labor these authors describe presciently characterizes the distribution of responsibilities between the PA and the Lower Manhattan Development Corporation (LMDC), which was entrusted with the chore of working with the surrounding communities in developing plans for reviving downtown.

At the same time, the PA's operations are subject to political pressures from which private corporations are normally exempt. These pressures are political in both the narrow sense of personal influence and in the broader one of policy directions. The governors of New York and New Jersey make appointments to the PA board and hire high-level staff, within a tradition whereby the executive director is a New York appointee and the board chair comes from New Jersey. Increasingly, and in contrast to the days of Austin Tobin, appointments are rewards for political service.[5] According to many observers, the quality of the Authority's investments and operations has correspondingly suffered. In the words of one longtime staff member, "The breadth and depth of political appointments was unprecedented [once Pataki became governor of New York]." Furthermore, the Authority's research and forecasting department was cut back drastically in the 1990s, and staff members were restrained from speaking to outsiders.

In terms of policy, decisions are responsive to the competition between New York and New Jersey. The buffeting over questions of which state was being favored reached fever pitch during the late 1990s, with Mayor Rudolph Giuliani of New York demanding that control of LaGuardia and Kennedy Airports be returned to the city and with the two governors at loggerheads to the extent that for eighteen months no new projects were approved (Smothers 2000a). Caught up in the dispute was the effort by the Authority to lease the World Trade Center structures to private interests, which was delayed for more than a year owing to the obduracy of the governors (Smothers 2000b).[6]

These factors—personal politics and the New York–New Jersey rivalry— were key to the original deal that had culminated in the construction of the Trade Center. In a now often-told story, David Rockefeller, president of Chase Bank, persuaded his brother, Nelson Rockefeller, governor of New York, to consider a proposal to build a world trade center along the Hudson in downtown Manhattan. The Port Authority was designated as the developer of the site, marking its first move into taking on what is normally a private-sector function: the speculative development of a large office complex.

The Port Authority was chosen as the vehicle for implementing the project because it possessed the right of eminent domain, it had access to financing capital, and it was subject to control by New York's governor. At first, then Governor Robert Meyner of New Jersey could see no benefit to his state from this proposition, but he agreed to sign off on it in return for the Port Authority acquiring and upgrading the bankrupt Hudson and Manhattan Railroad, renamed the PATH (Port Authority Trans-Hudson), a line connecting Manhattan and New Jersey (Gillespie 2002). The Authority had until then resisted taking on any mass transit responsibilities, and to ensure that it would not be called upon to do so again, it wrote into the bonds financing the Trade Center a proviso prohibiting it from funding mass transit for their lifetime. In a development wholly unforeseen at that time, the extension of the financial district westward combined with the convenience of the PATH connection to stimulate the growth of an enormous office district in Jersey City. This complex, in fact if not in name, is an extension of the downtown central business district (CBD) and should be seen in this light rather than only as a competitor to Manhattan.

After the completion of the twin towers and adjacent structures during the 1970s, the Authority engaged in various other property developments aimed at stimulating economic development within the bistate area. Not all of these were successes, however. Within the nation, privatization increasingly became the mantra for the conduct of governmental functions, and the 1994 election of a Republican, George Pataki, as governor brought to New York State a push to limit the role of government. With his urging, the PA returned to its earlier focus and began to shed its real estate ambitions. As part of this redirection, in September 2000 it issued a request for proposals (RFP) to real estate corporations calling for bids on a ninety-nine-year lease on the WTC property (Smothers 2000c). By this date, despite earlier difficulties in filling the buildings, the complex was fully rented and generating gross income of about $200 million a year (Bagli 2001a). After complex negotiations, the Authority awarded the lease to the developer Larry Silverstein for the office segment and to Westfield America, a shopping mall operator, for its retail portion. The bid was worth $3.2 billion (Bagli 2001b). When the deal closed in July 2001, New York governor Pataki declared: "When I came into office in 1995, the Port Authority had hotels, shopping malls, industrial parks and we asked why. We have worked hard to put those developments in the hands of the private sector experts who pay taxes. And today the Port Authority returns to the core mission of dealing with transportation" (Smothers 2001a).

Thus, at the time of the attacks on the twin towers, only six weeks later, the Authority no longer controlled the management of the buildings and was limited by the lease in its powers over the land to which it retained ownership. In line with its renewed mission to focus on transportation, it redeployed or divested itself of many of the personnel who had been involved with managing its real estate holdings. Because the transfer of control was so recent, the insurance arrangements relating to the structures had not been fully formalized by September 11. The insurance carried by Silverstein and Westfield, however, in providing compensation of at least $3.5 billion, greatly exceeded the amount ($1.5 billion) that the Port Authority would have received from its insurers if it had not leased the buildings.

THE IMPACT OF 9/11

The Port Authority suffered the shock of 9/11 in multiple ways. With its headquarters housed in the Trade Center and its police force responsible for patrolling the buildings, it took a direct hit. Its executive director, Neil Levin, was among the seventy-four PA employees killed in the attack. The remaining personnel, traumatized by the event, nevertheless faced the urgent job of dealing with the aftermath of the disaster. The tasks they faced included appointing new leadership, making a plan to clean up the site, providing grief counseling for survivors, providing utilities and emergency services, and acquiring new offices. In the words of one staff member:

> The immediate impact was intensely personal. [On September 11] some people left the building right away, others stayed and didn't get out. Top

executives and public safety staff were immediately on the scene and stayed for days. There were so many emergency needs—staff were on the phone responding to miscellaneous calls. They set up command centers. But even in the first few days, when most of the staff were in rescue and recovery mode, the law department had to start dealing with insurance issues, and the engineering department, which knew the infrastructure of the site, directed rescue teams. And we still had to deal with the airports, the tunnels, payroll.

In addition to the pressing tasks associated with the rescue operation and with securing the city's tunnels, bridges, airports, and harbor, the Authority had to begin planning the rebuilding effort. Its role in carrying out this task, however, was complicated by the parallel function of the LMDC. Appointed by the governor and the mayor, the LMDC was supposed to work "in cooperation with its partners in the public and private sectors to coordinate long-term planning for the World Trade Center site and surrounding communities" (Lower Manhattan Development Corporation 2004). The LMDC's website indicates its commitment to a "transparent planning process" in which the public would have "a central role in shaping the future of Lower Manhattan." In contrast to the Port Authority, with its technocratic, engineering mentality, the LMDC has acted as the principal liaison with the various constituencies among the public having an interest in the rebuilding process. A Port Authority staff member commented that the "LMDC was created in part because the Port Authority was not in a position to engage the public in a discussion of design issues, economic issues." Moreover, while the PA's interest was limited to the WTC site, the LMDC concerned itself with the entire downtown district.

PLANNING THE REBUILDING OF GROUND ZERO

The differing approaches and mandates of the LMDC and the Port Authority became apparent at the inception of the planning process. The LMDC began by promoting the idea of a mixed-use development on the site, including residential occupancy and cultural institutions. The Port Authority dismissed the concept of housing construction, arguing that "it is part of the organization's charter that they cannot develop and manage residential buildings" (McGeveran 2002). Enlarging its mandate to include housing would have required legislative action by both states, and the Authority never showed any interest in mounting the necessary lobbying effort, even though, at the time, New York had stronger market demand for housing than for office space. Although the Authority did not dismiss the possibility of developing cultural institutions, which could be justified under its mandate to promote economic development, its spokesperson expressed concern over the financial prospects of such projects, noting that "somehow the Port Authority has to receive revenues" (McGeveran 2002). Further differences surfaced when the LMDC issued an RFP for planning of the site without coordinating its action with the Port Authority. At the behest of the PA, the LMDC withdrew its request, and subsequently a joint RFP went out. Within two weeks of its issuance, the agencies announced the selection of the design firm Beyer Blinder Belle (BBB), causing the *Times* architectural critic, Herbert Muschamp (2002), to declare: "We have been witnessing the construction of mediocrity in Lower Manhattan."

The release of the Beyer Blinder Belle plans provoked a loud, negative outcry from civic groups and editorialists. The firm had responded to a program mandated by the sponsors calling for 11 million square feet of office space, 600,000 square feet of retail space, and a 600,000-square-foot hotel, in addition to a memorial for those who died in the collapse of the buildings and transit facilities (Wyatt and Bagli 2002). Much of the criticism centered on the height and density of the proposed structures, which were crowded onto the space remaining after the footprints of the original towers were left clear. The six slightly varied "development scenarios" were intended only to indicate the placement of buildings, not their architecture, but many people interpreted the blank, modernist structures used as "placeholders" in the site plans as indicating their final appearance. The ensuing avalanche of criticism prompted the LMDC, in conjunction with the Civic Alliance to Rebuild Downtown New York (a coalition of civic groups) and a reluctant Port Authority, to sponsor an exercise called "Listening to the City."[7]

On July 20, nearly five thousand people, each provided with access to a laptop computer, gathered at the Jacob K. Javits Convention Center to register their opinions on the future design of Ground Zero. The Regional Plan Association (RPA), which was responsible for convening the gathering, summarized the main concerns of the participants:

> Central to ... the rebuilding mission was a desire to ensure that the needs of low- and moderate-income people and new immigrants are not forgotten. The idea of including poor and moderate-income New Yorkers permeated "Listening to the City"; participants repeatedly reminded decision makers to make affordable housing a priority, to promote job-training and development programs for those who lost jobs or were left underemployed ... to provide adequate public facilities such as childcare centers and schools. ... 55 percent of the July 20 participants identified housing for all income levels and ages as most important. (Civic Alliance 2002, 8)

Besides their hopes, "Listening to the City" participants articulated additional concerns. They feared that business interests would dominate the redevelopment process and that undue attention would be paid to the needs of the Trade Center leaseholders at the expense of the public's interests (Civic Alliance 2002, 9).

Reaction to criticisms of density was minimal—the office component was reduced from eleven million to ten million square feet. Joseph Seymour, the Authority's new executive director, noted that by acquiring the Deutsche Bank building across the street from Ground Zero and thereby enlarging the site, densities would be reduced to a more tolerable level.[8] Speaking on November 14, 2003, before a breakfast forum sponsored by *Crain's New York Business*, he stated that "the Port Authority has an obligation to restore 10 million square feet" (Matthews 2003). The Authority justified this obligation in terms of the Silverstein lease, but the lease provided it with cover for doing what it wanted to do anyway—build structures that would relieve the pressure to realize maximum revenue by promising the highest rate of return. The call for affordable housing received no attention; as mentioned earlier, the Port Authority's charter prohibits it from acting as a housing developer.[9] There were incentives in place to encourage housing elsewhere downtown, but essentially the Port Authority's ownership of the WTC land offered less rather than more flexibility, as might have been expected of land owned by governmental institution.

On the other hand, the desire for arts venues on the site evoked a positive response (Salamon 2003). Evidently decisionmakers have become persuaded that arts clusters promote economic development even when not themselves moneymakers. This perspective, along with a favoring of the arts by elite groups, has outweighed the Authority's reluctance to yield space to activities with low revenue potential. A *New York Times* (2004) editorial reflected this viewpoint:

> Ever since 9/11, there has been serious talk of including a strong cultural presence in the rebuilding at ground zero. It's worth remembering why. For all the gravity of the site itself, and for all the dignity of Michael Arad's memorial design, ground zero is about more than remembering the lives of those who died in terrorist attacks or the events that caused their deaths. It is also about the creation of new vitality. The emergence of a new cultural hub in Lower Manhattan is a way of going beyond memory, a way of enriching, fulfilling and reinterpreting the emotional context of 9/11 itself. We should visit ground zero to honor the victims and remember that day, but we should stay to celebrate life itself in a way that only the arts allow us to do.

Despite much rhetoric concerning the triumph of democracy embodied in the rejection of the Beyer Blinder Belle plan by the Port Authority and the LMDC after "Listening to the City," the program on which the firm had developed its proposals remained largely unchanged. In a report that gave mixed reviews to the lower Manhattan planning process, the RPA commented that despite public opinion, "plans for the site were too dense, too dominated by office space, and too boring. Yet an office space program of ten million square feet continued to shape the World Trade Center master plan, despite lack of funding, unsupportive market conditions and a united civic community calling for a different approach" (Regional Plan Association 2004, 6). Generally real-estate experts identified slack demand for offices as a serious problem. One informed observer, who had advised the governor against moving rapidly to build new office space, asserted that no firm would be willing to lease space in a building so readily identified as a target: "There won't be tenants in the near future. Even the Port Authority staff won't go there very quickly. They are frightened."

The principal response of the Port Authority to criticism was to raise its architectural aspirations. Thus, it cosponsored with the LMDC an architectural competition for the design of the site, eventually won by Studio Daniel Libeskind (Wyatt 2003; Todorovich 2003). Further, it selected on its own, to the surprise of architectural critics, Santiago Calatrava, a highly praised, imaginative architect who specializes in transportation facilities, as the designer of the permanent transportation center to be located on the site (Port Authority of New York and New Jersey 2004; Todorovich 2003).[10]

The selection of Daniel Libeskind reflected the power of Governor Pataki in those decisions where he felt the need to involve himself. According to a member of the LMDC who had been heavily involved in it, the selection process was conducted by a "site working plan group" headed by Roland Betts, a member of the LMDC board who had a close relationship with President Bush. The members of the board had narrowed the choice of designers down to two architects—Studio Daniel Libeskind and Rafael Viñoly's architectural team, called THINK—and then had unanimously decided on Viñoly. The governor, however, reversed this decision in response to some of the family members of the victims who liked the mournful aspects of the Libeskind plan. From the PA's viewpoint, this was a highly risky move, since Betts, who was enraged by the decision, nearly departed the scene. Since the PA depended on federal money for construction of transportation facilities, angering Betts put that money in jeopardy (Goldberger 2004).

The Silverstein lease has acted as a significant constraint on the Authority's choices in planning for the site. Silverstein's insurance provided for the replacement of office space but not for residential construction, and the size of the award depended partly on a commitment to replace the amount of space lost. Central to the issue of the lease was Silverstein's argument that the attacks constituted two incidents and thus his insurers owed him $7 billion, or twice the value of a single destructive event (*WTC Properties LLC v. Hartford Fire Insur-*

ance Co., et al. [September 26, 2003], *New York Law Journal* [October 1, 2003], 18). While Silverstein's case was in court, no one wished to jeopardize the possibility of his receiving the larger sum since it would provide the money for rebuilding. Using the insurance proceeds would allow for construction without borrowing, thereby lowering projected rents and making the building more attractive to prospective tenants. Moreover, given the slack demand for downtown office space and the absence of a committed tenant, Silverstein would have serious difficulty obtaining debt financing. As of March 2005, the outcome of the court proceedings was mixed: Silverstein lost his case against one insurance company but won a smaller sum against another insurance group. If his insurance payments add up to only $3.5 billion, he will have funds sufficient to build only one of the proposed office towers (Golson 2004). Construction on the iconic, 2.6-million-square-foot Freedom Tower commenced in the summer of 2004, with the laying of a cornerstone by Governor Pataki, but subsequently stalled.

The court decisions left an opening for the Port Authority to renegotiate the lease or to buy out Silverstein's interest in the remainder of the area:

"There was this hold-your-breath attitude until one could see if the money was going to be double or not, and no one wanted to jinx the ability to get a lot of money to do ultimately whatever the program would be," said Rick Bell, executive director the New York Chapter of the American Institute of Architects. "This [the court decision on the larger sum] gives us the opportunity to rethink the programming of the site.... What never made sense was 10 million square feet of office space." (Golson 2004)

The PA had already sought more flexibility in planning the retail portion of the site by purchasing the interest of the leaseholder, Westfield America. Westfield initially paid $127 million for a ninety-nine-year lease on the shopping mall in May 2001 and received $140 million in the buyback (*Canberra Times*, September 16, 2003).[11] Westfield had earlier expressed unhappiness with the Libeskind plan, which moved a considerable proportion of the formerly underground retail space to the surface and broke up the continuous row of stores deemed essential to shopping mall success. According to Frank Lowy, Westfield's chairman, "While Westfield wanted to be a part of the future of the World Trade Center, we recognized the conflict between the interests of the public and the needs of our commercial/net lease rights. Selling our interest back to the Port will allow the public interest to take precedence" (quoted in *Canberra Times*, September 16, 2003). For Westfield, now the largest shopping mall operator in the world, abandoning what had formerly been its highest-revenue-grossing site freed it from negotiations about the site and gave it immediate use of the capital otherwise tied up in it. In the words of the financial analyst Mark Ebbinghaus: "From an earnings point of view... it's a negligible impact. They probably got a bit more than their holding cost on the whole thing and can redeploy the capital to a higher use.... I think it would take some time for it to become clear as to what exactly is going to happen with that site.... [They] just weren't prepared to continue to devote time and resources to something that was actually pretty marginal anyway" (*Canberra Times*, September 16, 2003).

Until there is a full build-out of the anticipated office space, the Authority is considering building low-rise structures for shops. According to its executive director, "We want to fill the voids.... We want to create street activity [in the meanwhile]" (Dunlap 2004a). Although the master plan allows for up to one million square feet of retail space, the Authority is projecting only 650,000 square feet. Its director disavows any intention of having his organization control the tenant mix, "because that's not our expertise" (Dunlap 2004b), and therefore it expects to put out an RFP for bids on a new retail lease.

Also in the interest of having increased room to maneuver, the Authority freed Silverstein from stipulations imposed by his mortgagor, GMAC, on the payoff of the loan that financed his purchase of the buildings (Bagli 2003). As a result of the GMAC settlement, Silverstein and his investment partners received almost all of their own equity back, even while they retained control of the right to build on the property (Starkman and Frangos 2004a). The financial relationship supporting Silverstein's continued role thus really only existed between the Port Authority and his insurers, since the PA continued to receive annual rental payments of $120 million from his business interruption insurance. Silverstein himself was not spending his own money, and his insurance money could not be used for some other purpose. The PA estimated that as a result of prepaying the loans to Westfield and Silverstein, it would be saving $500 million in interest and fees that could be applied to the restoration process (Port Authority board meeting minutes, September 10, 2003).

It was rumored that the Authority was going to try to limit Silverstein's role to construction of the Freedom Tower and seek other developers for the rest of the site (Starkman and Frangos 2004b). According to the *New York Post*, the PA had demanded a detailed accounting from Silverstein of his rebuilding plans. The Authority expected the developer to pay not only the costs of construction of the Freedom Tower but part of the infrastructure costs for the complex as a whole, which, for the first phase of reconstruction, were estimated at more than $1 billion (Neuman 2004).[12] In the agreement between the PA and Silverstein pursuant to the retiring of the GMAC debt, the Authority required the developer to use all insurance proceeds, including the money (amounting already to $100 million at that time) he had spent on his legal fees in connection with the insurance litigation (Port Authority board meeting minutes, November 20, 2003).

Adhering to the terms of the lease meant remaining committed to the initial program of constructing a very large amount of office space despite considerable criticism on various grounds, both practical and idealistic. The practical consideration was that demand for new office space downtown was weak and that competing with downtown would be other enterprises on which the city was embarking in—west midtown, Brooklyn, and Queens (Clark 2004; Vitullo-Martin 2004). There is considerable disagreement among experts concerning how much office space the city is likely to absorb in the future. Those who base their prognosis on past performance say that the present weakness in the office market is cyclical, all the excess space will be absorbed, and there will be demand for all the new space that comes on the market if it is added gradually. Even much of the existing vacant space is the result not so much of an overall surplus but of offices being unsuitable for contemporary uses. With new technologies, however, it is unclear whether employment expansion will necessarily give rise to the space demands of former times. Even though there has been a reconcentration of employment in the urban core of the New York metro area, employees have less need than in the past to be physically in the office, and therefore in the future the same number of employees may require less space.[13]

Nonmarket considerations include a concern about the environmental impact of so many huge structures, revulsion against so much commercialization, and a desire for low- and moderate-income housing. Some of the criticism was summarized in a *New York Times* article (Dunlap 2003a):

What may have been lost in the transition are voices; voices that might have questioned basic assumptions about a program in which skyscraping commercial development is to accompany the memorial, cultural and open spaces; voices that might have asked whether a public domain under tight control is truly public.

"It does make a huge difference," said J. Max Bond Jr. of the architectural firm of Davis Brody Bond. "No one really took exception to the program, in a profound sense. . . . The rush to get to a building almost inevitably set up a process that was exclusive and elitist." He added: "All these public spaces are going to be like shopping malls: privately controlled" (Dunlap 2003a).

According to a PA staff member, buying out Silverstein was too expensive for the Authority to contemplate, given its straitened budgetary circumstances. As a consequence of renegotiating the leases the Port Authority held with the city for the airports, it was now giving up a substantial proportion of the revenues it had received from the airports under the former lease terms. Silverstein's payments under the lease amounted to 10 percent of the Authority's revenues, and it would be extremely difficult to find another developer willing to build on the site, given the soft market for office space downtown. This staff member noted that "it's easier . . . [to keep Silverstein as] a kind of fall guy on the number of square feet." In addition, unlike Westfield America, Silverstein did not regard loss of the site with indifference, and Port Authority staff felt a moral obligation toward the developer.

If the Authority did buy out Silverstein's remaining interest, it could much more easily respond to public demands for less density and a greater mix of uses. But it would also be more vulnerable to popular pressure and would lack the excuse of the lease to support its preference for the highest possible revenue producers. A financial incentive to maintain Silverstein's position exists as long as his business interruption insurance continues to pay his $120 million per year rent. But subtracting the payouts for this rent correspondingly reduces the amount available for future rebuilding.

TRANSPORTATION INVESTMENTS

Much less public discussion has surrounded the transportation issues raised by the rebuilding. The Port Authority, in this area of its core expertise, has proceeded rapidly with reconstruction and has evaded challenges to its efforts. The only significant controversy surrounds the question of a rail connection to Long Island and Kennedy Airport (see Moss, this volume). As part of its new lease agreement with the city for Kennedy and LaGuardia Airports, the PA committed $560 million to the Kennedy access project; however, this amount would probably constitute no more than 7 percent of the final cost (Zupan 2003; Luo 2004; *Gotham Gazette* 2004).[14] As of this writing, the source of the remaining funding remains unclear.

Almost at once after the destruction of the WTC, the Authority began rebuilding the PATH tracks and an adjacent $500 million "temporary" station, which forms the base for the Calatrava terminal described earlier. Although the PATH tracks traversed the supposedly sacrosanct footprints of the twin towers, the PA ignored any sentiment opposing the route. Even the governor, who had involved himself in other decisions concerning the site in order to respect the wishes of the victims' families, did not interject himself into this issue. The Authority located the terminal and tracks where it did because of time and cost considerations: any attempt to move the right-of-way from its existing location would involve extensive reengineering that would delay transit restoration and be extremely expensive. A member of the LMDC board commented to me:

I don't know how judgments are made as to what gets to public forums and what does not. . . . [Allowing public discussion of the PATH station] would have delayed the reopening. The decision [on the station] was a little bit extra-process. By far the logical decision was to keep the same route. [But] there was a lot of emotion over this. The staffs of the Port Authority and the LMDC conspired to keep that decision from being taken by either board.

There have been protests from relatives of the attack victims, but they have received little attention. The lavish praise for the Calatrava station and general acknowledgment of the improved connections that will occur downtown after the WTC transportation center is linked to the proposed new Fulton Street subway station have outweighed any objections to this endeavor. Whereas the Regional Plan Association criticized the Port Authority for its office-building program, it has had nothing but praise for its approach to rebuilding transport facilities:

It [along with the other transportation agencies] repaired and restored Lower Manhattan's infrastructure and public space with unprecedented speed and efficiency. . . . PATH service [was] . . . restored and the Trade Center site was cleaned up far earlier than nearly anyone anticipated. . . . The Port Authority's selection of Santiago Calatrava's inspiring design for a new PATH station and the MTA's planning and design for the Fulton Street Transit Center should change the image of Lower Manhattan. (Regional Plan Association 2004, 6)

In the meanwhile, the PA was upgrading the PATH train fleet and stations. It could do so expeditiously because it already had plans in place for improving the system before the attack on the Trade Center. It was also planning an extension of the railroad to Newark Airport, thus ensuring a one-seat airport connection from downtown (Weisbrod 2003). Therefore, even without the huge expenditure on a Long Island airport connection, downtown businesses would already have relatively easy access to an airport with a full range of both international and national routes. The PATH extension, however, would not address the problem of bringing in commuters from the Long Island suburbs, and if carried out without a parallel project for Long Island, it would probably be viewed as favoritism by the PA of New Jersey over New York.

INSTITUTIONAL RELATIONSHIPS AND PLANNING DOWNTOWN

The involvement of the Port Authority in planning the reconstruction of downtown is in many respects an accident of history. If it had stuck to its original

mission of developing the port, if it had not been designated by Nelson Rockefeller as the vehicle for building the World Trade Center, and if it had not
taken on the PATH system as a consequence of the bargaining between New
York and New Jersey over the buildings' construction, then it would have had
no role to play in the reconstruction of downtown. But as fate would have it,
this public entity, which operates according to private-sector rules, is the central player in the reconstruction enterprise. At the same time, there are other
significant institutional actors, including the city of New York, the Empire
State Development Corporation (ESDC), the governors of New York and New
Jersey, the federal government, the Metropolitan Transportation Authority
(MTA), and the Lower Manhattan Development Corporation (LMDC). These
institutions have interlocking directorates, but they also have different constituencies and varying abilities to impose their will on each other. The federal
government, the PA, the MTA, and the LMDC all have funds at their disposal
that give them leverage in the development process. The mayor and the governors have powers of appointment over the officers and boards of the quasi-
public agencies, but the governor of New York State is in a much stronger
position than the mayor of New York City in this respect. According to one
high-placed informant:

> It's a jumble of who's in charge. Nobody's in charge. The governor's office
> lacks the skills. The LMDC can't do it, and the mayor's office is too
> preoccupied [over the West Side]. The Port Authority has the right
> skills. It should be the governor's entity . . . but they lay back and look
> for guidance [from the governor]. It's a result of poor leadership [within
> the agency], but it's the governor's fault.

Governor Pataki's ultimate authority has been acknowledged by several of
the authors in this volume, and it is somewhat unclear the extent to which
the Port Authority is responding to its own internal institutional culture or
the governor's prerogatives in the decisions it has made. The speed with which
reconstruction has proceeded, the choice of the Libeskind plan, and adherence
to Libeskind's siting of the Freedom Tower are all actions that reflect the
governor's role.[15] The most significant decision—the commitment to rebuild
ten million square feet of office space—served the interests of both the governor and the Authority in its potential to bring in the largest amount of future
revenue; thus, it cannot be said that either was the dominant force. The irony
of the governor's position is that his commitment to an office-building program
contradicts his frequent claim that market forces rather than government planning should determine the trajectory of real estate development. Overcoming
the strictures of the Silverstein lease in regard to the amount of office space,

however, would have required opposing the wishes of the developer and undoubtedly would also have produced litigation and delay. In this regard, there is a contrast between the calculations of Westfield America, which is an Australia-based, public, multinational corporation with no particular affiliation to New York City, and Silverstein Properties, which is a privately held company whose principal investor prides himself on his commitment to the city. Larry Silverstein reportedly has told the governor, "I really feel we have an obligation to rebuild. If we don't, the terrorists will have won" (quoted in Bagli and Wyatt 2003).

Many of the decisions that have pushed the siting of various elements in the reconstruction have failed to reach the political level, have not been of particular interest to the governor, or have been resolved by allowing engineering considerations to drive the final determination. These include the location of ventilating towers for the PATH station and various encroachments on the footprints of the towers, including ramps, underground circulation areas, and the PATH tracks. Urging by the LMDC, the Civic Alliance, and various members of the city's elite groups seems to have overcome the reluctance of the Port Authority to support cultural facilities on the site.

Even though the WTC is within the boundaries of New York City and traditionally city governments have determined land uses within their jurisdictions, planning for downtown has largely been outside mayoral control. In December 2002, the mayor outlined a plan for the redesign of lower Manhattan that encompassed the whole area between the two rivers rather than just focusing on the WTC site (Blake 2002). Estimated to cost $10.6 billion, the mayor's plan would transform downtown from a financial center into a diverse community of residences, schools, libraries, movie theaters, and other types of businesses. According to the *New York Times*:

> The mayor's plan is in many ways a direct challenge to the Port Authority of New York and New Jersey, the Metropolitan Transportation Authority, and the Lower Manhattan Development Corporation, which have led the rebuilding efforts at ground zero. For example, Mr. Bloomberg began his remarks deriding the original World Trade Center, saying, "The twin towers' voracious appetite for tenants weakened the entire downtown real estate market," a clear poke at the plans released ... by the development corporation, which called for substantial commercial development at the site. (Steinhauer 2002)

The Regional Plan Association (2004, 7) praised the mayor's conceptions but complained that "efforts to build Lower Manhattan's civic amenities to create a more attractive and livable community [as envisioned by the mayor] ... are lagging." According to Port Authority staff, however, the mayor's office never followed up on his original proposals, and they were never fleshed out. Moreover, the $10.6 billion for the mayor's plan, to be drawn from insurance money, federal funds, proceeds from the sale of development rights, and liberty bonds, had already mostly been spoken for by other agencies for other purposes.[16]

The most common explanation for the mayor's seeming lack of enthusiasm for involving himself in rebuilding downtown after he originally announced his plan has been his preoccupation with plans for the redevelopment of west midtown. As a consequence, he has ceded the lead on downtown to the governor and the state agencies: "While the two have not actually taken out a map and divided up the city with tiny push pins, their staffs have come to an agreement that each will do much of the work—and, their aides hope, get the credit—for their area of interest" (Steinhauer 2004). Although this arrangement appeared amicable, it did not confront the competition for funding and office tenants between the two development areas, both of which, as presently planned, will require huge transportation and infrastructure investments and both of which will add many millions of square feet of office space to the city's stock.

The mayor's office does occasionally express an opinion about the WTC site. In October 2003, Deputy Mayor Daniel Doctoroff wrote a letter to the Port Authority and the LMDC calling for more street-level retail than was in the plan (Dunlap 2003b). The Port Authority's public response did not reject the demand out of hand, but staff members privately indicated to me that they considered below-ground retail a convenience for PATH commuters and were not worried that it would destroy street life on the surface. After this expression of concern by the mayor's office, its interest in planning the site apparently again subsided until six months later. Then, evidently to gain more leverage in the ultimate design, the mayor's office drew attention to the fact that the city still owns some of the mapped streets within the sixteen-acre site. The *Times* quoted former Bronx borough president Herman Badillo, who voted against the original Trade Center agreement when he was a member of the Board of Estimate, as saying: "The more the city is involved . . . the better, because I've never found that the Port Authority is interested in looking after the interests of the people of New York City" (Dunlap 2004c).[17]

A further complicating factor is the involvement of the state of New Jersey as a consequence of its power within the Port Authority. The governor of New Jersey did not play a noticeable role in the discussions over downtown, perhaps partly because he was preoccupied with a series of scandals that culminated in his resignation from office. The Port Authority, however, has been sensitive to New Jersey's interest in the outcome. Essentially New Jersey has direct stakes in three aspects of the reconstruction: the creation of a memorial that satisfies the families of Jersey residents who lost their lives in the destruction of the towers; improvement in PATH train operations, including its exten-sion to Newark Airport; and the continuing importance of the Hudson River side of downtown as a financial center. The Jersey City office complex is sym-biotic with the downtown CBD even while, as an artifact of jurisdictional lines, it competes with it. Less directly but equally consequentially, the fund-ing of New Jersey's ambitious mass transit plans depends on revenues supplied by the Port Authority. Any shrinkage in PA income from its downtown source would therefore limit New Jersey's ability to spend on capital projects.

MISSED OPPORTUNITIES?

Many observers have commented that the destruction of the World Trade Center complex offered planners the opportunity to remedy the mistakes in-corporated into the original construction. The modernist buildings placed on superblocks represented the planning orthodoxy of the time. Since then, how-ever, norms have changed and the prescriptions of Jane Jacobs for urban suc-cess have been widely accepted; a normal road grid and active street life are now the new desiderata. What has not changed, however, is the pressure to use land to its most remunerative potential, whatever the externalities of this choice. In the case of the WTC, this pressure existed regardless of whether the structures were publicly or privately controlled. The Port Authority, although ostensibly a governmental agency, acted as a profit maximizer, and the effect of the original WTC was to absorb much of the growth of downtown within its walls, weakening the rental market around it.

The mayor's approach—that of seeing the WTC site within the context of all of downtown Manhattan and aiming at a more balanced form of develop-ment—represented an effort at more rational, comprehensive planning. But the mayor did not control the resources necessary to effectuate his plan. Rather, the LMDC, as the recipient of $1.3 billion in federal rebuilding funds, the Port Authority and the MTA, which were under gubernatorial control and backed by federal transportation financing, and Larry Silverstein, who had his insurance proceeds, called the tune. Furthermore, the mayor, after his initial pronouncements, mostly withdrew from discussions about the site, except for occasional interjections. In any event, even though his plan offered a broader vision for downtown, it did not go much further than the PA-LMDC plan in addressing equity issues.[18]

Until the Trade Center land was taken by eminent domain, Radio Row, a congeries of small businesses, occupied the site. (The pre-WTC organization of the area could be described as either pre-Fordist or post-Fordist.) Although it was in private hands, the area conformed to the model of the lively street scene prescribed by Jane Jacobs and contemporary new urbanists, and it pro-vided an accessible location to diverse small businesses. Takeover by the public sector displaced this low-rise district and substituted high-rise modernism dominated by financial firms and chain retailing. With the transfer of management to the private-sector developer Larry Silverstein, there was little likelihood that land use in the area would change in character.

At the moment, control of the site rests primarily with the Port Authority, a public agency, but the driving force behind its plans is the pressure to raise maximum revenues. Although theoretically public ownership could cause decisionmaking to tilt toward equity considerations, this is unlikely in the case of agencies whose explicit purpose is infrastructure development. Presumably the public at large benefits from investments in ports and transportation facilities, but such investments in fact provide direct benefits to shippers and truckers and do little, if anything, to redress distributional inequities. Currently a great deal of Port Authority investment is going to enlargement of the New Jersey port to accommodate the latest generation of gigantic container ships. This upgrade is necessary to meet the competition from other ports, which are similarly expanding. The shipping companies will reduce their costs as a consequence of using larger ships, but the huge expenses involved in port improvements as externalities of the greater efficiencies for the companies are borne by the public. Interestingly, objections to this cost shifting are rarely voiced; rather, it appears simply to be assumed that growth in the size of ships is a force of nature to which public institutions must respond.

The story then of the Port Authority and the World Trade Center indicates that insulated public institutions whose aim is economic development do "get things done." They form part of a national policy community that relies on the same consultants and shares the priorities of promoting traffic circulation, tourism, and large-scale office projects (Judd 2003). These institutions act largely according to the same norms that drive the private sector, even if their staffing is more politicized and they are potentially more susceptible to popular pressure. Although they are under the control of elected officials, their goals largely coincide with the goals of those politicians, who thus usually do not feel the need to exercise much supervision. The motives of politicians and public authorities may differ in that the primary concern of politicians is reelection rather than the creation of revenue producers, especially when the revenue stream goes elsewhere. But the construction of visible projects serves their common interests. Since public authorities can evade the kinds of reviews by councils and legislative bodies to which executive officers must submit if they are carrying out projects directly, elected executive officials frequently turn to such authorities to implement programs, thereby sparing themselves the expenditure of political capital involved with executing them themselves. Throughout its history, the Port Authority has at times bowed to the will of the governors of New York and New Jersey, and it has shrewdly allowed them to take credit for its projects. But while it is by no means completely autonomous, it nevertheless escapes direct legislative oversight and frequently avoids interference from the governors, who find it a convenient resource.

In the reconstruction of the World Trade Center, Governor Pataki, city agencies, civic associations, and the Port Authority have all shaped the outcome, but outside influences have not fully permeated the Authority's decisionmaking structure. Technical problem-solving, the capacity to make future investments, and protection of bondholders still prevail as the primary considerations at the Port Authority.

NOTES

1. Information sources for this chapter include published documents, newspapers, and interviews with public officials, civic leaders, and knowledgeable informants. Interviews were granted to me under the condition of anonymity with the assurance that informants would neither be mentioned by name nor easily identified from my descriptions. Thanks to Peter Marcuse for his helpful comments and those of readers with close connections to the Port Authority who prefer to remain anonymous.
2. "New Jersey" became part of the Authority's official name in 1972.
3. A brief history of the Port Authority is available at www.panynj.gov. For a historical account, focusing primarily on the period of Austin Tobin's directorship, see Doig (2001). For excellent descriptions of the workings of authorities with high revenue-raising capacities and the power to spend their proceeds on facilities other than those that produce these revenues, see Caro (1974) and Perry (1995).
4. The Port Authority receives tolls and fees from the George Washington, Outerbridge, Goethals, and Bayonne Bridges, the Lincoln and Holland Tunnels, the metropolitan area's four airports, the container ports at Port Newark, Howland Hook, and Port Elizabeth, the two Manhattan bus terminals, and the PATH trains.
5. Austin Tobin was executive director of the PANYNJ from 1942 to 1971. It was under his entrepreneurial leadership that the organization carried out most of its major projects. While criticized for high-handedness and overcommitment to the automobile, he nonetheless was widely admired for his effectiveness; see Doig (2001).
6. The governor of New Jersey was Christine Todd Whitman; New York's was George E. Pataki. Other projects delayed included leasing of the air rights over the Port Authority Bus Terminal and leasing of space in Port Elizabeth for a major tenant (Smothers 2000b).
7. For an excellent account and critique of the planning process leading up to this point, see Beauregard (2004).
8. Inclusion of the Deutsche Bank site did in fact reduce the projected number of square feet on the WTC property by about 20 percent and overall densities in the area by even more.
9. At the breakfast sponsored by *Crain's New York Business*, where Seymour was the principal speaker, security was called to suppress interruptions by affordable housing advocates. At one time these breakfasts, at which prominent figures in the city make presentations, entertained questions from the floor, but they are no longer allowed.

10. Herbert Muschamp (2002), who had been extremely critical of the Libeskind plans, extolled Calatrava's design: "In place of suburban shopping-mall atrium design, there emerged civic architecture of the highest order. . . . With deep appreciation I congratulate the Port Authority for commissioning Mr. Calatrava, the great Spanish architect and engineer, to design a building with the power to shape the future of New York. It is a pleasure to report, for once, that public officials are not overstating the case when they describe a design as breathtaking." Nevertheless, praise for the station was not quite universal. Thus, the *Daily News* editorialized: "The PA persists in its boondoggle plan to sink nearly $2 billion in federal disaster funds into a lavish PATH station to handle just one-seventh the passengers that Grand Central does. A pared-down $1 billion station, still mighty lavish, would leave enough funds to build the Freedom Tower plus two more" (Schwartz 2004).

11. Westfield America is a subsidiary of the Australian firm Westfield Holdings Ltd.

12. As of May 13, 2004, a total of $1.5 billion of the projected $3.5 billion in insurance proceeds had been spent. The PA had received $320 million in lease payments, which it used to support its various capital programs, including the expansion of Port Elizabeth; $343 million had gone to Silverstein's legal and management fees.

13. For an analysis of the location of employment in the tristate region, see Hughes and Seneca (2004).

14. For a while the city was investigating a swap that would have given it ownership of the WTC site in return for ceding ownership of its Long Island airports to the Port Authority. In the end, however, it became clear that receiving the much higher rents from holding on to the airports was greatly to its advantage.

15. Larry Silverstein had wished to place the Freedom Tower further east, where it would be closer to the subway station, but was forced to keep it where the Libeskind plan had put it.

16. Liberty bonds are tax-free bonds authorized by the federal government to assist the rebuilding effort.

17. The Board of Estimate consisted of the five borough presidents, the mayor, the City Council president, and the comptroller. It was eliminated by a U.S. Supreme Court decision that judged it to contravene the principle of one person, one vote.

18. New apartment buildings and conversions of old office structures into residences have proceeded apace downtown, with the assistance of liberty bonds and city subsidies. Developers using the city's program are required to contribute to the construction of low- and moderate-income housing; however, they have built this housing elsewhere, and as a result, homogeneously luxury buildings prevail downtown. A New York State program does require a minimal number of units to be "affordable."

REFERENCES

Bagli, Charles V. 2001a. "Developer Scrambles to Save World Trade Center Deal." *New York Times*, April 26.

———. 2001b. "Deal Is Signed to Take over Trade Center." *New York Times*, April 27.

———. 2003. "Silverstein Will Get Most of His Cash Back in Trade Center Deal." *New York Times*, November 22.

Bagli, Charles V., and Edward Wyatt. 2003. "At Helm of Trade Center Site, as He Always Planned to Be." *New York Times*, July 21.

Beauregard, Robert A. 2004. "Mistakes Were Made: Rebuilding the World Trade Center, Phase 1." *International Planning Studies* 9(2–3, May–August): 139–54.

Blake, Wendy. 2002. "Mayor's $10.6 Billion Plan for Downtown." *Crain's New York Business*, December 12. Available at: www.crainsny.com/new.cms?newsId=4748.

Caro, Robert. 1974. *The Power Broker: Robert Moses and the Fall of New York*. New York: Alfred A. Knopf.

Civic Alliance to Rebuild Downtown New York. 2002. *Listening to the City: Report of Proceedings, July 20 and July 22, 2002, Jacob Javits Center, New York City*. New York: Regional Plan Association.

Clark, Mary L. 2004. "A Fresh Start at Ground Zero." *New York Times*, May 5.

Doig, Jameson W. 2001. *Empire on the Hudson: Entrepreneurial Vision and Political Power at the Port of New York Authority*. New York: Columbia University Press.

Dunlap, David W. 2003a. "Unheard Voices on Planning New Trade Center." *New York Times*, October 16.

———. 2003b. "Mayor's Office Seeks More Retail Space at Ground Zero." *New York Times*, October 29.

———. 2004a. "Ground Zero Will Wait to Grow to Its Full Height." *New York Times*, March 11.

———. 2004b. "At 9/11 Site, Balancing Reverence and Retailing." *New York Times*, March 29.

———. 2004c. "The Fine Print on the Trade Center Site." *New York Times*, April 22.

Friedland, Roger, Frances Piven, and Robert Alford. 1978. "Political Conflict, Urban Structure, and the Fiscal Crisis." In *Comparing Public Policies*, edited by Douglas E. Ashford. Beverly Hills, Calif.: Sage Publications.

Gillespie, Angus Kress. 2002. *Twin Towers: The Life of New York City's World Trade Center*. Rev. ed. New York: New American Library.

Goldberger, Paul. 2004. *Up from Zero: Politics, Architecture, and the Rebuilding of New York*. New York: Random House.

Golson, Blair. 2004. "Is Silverstein Down to One at Zero Site?" *New York Observer*, May 7.

Gotham Gazette. 2004. "Rebuilding Roundup." May 7. Available at: www.rebuilding. gothamgazette.com. Downloaded on May 7, 2004.

Hughes, James W., and Joseph J. Seneca. 2004. *The Beginning of the End of Sprawl?* Issue paper 21. New Brunswick, N.J.: Rutgers Regional Report (May).

Judd, Dennis R. 2003. *Reconstructing Regional Politics: Special-Purpose Authorities and Municipal Governments*. Working paper GCP-03-01. Chicago: University of Illinois, Great Cities Institute (June).

Lower Manhattan Development Corporation (LMDC). 2004. (May 22). Available at: http://www.renewnyc.com/AboutUs/index.shtml.htm.

Luo, Michael. 2004. "Four Options Presented for Airport Rail Link." *New York Times*, February 5.

Matthews, Karen. 2003. "Bank Tower Joining in WTC Redevelopment." Associated Press Online, August 28.

McGeveran, Tom. 2002. "Port Authority Reasserts Grip on Towers Site." *New York Observer*, May 8.

Muschamp, Herbert. 2002. "Marginal Role for Architecture at Ground Zero." *New York Times*, May 23.

Neuman, William. 2004. "PA Is Leery About Larry—Wants WTC Funding Plan." *New York Post*, May 13.

New York Times. 2004. "Culture in Lower Manhattan" (editorial). May 27.

Perry, David C. 1995. "Building Through the Back Door: The Politics of Debt, Law, and Public Infrastructure." In *Building the Public City*, edited by David C. Perry. Thousand Oaks, Calif.: Sage Publications.

Port Authority of New York and New Jersey (PANYNJ). 2004. "A Glimpse of the Future in Lower Manhattan: Renowned Architect Santiago Calatrava Unveils Design Concepts of Port Authority's World Trade Center Transportation Hub" (press release 7–2004). January 22. New York: PANYNJ.

Regional Plan Association (RPA). 2004. *A Civic Assessment of the Lower Manhattan Planning Process*. Report to the Civic Alliance. New York: RPA (October).

Salamon, Julie. 2003. "Following a Trend, Downtown Looks to the Arts." *New York Times*, September 15.

Schwartz, Richard. 2004. "Downtown Funds Go Pffft; There'll Be Little Left for Rebuilding After PA and Lawyers Get Paid." *New York Daily News*, May 11.

Smothers, Ronald. 2000a. "Governors End Port Authority Rift That Blocked Billions in Projects." *New York Times*, June 2.

———. 2000b. "Trade Center Leasing Project Goes Forward." *New York Times*, June 28.

———. 2000c. "Six Real Estate Companies Submit Bids on 99-Year Lease for the World Trade Center." *New York Times*, September 1.

———. 2001a. "Leasing of Trade Center May Help Transit Projects, Pataki Says." *New York Times*, July 25.

Starkman, Dean, and Alex Frangos. 2004a. "Before Ground Zero Rebuilding $1.3 Billion Has Already Been Spent." *Wall Street Journal*, February 25.

———. 2004b. "Jury's Decision Leaves Rebuilding of World Trade Center in Turmoil." *Wall Street Journal*, April 29.

Steinhauer, Jennifer. 2002. "Mayor's Proposal Envisions Lower Manhattan as an Urban Hamlet." *New York Times*, December 13.

———. 2004. "The West Side's Yours, Ground Zero Mine." *New York Times*, March 27.

Todorovich, Petra. 2003. "At the Heart of Ground Zero, Still a Questionable Program." *Spotlight on the Region* (Regional Plan Association) 2(17, September 5).

Vitullo-Martin, Julie. 2004. "In the Fray: Jury's Decision Hinders Leaseholder's Ground Zero Plan—Perhaps It's All for the Best." *Wall Street Journal*, May 6.

Weisbrod, Carl. 2003. "Airport Access Is a Key to Downtown's Future." *Downtown Express*, April 9.

Wyatt, Edward. 2003. "Ground Zero Plan Seems to Circle Back." *New York Times*, September 13.

Wyatt, Edward, and Charles V. Bagli. 2002. "Officials Rethink Building Proposal for Ground Zero." *New York Times*, July 21.

Zupan, Jeffrey M. 2003. "Transportation and Lower Manhattan: Where Do We Go from Here?" *Gotham Gazette*, May 12. Available at: www.gothamgazette.com/article/feature-commentary/20030512/202/386.

CHAPTER 4

The Redevelopment of Lower Manhattan: The Role of the City

Mitchell L. Moss

THE ATTACK on the World Trade Center reinforced a process of change in lower Manhattan that had been under way for at least the past fifty years. The public and private responses to the destruction wrought on September 11 have provided the funds, organizational capacity, and public commitment to do what a previous generation of municipal planners tried to accomplish, with only partial success: creating a mixed residential and office community in what was once New York City's dominant financial and business district. Federal aid to rebuild lower Manhattan has been the catalyst for modernizing and expanding its mass transit systems and facilities, providing low-cost financing for converting obsolete office buildings into housing, improving pedestrian movement, investing public funds in parks and cultural institutions, and subsidizing the creation of new public schools. This chapter examines the key public and private organizations that have shaped this redevelopment and the implications for the future of lower Manhattan and for office development in the rest of New York City.

RECENT PLANNING EFFORTS

For almost half a century, major law firms, securities firms, and insurance companies have been moving out of lower Manhattan to midtown Manhattan and suburban locations. With 90 million square feet of office space, lower

Manhattan is the third-largest central business district in the nation. More than 40 percent of this space was built before World War II, however, and the older space lacks the technological and physical infrastructure essential for modern office activities. Although lower Manhattan remains the home of major financial firms and the nation's leading stock exchanges, it has just one-fourth of New York City's total office space. Today "Wall Street" is a metaphor for New York City's preeminence as a world financial capital, not the physical center of the city's financial industry. Within lower Manhattan, the share of jobs in the FIRE (finance, insurance, and real estate) sector has declined from 57 percent in 1996 to 52 percent in 2003, while professional services employment rose from 28 to 34 percent (Alliance for Downtown New York 2003, 10).

During the 1990s the residential population of lower Manhattan grew from 14,000 to 31,000. A study prepared by the Lower Manhattan Development Corporation (LMDC) (2002) stated: "Lower Manhattan has enjoyed stronger residential population growth than the rest of Manhattan over the last decade. ... Growth in lower Manhattan was strongest south of Liberty Street, as the result of conversions of obsolete office buildings." The population of lower Manhattan is also more affluent than that of New York City as a whole. In 2000 the annual average household income in the area was $138,852, almost 60 percent of the population was between twenty and fifty-nine years of age, and the average household size was 1.76 individuals (Alliance for Downtown New York 2003, 12).

Over the past fifty years, numerous proposals have been advanced to stimulate development in lower Manhattan, starting in 1956 when the Rockefeller family commissioned a 64-story tower to serve as the new headquarters for the Chase Manhattan Bank—the sixth-tallest building in the world when it opened in 1961. A subsequent plan by the Downtown–Lower Manhattan Association (the forerunner to the Alliance for Downtown New York) called for razing and redeveloping 564 acres below Chambers Street. Though not implemented, this plan inspired a 1966 lower Manhattan plan issued by the city that called for the construction of new office towers and the creation of new residential neighborhoods on both the Hudson and East Rivers to make lower Manhattan a place of residence as well as employment. In 1993 Mayor David Dinkins' administration issued a plan for lower Manhattan that recommended the use of tax incentives to encourage the renovation of lower Manhattan commercial buildings, while also highlighting the need to attract tourists and redevelop the waterfront in lower Manhattan (New York City Department of City Planning 1993). In 1995 the city and the state approved the use of tax incentives to stimulate the renovation of commercial buildings and the residential conversion of obsolete office buildings in lower Manhattan. The success of this program in attracting 110 new businesses, creating 3000 new residential units, and reducing the downtown office vacancy rate by 40 percent led the

Downtown–Lower Manhattan Association to name then-mayor Rudolph Giuliani as the "Hero of Downtown" in 1997 (New York City Office of the Mayor 1997).

GROUND ZERO AND LOWER MANHATTAN

Enormous public attention has been given to the rebuilding of the World Trade Center site, popularly known as "Ground Zero," and to the debate over the future of the sixteen-acre site. As Lynne Sagalyn and Susan Fainstein detail elsewhere in this volume, that site is located within New York City but owned by the Port Authority of New York and New Jersey (PANYNJ). Fainstein analyzes the Port Authority's powerful role as the owner of the site, and Sagalyn details the intricate process of policymaking for Ground Zero. However important, this site is only one part of a larger context. The portion of lower Manhattan below Canal Street, bounded by the East and Hudson Rivers, is far more diverse and complex. While the states of New York and New Jersey control the planning and development of the WTC site, the city's authority to regulate land use and historic landmarks and to provide parks, schools, and surface transportation systems places the city of New York in the role of planning and redeveloping the larger community surrounding the WTC site (Regional Plan Association 2004).

While the governors of New York and New Jersey have appointing power for the Port Authority board—and therefore ultimate responsibility for its decisionmaking regarding the World Trade Center—the mayor of New York City, as the elected official responsible for the city's land use and economic development policies, is responsible for the larger community surrounding the WTC site. As mayor, Michael R. Bloomberg has aggressively pursued a policy of transforming lower Manhattan from a business district that closed up after the end of the business day into a twenty-four-hour community that mixes residential activities with commercial uses. The Bloomberg administration has strongly advocated the construction of new parks, schools, and cultural facilities that will push this transformation forward.

Lower Manhattan consists of a number of quite distinct neighborhoods and business districts. It is neither a homogeneous community nor a highly cohesive and economically integrated one. The historic financial district stretches from the southern tip of Manhattan north to about Fulton Street, encompassing the New York Stock Exchange, the Federal Reserve Bank of New York, and major banks, insurance companies, and securities firms. In recent years, corporate service firms, such as architecture and consulting firms, as well as nonprofit organizations have gradually moved into what was formerly a predominantly financial and legal complex. North of Fulton Street, on the east side of Broadway, are city hall, state and local government offices, courthouses, with the South Street seaport and the Fulton fish market on the East River. To the west is the World Trade Center site and Battery Park City, home to more than eight thousand residents and approximately seven million square feet of office space. From Chambers Street north to Canal Street and from Broadway west to the Hudson River is Tribeca, a trendy area now home to converted lofts, restaurants, galleries, and film companies. Two of Zagat's top-ranked restaurants, Nobu and Chanterelle, are in Tribeca, while none are located in the financial district (Zagat Survey 2003, 10). East of Broadway, from just north and east of the municipal and court complex, running up to and beyond Canal Street, is Chinatown, home to a large concentration of garment manufacturing firms, tourist-oriented establishments, and a substantial residential population (for studies of these neighborhoods, see Foner 2005).

Although the September 11 attack had a distinct effect on each of these communities, New York government mobilized quickly to respond to the disruption of day-to-day life within all of them. In the weeks after the attack, the authorities first prohibited access to all of lower Manhattan below Houston Street; they later moved that barrier down to Canal Street. Severe restrictions remained in place until October 28, 2001. The need to remove debris from the WTC site also led to a ban on all trucks and buses through the Holland and Battery Tunnels for the first six months of 2002, and PATH service to lower Manhattan was knocked out until November 2003.

The destruction of 13.4 million square feet of office space at the World Trade Center and related damage to an additional 8 million square feet of office space in the area immediately surrounding it displaced 110 firms with about 114,000 workers—almost one-third of the lower Manhattan workforce. A year later more than 80 percent of those jobs were in Manhattan, but only about half, 53,500, had returned to downtown (Battery Park City Authority 2003). In early 2005 lower Manhattan had 50,000 fewer workers than had been there on September 10, 2001. This decline in the economic base also led to a reduction of retail activity downtown and less demand for business services.

The response of the residential population in lower Manhattan to the September 11 attack was initially less well organized than that of the families of the victims of the attack or the area's commercial property owners. In the days after September 11, Mayor Giuliani emerged as a strong advocate for the families who had lost a loved one at Ground Zero, and he continued to argue forcefully for honoring those who had died there, often suggesting that the entire sixteen-acre WTC site be preserved as a memorial. The commercial property owners in lower Manhattan relied on three politically adept and influential organizations—the Partnership for New York City and Chamber of Commerce (the Partnership), the Real Estate Board of New York (REBNY), and the Alliance for Downtown New York (the Alliance)—to convey their preference for rebuilding lower Manhattan's transportation systems as quickly as possible. In comparison, the residents of lower Manhattan, including the affluent community living in Battery Park City, initially struggled to make their voices heard by public officials (Wils 2004). Many residents thought the federal government had responded poorly to their concerns about the air pollution caused by the destruction of the twin towers and the potential environmental hazards it caused, and they ultimately raised funds to hire independent scientists to establish the need for a federal cleanup of downtown housing. Small businesses in and near the WTC also suffered severe losses from the destruction of equipment and records and a decline in foot traffic downtown. These conditions forced many retail stores to close, while others managed to cope with assistance in the form of grants and loans provided by New York-based foundations (Seedco 2004).

Chinatown's tourist and manufacturing industries suffered as a result of the shutdown of Park Row for security reasons and the ban on trucks over the Manhattan Bridge. The need to rebuild essential energy, telecommunications, and transportation systems without disrupting the flow of people in, through, and out of lower Manhattan led to the creation of a Lower Manhattan Construction Command Center in February 2005.

GOVERNMENT, BUSINESS, AND THE NONPROFIT SECTOR

The attack on the World Trade Center generated a remarkable level of cooperation among the federal, state, and local government agencies participating in the rescue and recovery efforts at Ground Zero. Led by the city of New York, public agencies worked rapidly and closely to mobilize resources to clean up the WTC site, a task accomplished by May 2002. (As Fainstein notes in her chapter in this volume, the deep trauma sustained by the Port Authority, including the loss of its executive director and its physical premises, made it a secondary player in this activity.) Although the Federal Emergency Management Agency (FEMA) often plays the principal role in responses to large-scale disasters, in this case the city of New York, not FEMA or the Port Authority, served as the principal public-sector entity responsible for the rescue and recovery efforts at Ground Zero. New York City's Police Department assumed responsibility for security around the site, while the city's Department of Design and Construction (DCC) coordinated the management of the recovery efforts. As one municipal official noted, "There was no way to reach anyone at the Port Authority" (Monahan and Holden 2002).

The Department of Design and Construction, a new municipal agency, was created by the Giuliani administration to manage most, though not all, municipal design and construction projects. It centralized design, engineering, and construction staffs that had previously been spread across several agencies. By default, this agency assumed control over the removal of debris and the recovery of remains at Ground Zero. Because DCC had working relationships with the leading contractors in the New York metropolitan region, it was immediately able to harness private and public resources to advance the recovery effort at Ground Zero, such as installing portable light towers before natural light was lost at the end of the day, bringing in heavy equipment to lift steel to search for survivors, spreading one million square feet of net over the surrounding buildings, and making arrangements to ship WTC debris and steel by barge from pier 25 on the Hudson River. The city successfully resisted pressures from the federal government to give total control of the recovery efforts to Bechtel, a San Francisco–based firm with global expertise in disaster recovery projects, and DCC maintained control over the recovery effort through its completion in May 2002. (Bechtel did receive a major contract as part of the recovery at Ground Zero.)

In addition to this cleanup effort, a number of civic organizations moved quickly to plan for the future of the WTC site and surrounding area (see Goldberg, this volume). The Regional Plan Association (RPA) took the lead in forming the Civic Alliance, a coalition of academic, labor, and planning groups, while local residents, particularly those living in Battery Park City and Tribeca, worked through Community Board 1 and residents' groups to advocate for reopening public schools as quickly as possible, monitoring downtown air quality, and lifting restrictions on downtown streets. Within days, differences had emerged between the priorities of the residents of lower Manhattan and those of the families of the victims. Local residents were eager to rebuild the WTC site and rekindle an active commercial and cultural life, while many of the victims' families felt that the WTC was "sacred ground" and that the entire site should be treated as a cemetery.

THE PRIVATE SECTOR SHAPES POLICY

While the physical rescue and recovery efforts were under way, leading New York business and civic groups launched a separate effort to "get lower Manhattan opened as soon as possible" (Spinola 2004). In the days immediately after the attack, the Real Estate Board of New York, representing New York's leading commercial and residential property owners, the New York City Partnership and Chamber of Commerce, representing its major corporations, and the Alliance for Downtown New York, representing downtown property owners, worked to put together a plan to obtain federal assistance to rebuild lower Manhattan's office space and fund incentives for businesses and residents to remain in, or locate to, lower Manhattan.

Recognizing that a new mayor would take office on January 1, 2002, members of the business community in New York City felt strongly that a state entity under the auspices of Republican governor George Pataki should oversee the rebuilding efforts in lower Manhattan. They were motivated partly by the worry that the Democratic candidate for mayor, probably either Mark Green or Fernando Ferrer, would defeat Michael Bloomberg, the likely Republican nominee, and that either Democrat would be less responsive to commercial property interests than the governor. More important, an existing state public authority, the Empire State Development Corporation (ESDC), had the legislative authority to create subsidiaries that could supersede the land use and development rules of local government. Finally, real-estate industry leaders had a deep desire to prevent the New York City Council from playing a serious role in the rebuilding effort.

A critical meeting to formulate an agenda for federal aid to New York City was held on Sunday, September 16, 2001, following a large public memorial service at Yankee Stadium. In attendance were senators Charles Schumer (D-N.Y.) and Hillary Clinton (D-N.Y.); Kathy Wylde, president of the Partnership; Jerry Speyer, chairman of the Partnership; Steve Spinola, president of the Real Estate Board; Brad Race, secretary to the governor; and a top aide to assembly speaker Sheldon Silver, who represented lower Manhattan in the State Assembly. Earlier in the week the senatorial staffs of Clinton and Schumer had begun working closely with the staff of Mayor Giuliani to prepare a program of federal assistance for New York City.

Two days after the attack, Governor Pataki had called a meeting of thirty leaders from the real estate and finance industries to seek their ideas for rebuilding priorities in lower Manhattan. In addition, architects and planners had met independently to develop approaches to rebuilding lower Manhattan, leading to the formation of New Visions for New York (NVNY), an organization seeking to foster public amenities and strong design values in any redevelopment effort. (Many of the clients of these firms were members of the Partnership, REBNY, and the Alliance for Downtown New York.) Clearly, the Real Estate Board, the Partnership, and the Alliance were fashioning a new agenda for lower Manhattan and building the political alliances that would lead to federal support to rebuild its transportation systems and provide incentives to keep and attract businesses and residents.

As Arielle Goldberg (this volume) describes at greater length, the Civic Alliance, formed largely as a result of the initiative taken by the Regional Plan Association, developed a parallel agenda that emphasized the need for having the public participate in the rebuilding effort, for diversifying the lower Manhattan economy, for building environmentally sensitive structures, for promoting a high level of design in public spaces, buildings, and cultural facilities, and for encouraging a mix of residential development in lower Manhattan. The

Civic Alliance was especially active in identifying the transportation invest-ments that would be essential to the renewal of downtown, including a single new subway and commuter train facility, a version of Grand Central Terminal in lower Manhattan that would integrate the PATH system with the Fulton Street subway station, and the extension of the planned Second Avenue sub-way to lower Manhattan. Finally, John Zuccotti, chairman of Brookfield Prop-erties, which owned the office buildings in Battery Park City, called for con-structing a new high-speed train connection from lower Manhattan to the Long Island Railroad (LIRR) station in Jamaica so that the Airtrain that cur-rently linked it with JFK Airport could run all the way to downtown. Al-though the Second Avenue subway would have strengthened lower Manhat-tan's connection to Manhattan's Upper East Side workforce, neither the downtown property owners nor the LMDC included it in their agenda for rebuilding lower Manhattan's transportation infrastructure.

CREATING THE LOWER MANHATTAN
DEVELOPMENT CORPORATION

By October 4, 2001, less than a month after the attack and well before the November general election, the business community had developed a consen-sus about what should be done in lower Manhattan. In a letter to Robert Harding, then deputy mayor for economic development, REBNY called for the creation of "a reconstruction authority with private sector representation to handle the funds and rebuilding efforts for Lower Manhattan. The authority should have the power to expedite all approvals" (Spinola 2001). On October 9, 2001, the Partnership board adopted a resolution stating, in response to the 9/11 attack on the World Trade Center,

> the Governor and Legislature should create an authority to manage the reconstruction of lower Manhattan, with representation from the city and private sector. The authority should be the vehicle for investment of federal aid for recovery and redevelopment, and it should have broad powers over planning, permitting and the reconstruction of the power, transportation and telecommunications infrastructure.

Most important, the Partnership explicitly endorsed efforts to attract busi-nesses and residents to lower Manhattan and for economic development activi-ties beyond the lower Manhattan community.

> The redevelopment plans should be driven by an understanding of mar-ket forces, global and domestic. These plans ought to focus on projects

that will maximize the retention of financial services and technology sectors and also attract new businesses and residents to lower Manhattan. The authority should also have responsibility for construction of replacement commercial facilities and other economic stimulus activities outside lower Manhattan. (New York City Partnership 2001)

On November 2, 2001, the governor announced the establishment of the Lower Manhattan Development Corporation (LMDC), with eleven board members, seven appointed by him and four appointed by the sitting mayor of New York City, Rudolph W. Giuliani. After Republican Michael Bloomberg defeated the Democratic nominee Mark Green in November and took office in January 2002, these arrangements were slightly altered. On April 9, 2002, the governor expanded the LMDC board to sixteen members, with Mayor Bloomberg appointing the additional members, so that the board was evenly split between the governor's appointees and mayoral appointees.

As has been extensively described in the chapters by Sagalyn and Fainstein, the governor controls all the institutions responsible for rebuilding the site. Governor Pataki names half the members of the Port Authority board and its executive director (the governor of New Jersey appoints the other half and the board chairperson); most members of the Metropolitan Transportation Authority (MTA) board, which deploys federal funds to repair the damaged subway lines and stations; and all the board members and officials of the Empire State Development Corporation, which administers a large share of the federal funds for assisting firms and residents in lower Manhattan. As an ESDC subsidiary, the LMDC, which was responsible for planning and designing the rebuilding of the WTC site and allocating federal community development block grant (CDBG) funds for rebuilding lower Manhattan, was also a creature of the state and the governor.

Working through these state authorities, Governor Pataki formed an alliance with incoming mayor Michael Bloomberg. The new mayor had to cope with a looming budget crisis, the general economic decline worsened by the September 11 attack, and the loss of finance and technology jobs that had begun with the collapse of the dot-com sector in late 2000 (Chernick 2005). The mayor needed the governor's support to help resolve the city's fiscal crisis, while the governor needed the mayor's cooperation to rebuild at Ground Zero. The mayor also had to rebuild confidence in the face of a heightened sense of loss and vulnerability among New Yorkers. Less than two months after September 11, an American Airlines jet taking off from JFK Airport, destined for the Dominican Republic, crashed in the Rockaways, killing all passengers and crew along with residents of a single-family house that absorbed the bulk of the crash damage. The Rockaways, a community filled with families of firefighters who had died at Ground Zero, suddenly absorbed another shock, as did Washington Heights, where many of the airplane's passengers and their families lived (see Hildebrandt 2005). For many New Yorkers, this news reminded them that they remained vulnerable to terrorism, even though this crash was an accident.

THE MAYOR'S ROLE IN THE REDEVELOPMENT OF LOWER MANHATTAN

Within days of September 11, the Democratic and Republican candidates for mayor had offered their priorities for responding to the destruction of the twin towers. Democrat Mark Green, who argued that he would do a superior job in rebuilding lower Manhattan as a world financial district, narrowly defeated Fernando Ferrer in the September 25 runoff primary; Ferrer had suggested that financial and business services should be dispersed throughout the five boroughs. The Republican nominee, Michael Bloomberg, argued that lower Manhattan should be rebuilt to encompass a wide range of commercial and residential uses and not be confined to financial services industries. Although Bloomberg narrowly won the November election, many of these differences over what should be built on Ground Zero and how federal and local resources should be used for the development of lower Manhattan and the rest of New York City continued to reverberate through the city's politics.

Michael Bloomberg's narrow victory had a number of important consequences for planning the redevelopment of lower Manhattan. Most importantly, it enabled George Pataki to displace Rudy Giuliani as the leading public official concerned with the future of Ground Zero. From September 11 until the day Giuliani left office, the mayor had been the public official most visibly and powerfully involved in defining the recovery efforts at the twin towers. Giuliani continually emphasized the need to recognize the wishes of the families of the victims and make certain that "people did not forget what happened on September 11." Two years after the attack he called for a "soaring memorial" at the site. Governor George Pataki shared the Port Authority's goal of rebuilding commercial space at the World Trade Center site so that it would provide revenues to replace those lost by the WTC's destruction, while also wishing to be attentive to the desires of the victims' families. His decision to keep the footprints of the twin towers free of commercial development reflected the latter concern.

Upon taking office on January 1, 2002, Michael Bloomberg was faced with a serious budget crisis: how would he contain municipal costs while maintaining the basic public services so essential to New Yorkers' quality of life? He chose to address this task by reconsidering the city's economic development priorities; one of his first steps was to terminate the previous administration's plans to subsidize a new headquarters for the New York Stock Exchange (NYSE) on Wall Street. Even though he had been a leader in the financial services industry, the new mayor rejected the $750 million subsidy that the previous mayor had promised to Richard Grasso, then president of the New York Stock Exchange, who had been advocating the need for a new headquarters for many years. Mayor Bloomberg noted that the projected security needs of the proposed NYSE headquarters would disrupt the flow of traffic within the financial district. Today, as a result of the mayor's efforts, the buildings located on the proposed NYSE site are being converted into residential structures; even Wall Street's Regent Hotel, once the headquarters of the First National City Bank, has closed so that it can be turned into residential condominiums.

Mayor Bloomberg's agenda for lower Manhattan emphasized new housing, improved transportation, retaining major office tenants, increasing public access to the waterfront, and modifying the street grid so that pedestrians would have better access from river to river. While much public attention was focused on reviewing and evaluating the plans for Ground Zero, the mayor prepared a "new vision" for lower Manhattan that he presented at a December 12, 2002, meeting of the Association for a Better New York. The Bloomberg vision called for new waterfront parks and promenades on the East River, a revitalized Fulton Street, and a new subway station linking MTA lines with the proposed new PATH station at the WTC site. Most important, he proposed a high-speed rail link to JFK Airport through a reconstruction of a subway tunnel linking lower Manhattan with Brooklyn; he considered this new rail link essential for attracting Long Island commuters and international business travelers to New York City and lower Manhattan. The plan also proposed building new housing units for thirty thousand people. Although the plan included office towers at the World Trade Center site, the mayor's clear priority was to remake lower Manhattan into a twenty-four-hour residential and business community.

In short, the Bloomberg administration wanted to transform lower Manhattan, not rebuild what had once been there. It wanted to remake the old, bleak financial district into a profoundly different community. At the same time, the Bloomberg administration advanced a major initiative to create a new office and convention complex on the far West Side of midtown Manhattan, stretching from Twenty-ninth Street to Forty-second Street and from Tenth to Twelfth Avenues. This initiative gave the far West Side a new name ("Hudson Yards") and proposed that a new stadium and convention center be built over the storage tracks west of Penn Station along with the expansion of the Jacob Javits Convention Center, the construction of more than ten thousand housing units, and the creation of more than twenty million square feet of new commercial office space. It also proposed extending the 7 line of the subway west of the Avenue of the Americas to Eleventh Avenue along Forty-second Street and then south to Thirtieth Street, serving all these new facilities.

The Bloomberg administration timed its proposal for the far West Side to follow—not compete with—the rebuilding of lower Manhattan. Its rationale for office development on Manhattan's far West Side was based on long-term projections of office employment growth contained in a report issued by Senator Charles Schumer's Group of Thirty-five in 2000. While the governor gave public support to the mayor's downtown proposal, the mayor emphasized a development agenda for the broader areas of lower Manhattan and the far West Side. The mayor predicated his plans on the belief that fundamental technological and economic forces had reshaped lower Manhattan over the last half-century and that public policies should reflect and promote the evolution of lower Manhattan from a one-dimensional financial district into a mixed-use community.

The mayor also felt strongly that rebuilding the World Trade Center site would not meet all the projected demand for office space that New York would need to compete in the twenty-first century. Building on Senator Schumer's Group of Thirty-five report, the mayor's proposed massive rezoning of the far West Side would ensure that an adequate supply of office space was built. It was the administration's belief that the relative paucity of new office construction during the 1990s had enabled developers of new office space on the New Jersey side of the Hudson River to attract financial services jobs across the river. By planning for future office development on the West Side, the Bloomberg administration sought to ensure that the city did not suffer a similar loss in future decades.

TRANSPORTATION PRIORITIES FOR LOWER MANHATTAN

Reflecting its status as the original heart of the city, more mass transit lines serve lower Manhattan than any other area in New York City. Not only do fifteen subway lines converge there, but the PATH system links lower Manhattan to New Jersey, and twenty ferry routes and thirty bus routes provide additional access. Although vehicular tunnels connect it to New Jersey and Brooklyn, the area lacks direct commuter rail service to the northern suburbs. (The subway does provide service to the Long Island Railroad terminal at Atlantic Avenue in Brooklyn, where commuters can then board trains to Long Island suburbs.) Since the largest number of managerial and professional commuters to Manhattan live in Westchester and other areas north of the city, the absence of a direct commuter rail connection to lower Manhattan has often been cited as a source of its gradual loss of employment to midtown, which is served by both Grand Central and Penn Stations.

The Federal Transportation Authority is providing $4.5 billion for transportation projects as part of the overall $21 billion in federal assistance to rebuild New York. The MTA will use much of this money to modernize existing subway stations, not only rebuilding damaged infrastructure but creating long-sought improvements. The city and the state have agreed to let the MTA use approximately $500 million to realize its long-held goal of expanding the South Ferry subway station serving the 1 and 9 trains. It will also use $750 million to build a new Fulton Street transit hub to provide a new subway entrance on Broadway at Fulton Street. This new station will be located several hundred yards east of the new PATH station being built at the World Trade Center site; approximately $1.7 billion has been allocated for that project, while another $150 million is being used for street reconstruction surrounding the WTC site.

It is a reflection of the division of authority across separate transit agencies and the strength of bureaucratic momentum that the Port Authority and the Metropolitan Transportation Authority will build two new train stations in lower Manhattan rather than one fully integrated commuter and subway facility. Instead of achieving all the efficiencies that might come from building one central intermodal facility, PATH and the subway system will each have a new station to serve their riders. The only newly proposed transit line will be the express train to JFK designed to attract Long Island and southern Queens commuters to lower Manhattan. Downtown commercial property owners strongly believe that this new express train is essential for the future of their businesses. Under a project known as East Side Access, the MTA also plans to bring Long Island Railroad service into Grand Central Terminal. This project would strengthen the midtown office complex, and downtown property owners view it as a potential threat. Rather than take the LIRR to Brooklyn and switch to the subway, most Long Island commuters go to Penn Station and take the subway from there to downtown or midtown.

Downtown businesses also believe that the proposed express will afford international travelers a quick and reliable way into Manhattan from JFK. The availability of rail service from the airport to the city's central business district in such global competitors as London, Paris, and Tokyo has fostered the belief that a similar link would attract international business to lower Manhattan. The continuing strength of this perspective among business leaders and elected officials is reflected in their support for converting $2 billion in unused federal depreciation tax credits into direct federal help in financing the estimated $6 billion cost of the link. The Regional Plan Association (2004, 22) has emphasized that any new rail link to lower Manhattan should connect well with the rest of the regional mass transit system, including the proposed Second Avenue subway, and not divert funds from existing transit projects.

RESIDENTIAL GROWTH IN LOWER MANHATTAN

Long before September 11, New York City had adopted a program of granting incentives to encourage owners of older commercial buildings to convert them into housing. Though the attack temporarily weakened lower Manhattan's housing market, REBNY successfully urged the Lower Manhattan Development Corporation to provide cash incentives to retain residential tenants or attract new ones to lower Manhattan. Those who signed two-year leases in downtown apartment buildings received cash payments of 15 to 30 percent of their rent, up to a maximum of $12,000. This program proved to be remarkably successful and led to a reduction in the vacancy rate from more than 10 percent soon after September 11, 2001, to 5.4 percent by mid-2003.

The liberty bonds that were part of the federal aid to New York included $1.6 billion of triple tax-free financing (federal, state, and local) for residential development, leading to a substantial increase in new rental housing in lower Manhattan, since the liberty bonds (which were modeled on existing federal programs) could not be used for owner-occupied housing. The city of New York has required developers who received financing through liberty bonds to pay a 3 percent fee to subsidize affordable housing in other areas of the city. The state has required developers to make 5 percent of the units in their residential developments downtown available as affordable housing. Civic groups such as the Regional Plan Association and the Fiscal Policy Institute, along with City Council member Alan Gerson, have pointed out, however, that low- and middle-income households cannot afford most of the new housing downtown. Prior to September 11, affordable housing in the area was largely limited to Southbridge Towers and Independence Plaza, two major projects built more than twenty years ago.

Over the last decade more than seven million square feet of office space have been converted to housing in lower Manhattan, and conversion of an additional one million square feet has been proposed. Approximately fifteen hundred units of housing are already being built in the Wall Street, Maiden Lane, and John Street corridors, east of Broadway. By 2010 almost twenty thousand new or converted housing units will have been developed in Tribeca, Battery Park City, and the Seaport-financial district. The rapid growth of housing in these areas has generated concerns among commercial property owners that residential buildings cannot peacefully coexist with commercial buildings in lower Manhattan. Residents do not like the nighttime noise and truck traffic required to service commercial buildings, although commercial and residential buildings manage to exist next to each other in east midtown from Forty-second Street to Sixtieth Street and in SoHo. In fact, the highest-value office building in Manhattan, the GM Building on Fifth Avenue at Fifty-ninth Street, is situated near residential buildings.

The surge in residential population has also raised the need for additional off-street parking, since upper-income residents own automobiles, even in Manhattan. ICON Parking, a major parking garage operator in Manhattan, has indicated that the shift in the lower Manhattan economy has produced a growing number of monthly tenants—typically residents—and that the number of daily commuters driving from suburban locations to park in its facilities in the area has declined (Mallah 2004).

THE CHANGING PATTERN OF OFFICE LOCATION IN LOWER MANHATTAN

The new transportation nodes in lower Manhattan and the potential new connections to JFK Airport and the Long Island Railroad will enhance the value and potential for commercial office buildings located in the corridor running from Broadway west to Church Street and from Fulton Street down to Vesey Street. This movement westward and northward from the traditional financial district began more than thirty years ago with the opening of the World Trade Center and the subsequent development of the World Financial Center at Battery Park City. The strength of the residential conversion market in the Wall Street corridor and the South Street Seaport area has caused residential communities to emerge in those downtown areas and take over space formerly occupied by finance and insurance firms and their ancillaries. New office space downtown will be developed next to the new transportation facilities that offer the best access to the regional labor force, not in the historic core of the financial district. In a prescient report prepared for the Civic Alliance, Hugh Kelly (2004) has pointed out that "new commercial buildings are especially appropriate on the World Trade Center site, above major transportation facilities." Its geographic location near critical regional transportation hubs makes the former World Trade Center site "best suited to provide the needed commercial space in an anticipated recovery later this decade." Kelly also suggests that new commercial buildings will attract people to the growing residential areas downtown because some people will want to live near their places of employment.

The decision by Goldman Sachs to consolidate its lower Manhattan offices by building a new office tower in Battery Park City at the corner of West and Vesey Streets will also reinforce the new financial services hub emerging at the northern and western edges of lower Manhattan. The older office buildings in the old financial district on Broad Street, William Street, and Water Street are increasingly attracting professional services firms, nonprofit organizations, and health care organizations, drawn by accessible Manhattan locations at lower rents than prevail in midtown. In fact, long before September 11, Skidmore, Owings & Merrill, a leading architectural firm, had moved into the former headquarters of Bankers Trust at 14 Wall Street, opposite the New York Stock Exchange. Since September 11, the United Federation of Teachers has decided to relocate to 50–52 Broadway, the Health Insurance Plan of New York will move into 55 Water Street, the new Millennium High School opened at 90 Broad Street, and Claremont Preparatory School is at 43 Broad Street. Lower Manhattan—with office rents that are one-third or more lower than midtown Manhattan rents—is reinventing itself with a new group of office tenants who prefer Manhattan but not midtown Manhattan rents. Educational institutions such as New York University and New York Law School have also expanded their presence in lower Manhattan.

LOWER MANHATTAN IN NEW YORK CITY

Lower Manhattan has three great assets: superior mass transit access, proximity to the waterfronts of the Hudson and East Rivers, and a dense mix of historic buildings that can serve both residents and small firms. Lower Manhattan has not often built on these advantages in the past, but the scale of new public investment in transit infrastructure, streets, and parks will further transform the area by the end of this decade. Many fewer people may work in lower Manhattan than in 2000, but many more will live there and thousands more tourists will visit the memorial and PATH station at the WTC site. The relocation of the Fulton Fish Market to Hunts Point in the Bronx and further redevelopment of the South Street Seaport will open up the East River waterfront for many more sites for housing and cultural activities. Since September 11, 2001, the New York City Planning Commission and the New York City Landmarks Preservation Commission have approved new housing in the South Street Seaport Historic District, and bold new residential projects have been proposed on the East River waterfront.

The proximity of new housing to both the downtown waterfront and major financial institutions is difficult to match anywhere else in New York City. Moreover, this development will occur well before the time horizon set for the development of the far West Side after 2010. Although the September 11 attack killed 2,749 people at Ground Zero, it also provided further impetus to the fundamental realignment taking place in lower Manhattan's role in the economic geography of the New York region. Lower Manhattan is emerging as a far more dynamic and diverse community than was provided by the collection of office buildings that once dominated its economy. One important way 9/11 will be memorialized is in a physical and economic transformation that will be far more rapid and pervasive than could have been anticipated before the attack.

REFERENCES

Alliance for Downtown New York. 2003. *State of Lower Manhattan*. New York: Alliance for Downtown New York.

Battery Park City Authority. 2003. *$406,350,000 Battery Park City Authority Senior Revenue Bonds, Series 2003A, Real Estate Consultant's Report, Pro Forma Revenue Forecast Study*. New York: Battery Park City Authority (September 1).

Chernick, Howard, ed. 2005. *Resilient City: The Economic Impact of 9/11*. New York: Russell Sage Foundation.

Foner, Nancy, ed. 2005. *Wounded City: The Social Impact of 9/11*. New York: Russell Sage Foundation.

Hildebrandt, Melanie D. 2005. "Double Trauma in Belle Harbor: The Aftermath of September 11 and November 12 in the Rockaways." In *Wounded City: The Social Impact of 9/11*, edited by Nancy Foner. New York: Russell Sage Foundation.

Kelly, Hugh. 2004. *The New York Regional and Downtown Office Market: History and Prospects After 9/11*. New York: Civic Alliance Committee for Economic Development. Available at: www.civic-alliance.org/pdf/econdev-book-kelly.pdf.

Lower Manhattan Development Corporation (LMDC). 2002. *Revitalization Strategy for Lower Manhattan*. New York: LMDC (November).

Mallah, Sheldon (president and CEO, Icon Parking, Inc.). 2004. Interview with the author. August 2.

Monahan, Matthew (deputy commissioner, New York City Department of Design and Construction) and M. Holden (commissioner, New York City Department of Design and Construction). 2002. Interview with the author. July 11.

New York City Department of City Planning. 1993. *Plan for Lower Manhattan*. New York: New York City Department of City Planning (October).

New York City Office of the Mayor. 1997. "Mayor Giuliani Receives Hero of Downtown Award" (press release). November 17.

———. 2002. "Mayor Michael R. Bloomberg Outlines Vision for Twenty-first Century Lower Manhattan" (press release). December 12.

Regional Plan Association (RPA). 2004. *A Civic Assessment of the Lower Manhattan Planning Process: A Regional Plan Association Report to the Civic Alliance*. New York: RPA (September).

Seedco. 2004. *A Support Strategy for Small Businesses*. New York: Seedco (June).

Spinola, Stephen. 2001. Letter to Robert Harding (deputy mayor for economic development). October 4.

Spinola, Stephen (president, Real Estate Board of New York). 2004. Interview with the author. June 25.

Wils, Madelyn (chairperson, Community Board 1). 2004. Interview with the author. June 22.

Zagat Survey. 2003. *New York City Restaurants*. Available at: zagat.com.

CHAPTER 5

Civic Engagement in the Rebuilding of the World Trade Center

Arielle Goldberg

ON SEPTEMBER 11, 2001, people around the world, most especially New Yorkers, shared a tragic human, financial, and emotional loss. Many New Yorkers emerged from this experience with a renewed sense of shared fate and a strong desire to contribute to revitalizing and rebuilding lower Manhattan and New York City. This new sense of community was manifested in both a wide range of individual voluntary efforts and the formation of new collaborations among social service organizations, such as the 9/11 United Services Group. Another dimension was widespread interest, especially within the planning, design, architecture, and urban studies professions, in the physical redevelopment of the World Trade Center (WTC) site and the symbolism of that effort. The loss of 2,749 individuals also catalyzed an unprecedented general public interest in the redevelopment project. Many New Yorkers felt that the public had a stake in how decisionmaking about the site played out and that the project had to strive to achieve a higher public interest, not simply reflect "business as usual."

This wide and deep interest posed a serious dilemma for rebuilding officials: how could they reconcile this sense of proprietorship over the site from a variety of constituencies with the legal rights of the Port Authority and the private firms that had leased the WTC to rebuild the site along lines that served their organizational interests and needs? Newly created civic coalitions sought to help them resolve their dilemma and pursue the public interest. Adept at slipping between their multiple roles as members, organizers, representatives of the "public," technical advisers to public officials, and watchdogs of the process, these coalitions sought to help frame the discussions and shape decisionmaking around rebuilding one of the most symbolically potent physical spaces in American history.

From Alexis de Tocqueville (1835/1988) in the 1830s to Robert Putnam (1993) and Theda Skocpol (2003) today, observers have assigned civic associations a central and respected place in American society and politics. A sign of a healthy democracy, associations enable myriad interests to shape policies that define physical and communal space. They provide forums for public participation and deliberation, and they engage individuals in processes that yield a collective voice. At the same time, some social scientists have raised concerns about just how representative these organizations are. They argue that although civic associations claim to represent the "public," they often mirror the hierarchies of race and class evident in the broader society. Their leaders tend to be white, middle-class, educated, and capable of gaining access to decisionmakers, but they are also more vulnerable to being co-opted by decisionmakers, who may use them to legitimate their decisions as reflecting public input (Gittell 1980; Reed 1999). Furthermore, those who believe that a hierarchical social structure inevitably shapes public policy outcomes doubt that these organizations can really influence decisions or significantly shift the agenda, especially given the pressure on cities to promote corporate investment as a way of raising revenues and spurring economic growth (Bachrach and Baratz 1962; Peterson 1981).

This chapter reports on five civic coalitions that engaged in the process of deciding how to rebuild the WTC and revitalize lower Manhattan. It seeks to elucidate how these civic coalitions—the Civic Alliance to Rebuild Downtown New York, Imagine New York, the Labor Community Advocacy Network, New York New Visions, and Rebuild Downtown Our Town—interacted within themselves, between each other, with the larger public, and with decisionmakers. I examine how these coalitions sought to facilitate public participation, speak for or represent the public, and interact with the rebuilding agencies and government decisionmakers as partners and critics. More specifically, it asks: How did the civic coalitions seek to facilitate public participation? Whom do these civic coalitions represent? If these coalitions were more diverse than their constituent organizations, how did they reconcile any internal differences? How did key decisionmakers relate to these civic coalitions? And what impact did these coalitions have on rebuilding decisions?

The public forums and monthly meetings launched by the civic coalitions certainly enriched the level and breadth of discussion about the rebuilding process. Ultimately, however, decisionmakers adopted policies that were significantly different from the ideas generated in these forums. Even those coalition members with insider access could not, in the end, challenge the institutional constraints described by Lynne Sagalyn and Susan Fainstein elsewhere in this volume. Perhaps if the coalitions had engaged the broader public more regularly, worked through some of their internal conflicts, and overcome their fear of being confrontational, they might have been more successful. Organizational culture, competing agenda priorities, and ideological differences sometimes prevented them from working together or speaking with a united voice. Nevertheless, these coalitions held real potential for developing a progressive agenda for New York City and creating a dialogue between polarized communities.

THE POST-9/11 CONTEXT

The public perception of the World Trade Center changed dramatically following the 9/11 attacks. Those who worked in the WTC enjoyed wide modern offices and spectacular views, but other New Yorkers had often ignored the towers, and some even despised the imposing complex, which had decimated the once-thriving radio district in lower Manhattan, as Sagalyn (this volume) explains. Nevertheless, the 1993 bombing, the frequent use of the towers as a backdrop in films and television series based in New York, their ever-present place in virtually any vista of the city, and an active program of cultural activities on its plaza seemed to ease some of the antagonisms expressed about the buildings after their completion in 1973.

Whatever their status before the 9/11 attack, the towers took on a quantitatively and qualitatively different meaning afterward (Goldberger 2004). Whether as a symbol of capitalism, democracy, or New York City, New Yorkers and other Americans embraced the fallen towers and bestowed a new importance on them. With that emotional investment came a sense of public proprietorship. New Yorkers, whether in the literal or the extended sense, wanted to have a meaningful role in deciding what would be rebuilt on this publicly owned but privately leased and extremely valuable commercial property. Many opinion leaders voiced a concern that the decisions not reflect politics or business "as usual." This was an opportunity through information sharing and candid public discussions to transcend conflicting private interests or professional differences and generate a world-class program for the rebuilding of the WTC site and revitalizing lower Manhattan. According to Robert Yaro (2004), president of the Regional Plan Association (RPA) and co-convener of the newly formed Civic Alliance for Downtown New York:

> New Yorkers are notorious for not agreeing on things and for being motivated by kind of crasser impulses—power, greed, lust, envy, all those things—and that kind of got put away for a while, and groups that

had never collaborated on anything or agreed on anything were working together. That lasted for several months, maybe a year.

For many, government had erred in the past by using unaccountable public agencies to make decisions that favored business and real estate interests over the public interest. They saw extensive public deliberation as the remedy. Those who engaged in the process of civic deliberation had high hopes that the rebuilding process would set new standards for public involvement, community planning, and design excellence. Their presence as mobilized constituencies put considerable pressure on decisionmakers, especially elected officials, to address these three goals. But who would do this and how?

WHO'S IN CHARGE? INSTITUTIONAL DYNAMICS

The Port Authority of New York and New Jersey (PANYNJ) and the Lower Manhattan Development Corporation (LMDC) both have jurisdiction over the sixteen-acre World Trade Center site. As Sagalyn and Fainstein have spelled out, the Republican governor of New York, George Pataki, appoints the boards of both organizations (he appoints only half the Port Authority board but has the dominant influence over its New York activities). As an elected official, it was incumbent on the governor to appear to be responsive to his constituents, especially to the grieving families who lost members on September 11. The Authority had owned and operated the World Trade Center complex and the commuter rail system connecting to it (PATH) for three decades before leasing the complex to Silverstein Properties and Westfield America in July 2001. Although a public authority, the Port Authority has little experience and perhaps less interest in encouraging public or civic input into its decisionmaking (Doig 2001; Fainstein, this volume; Walsh 1978).

After 9/11, the Port Authority and its leaseholders found themselves in the unenviable position of facing a public that wanted a meaningful say in what they regarded as their own business. The Port Authority was overwhelmed, however, by the loss of seventy-four members of its staff, including its promising new executive director, as well as the complete loss of its physical headquarters (Fainstein, this volume). Given its large financial stake in the site, the complexity of the legal situation with Silverstein, and its proclivity for insular decisionmaking, the Port Authority was not a good candidate for initiating a broad process of public deliberation leading to an inclusive decisionmaking process.

On November 2, 2001, Governor Pataki announced the creation of the city-state LMDC to plan the redevelopment of the WTC site, create a suitable memorial, and revitalize the adjacent areas of lower Manhattan. Four days after this announcement, the general election for New York City's mayor would be held, and, as Mitchell Moss (this volume) has indicated, the governor structured the LMDC board to prevent Democratic candidate Mark Green from influencing decisions regarding the WTC site if he won. At the same time, the LMDC needed to be solicitous of input from the public and the emerging civic coalitions. As a brand-new organization, it needed to establish its legitimacy as an important body in this terrain. Its board and staff were therefore preoccupied with establishing that its decisionmaking process would be seen to be transparent and responsive to a vast array of stakeholders, in stark contrast to the Port Authority.

At the same time, as a subsidiary of the Empire State Development Corporation (ESDC), the LMDC was not subject to any formal accountability mechanisms. The legislative authority for the ESDC descended from its precursor, the New York State Urban Development Corporation (UDC), which was created during the Rockefeller era to spearhead redevelopment in troubled urban areas. Endowed with the power to take property by eminent domain, raise funds in the bond market, and override local zoning regulations, the ESDC, successor to the UDC, had become a powerful state development agency. As a subsidiary, the LMDC could exercise these powers as well. Governor Pataki appointed the majority of the LMDC board, while then-mayor Rudolph W. Giuliani appointed the others. Many LMDC staff members, including its president, had been key aides to the governor.

The Port Authority, as owner of the sixteen-acre WTC site, may have had the greatest leverage over its fate, but the LMDC had a broader mandate—revitalizing the surrounding areas of lower Manhattan. Much of the money in the $21 billion federal recovery package granted to New York was earmarked as liberty bonds for residential and commercial development and for rebuilding transportation infrastructure, but $2 billion of that package flowed to the LMDC in the form of community development block grant funds. This money came with relatively few constraints on how it might be spent and was therefore in a certain sense the most valuable part of the federal aid. Although the LMDC spent its first few months simply getting organized, these responsibilities ultimately enabled it to play a seminal role in organizing the public involvement in the process.

In the months following 9/11, the Port Authority struggled to deal with its losses while the LMDC organized its board and recruited a staff. During this time, neither agency provided many formal opportunities for public discussion and input. New York City government could have been an alternative forum for public outreach and discussion, but it was not, owing to the pressing demands of cleaning up the site, the transition from the Giuliani to the Bloomberg administration, and the fiscal challenge facing the new administration. Instead, the governor's decision to create the LMDC established that it would be the ultimate venue for the debate. Its institutional need to establish its own influence meshed well with the civic coalitions' interest in fostering public deliberation and their professional savvy.

Interagency Competition and the "Scope of Conflict"

The institutional vacuum that opened up between the Port Authority, the LMDC, and the city government in the months after 9/11 was one factor explaining why the civic coalitions came to play an important role in the discussions over the rebuilding process. Other factors included the lack of a clear division in authority between the Authority and the LMDC and their competition—indeed, at times conflict—over which would play the predominant role in the rebuilding process. Overall, the Port Authority benefited from the fact that the LMDC served as the public face for most decisions related to the site; the Authority was thus shielded from direct public scorn. Underneath this surface unity, however, the LMDC and the Port Authority had important conflicts over what to do. As has been outlined by Sagalyn and Fainstein, the Authority owned the site, held the lease with Silverstein Properties and its partners, and drew critically important rental payments from this lease. As landlord and developer, the Authority and Silverstein shared a desire to restore a commercial arrangement. The LMDC, on the other hand, was custodian of a planning process that sought to direct and regulate what the landlord and developer would be allowed to do. Although Governor Pataki appointed the LMDC's top managers, its planning staff had ties to the City Planning Commission and tended to have a broader view of the redevelopment effort than the Authority. The LMDC was also charged with revitalizing all of lower Manhattan, not just rebuilding on the World Trade Center site. The potential for interagency conflict flowed from these differences in mission.

To increase its influence over the landlord and developer and strengthen its authority over the rebuilding process, the LMDC became a broker of public opinion. Given the high level of public interest, the LMDC sought to "widen the scope of conflict" (Schattschneider 1960) by organizing public hearings and private meetings with stakeholders and the civic coalitions on the planning and design of the redevelopment project and the creation of a memorial. It established numerous stakeholder advisory councils and created a committee to address the memorial and provide guidelines for an independent jury that would select the memorial design. In pursuit of its organizational goals, the LMDC therefore provided New Yorkers with many opportunities to participate in the rebuilding discussions. The LMDC planning staff also met regularly with the civic coalitions, especially New York New Visions and the Civic Alliance, to get feedback on technical issues and planning strategies.

The professional advice that the LMDC received through these interactions bolstered its hand in dealing with the bigger, more powerful, and longer-established organizations operating in its domain. Unlike the ESDC or the Port Authority, the LMDC had a small staff with large responsibilities. It therefore relied on consultants and civic coalition volunteers for technical expertise. Many of these volunteers invested time and energy in evaluating complex questions of urban design, architecture, and economic development. By drawing on and recognizing these efforts, the LMDC earned public support even when it did not respond to the substantive concerns that these volunteers raised. Its interactions with the public and with civic organizations may not have been purely instrumental, but it often structured them to strengthen support for its own positions. In short, the LMDC used civic engagement to enhance its authority, gain legitimacy, and compensate for its limited human capital.

Giving the Public a Voice

In the weeks after the 9/11 attack, a number of civic leaders from around the city reached out to their friends and colleagues to form several networks of professionals, community members, and even victims' family members. These "civic entrepreneurs" were able to attract foundation resources and had the experience to organize large-scale public meetings and events. Although limited in their capacity to help with the rescue and recovery efforts, the members of these emerging coalitions felt that they could contribute significantly to the inevitable discussions about how the city should rebuild. By temperament, they were inclined to address broad questions about the future of lower Manhattan and create general principles to guide responses to the technical issues of planning, architecture, sustainable and equitable community development, and economic revitalization.

Participants felt that these emerging coalitions would provide a forum for open debate and inform the public (or at least certain parts of it). Many coalitions began as informal brainstorming meetings or collective expressions of concern about what had befallen the city. They also sought to identify areas of consensus that would yield to a shared vision of how to rebuild the site and lower Manhattan. To achieve these goals, the coalitions held regular meetings of their inner circles as well as large-scale public events. Their regular meetings were designed to help participants pool their collective knowledge, learn from each other's insights, and deliberate on the best course of action. They considered their larger forums an alternative to the sometimes inadequate opportunities for articulating public concerns offered by the LMDC and the Port Authority.

The coalitions also sought to communicate or advocate for their emerging visions to shape the decisions that officials were making about the site and the surrounding area. They acted as watchdogs and gadflies, prodding the rebuilding agencies to make their decisionmaking more transparent and to gather more public input. Coalition members also helped the LMDC's growing staff to organize their own public meetings, and they offered formal and informal comments on the LMDC's work. As some civic coalitions became more critical of the LMDC, they were forced to stop playing an inside game and take a more vocal and confrontational stance. Others, however, continued to collaborate with the LMDC.

Regardless of the partial symbiosis between the LMDC and the civic coalitions or the benefits that some civic elites who organized these coalitions may have drawn from this relationship, it is also important to remember that their growth was driven by a strong collective spirit arising from below, especially in the first months after 9/11. That spirit stemmed from enthusiastic and sometimes broad-based public participation in their events, which brought a new level of energy and legitimacy to civic organizations that had sometimes been criticized in the past for being out of touch (Leicht 2005).

WHY FIVE CIVIC COALITIONS EMERGED

After 9/11, members of the public exercised their emotional claims to help decide what would happen to the site not only by participating in resident groups, family groups, and business associations but by forming five new civic coalitions. All of them engaged in similar activities and faced similar challenges in terms of providing forums for generating and exchanging information and advocating desired courses of action. Owing to diverse constituencies, each sometimes encountered difficulty in balancing these objectives. Five different coalitions emerged because, despite internal differences between their component organizations, they represented different "publics" with different priorities and outlooks.

The Civic Alliance to Rebuild Downtown New York

The Civic Alliance (CA) sought to forge a common perspective among professionals in planning, architecture, and environmental and sustainable design, as well as among those concerned with economic and social justice, members of the business community, area residents, and family members of the victims of 9/11. Top staff at the Regional Plan Association and the Pratt Institute Center for Community and Environmental Development (PICCED) and academics from the policy schools at New York University and the New School took the initiative to convene approximately eighty organizational representatives for the Alliance's first meeting in October 2001. The Rockefeller Brothers Fund, the Ford Foundation, the W. K. Kellogg Foundation, and Con Edison provided support for the Civic Alliance, which continues to convene monthly meetings for its member organizations and interested individuals. Other foundations and corporations funded the Alliance's "Listening to the City" initiative.

CA steering committee members Robert Yaro and Petra Todorovich of the RPA, Ron Shiffman of PICCED, and Paul Elston of the League of Conservation Voters played key roles in shaping the Civic Alliance's goals and keeping its members focused on lower Manhattan's role in the region. In the first year CA meetings drew a large attendance from a diverse membership, and many participated in its eight working groups on economic development; transportation and mobility; social, economic, and environmental justice; the memorial process; green buildings and sustainable systems; civic amenities; urban design; and the regulatory framework. These committees allowed members with different interests to develop policy ideas in a small setting and to resolve tensions between traditionally opposed groups.

Imagine New York

From its first meeting on December 20, 2001, its steering committee called Imagine New York (Imagine NY) a "project" to convey its temporary nature. The project was "intended to be different from but synergistic with the work being done [by other civic coalitions formed after 9/11]," according to the group's meeting minutes. Through a series of workshops, this project would "solicit opinions from the broadest possible public." The Municipal Arts Society (MAS) spearheaded the project, but its steering committee included planners and architects, family members, and Community Board 1 president Madelyn Wils, whom Governor Pataki had appointed to the LMDC board. Unlike the other coalitions, it did not meet monthly with a large membership group but operated through a small steering committee that planned its workshops. Imagine New York was therefore simultaneously centralized and decentralized. Its small central steering committee organized all of its workshop themes, but the actual workshops were conducted by volunteer facilitators, and participants came from many different communities.

The Labor Community Advocacy Network

With support from the Rockefeller Foundation and the Open Society Institute, the Fiscal Policy Institute and the Central Labor Council formed the Labor Community Advocacy Network (LCAN) after 9/11 to pursue issues important to community activists, labor unions, and environmental justice advocates. While it weighed in regularly on site plan discussions, its members focused on two main priorities—fostering high-paying jobs and building affordable housing—and it developed policy papers in these two areas. LCAN members suggested that equity and fair wage requirements be attached to the economic revitalization projects being carried out by the LMDC. Although many labor leaders were active in LCAN's first year, they became much less active afterwards. David Kallick and James Parrott of the Fiscal Policy Institute co-chair LCAN, and advocacy organizations representing people of color have become more involved in shaping the group's goals and strategies. LCAN pursued both an inside and outside strategy to promote the creation of better jobs and affordable housing. Committees made up of organizations with expertise in particular areas developed policy proposals and strategies for influencing decisionmakers. Unlike the other organizations, LCAN did not draw its membership primarily from architects and planners. Therefore, although it took positions on planning decisions, it focused more on whether the rules governing development practices would be inclusive and whether they would include equity requirements.

New York New Visions

New York New Visions (NYNV) members are architecture and planning professionals who focus on substantive and design issues. The coalition has twenty (originally twenty-one) constituent organizations and has provided a forum for New York's top design professionals to weigh in on the rebuilding. New York New Visions is a pro-bono organization operating without foundation support (Bell 2004). Member organizations have provided some in-kind support and financing for one intern. The American Institute of Architects (AIA) initiated and co-chairs the coalition. It and the American Planning Association (APA) played an important role in shaping the organization's agenda. Over time, the larger constituent organizations have participated less frequently, mainly attending presentations organized by the executive committee or simply lending their names to the coalition. As their participation waned, the executive committee organized more information meetings for its constituents and co-hosted some large events for design professionals whom NYNV seeks to represent. The coalition has resisted endorsing particular plans and tried instead to evaluate the alternative plans according to professional standards and guidelines.

Members are centrally concerned with applying their professional expertise, not raising issues of equity or social justice. Their frequent professional interactions with government agencies and corporate clients have made them acutely aware of the political nuances of the decisionmaking process. NYNV members face the dilemma of advocating for design excellence and rational planning while also recognizing the symbolic magnitude of the rebuilding. Although they routinely express concern about the importance of public input and argue for transparent decisionmaking, the coalition's professional culture, dedication to design excellence, and desire to maintain access to decisionmakers sometimes limit how vigorously they push for public participation.

Rebuild Downtown Our Town

Beverly Willis, director of the Architecture Research Institute, and Susan Szenasy, editor in chief of *Metropolis* magazine, formed and co-chaired Rebuild Downtown Our Town (R.Dot), a coalition that claims to be the "voice of lower Manhattan." R.Dot has received support from the Alfred P. Sloan Foundation and the Rockefeller Brothers Fund. The organization draws on a cross-section of downtown architects, planners, artists, residents, and business owners. Vocal members from Tribeca have advocated broadening the meaning of "downtown" beyond the WTC site, a position that sometimes brings them into conflict with the residents of the immediate area. With its varied membership, R.Dot has been concerned with how the site connects with the surrounding downtown area. R.Dot members have tended to focus on concrete local goals and a concern for government accountability. The coalition conducted several studies and published several position papers exploring how to revitalize downtown, focusing on issues like retail, street management, and cultural programs.

These brief descriptions identify how the coalitions differed in terms of organizational culture and values and orientation to decisionmakers and public opinion. Some coalitions, like New York New Visions, consciously chose to represent the design and planning professionals to decisionmakers rather than directly engage the public because they felt that others, especially the Civic Alliance, were fulfilling that need (Kesner 2005). One group, Imagine New York, did not see itself as a coalition at all, but rather as a "project" meant to develop a synergistic relationship among the other coalitions. Although the other groups also wanted to educate the public, Imagine NY focused on eliciting public views in ways that would not be channeled by any existing framework. Because one coalition, LCAN, focused on how the LMDC would allocate its federal funds, it had a different relationship with the LMDC than did New York New Visions, which focused on providing the LMDC with design advice. In short, each coalition has had its own purpose, membership, and structure. At the same time, the coalitions have collaborated with each other, and their leaders attend each other's meetings or at least nominally belong to the other coalitions (except for the leadership of LCAN and NYNV). While each coalition has had its own focus, they have all drawn strength from their participation in each other's activities.

CREATING A VISION AND AN AGENDA

In the weeks and months after 9/11, the civic coalitions provided forums for the expression of the tremendous and pervasive public concern that arose after the attacks. These forums showed that civil society was alive and engaged in

New York. By participating in these, civic associations that had been considered elite organizations seeking to impose their professional values on the public were also reinvigorated with a new sense of mission. Events like Imagine New York's workshops or "Listening to the City" were important departures for these organizations.

Imagining New York

Imagine New York organized several workshops in early 2002 to discuss the future of lower Manhattan and New York City. While planning for these workshops evolved over time, their intent—to give the public a voice—was forged at a staff meeting of the Municipal Arts Society (MAS) within days of the attacks. MAS has a long and distinguished history as an elite planning and design organization, but the exchange at this meeting showed the emotional impact of 9/11 on young New Yorkers. At the meeting the organization's president and executive director emphasized that it would provide an opportunity to replan downtown. The younger staff members seemed shocked by this suggestion and essentially rebelled. Organized advocacy seemed an inappropriate, almost blasphemous, response to the loss they had experienced on 9/11. The germ of the idea of Imagine New York emerged from this meeting and a subsequent board meeting. It would expand the community-based planning conducted by MAS's Planning Center on a much larger scale. A steering committee was established to reach out to civic, community, and governmental entities throughout the tristate area. With them, it organized an initial round of 230 workshops for 3,000 people between March and May 2002 (Imagine New York 2002). These workshops were very much a normative experiment in "imagining" how the city ought to look. They were conducted in Cantonese, Spanish, and American Sign Language, often in the neighborhoods where participants lived. The workshops brought individuals from different backgrounds and different interests together to foster deliberation among them. They yielded 19,000 ideas, which Imagine NY's steering committee separated into 49 themes or "visions."

Imagine New York sought to provide public information that non-experts could understand and to elicit public responses without manipulating support for a particular agenda. According to one Imagine NY steering committee member, "Since the whole point of our project was to find out what the public thinks should happen, no, we didn't have any principles prior to the forty-nine visions." Steering committee members thought carefully, however, about how to pose questions in the workshops so that participants would think "qualitatively" about the options for planning lower Manhattan and the WTC instead of just selecting an aesthetically appealing architectural design. They wanted to educate participants so they could critically evaluate the designs. This was a very direct kind of representation in that Imagine New York published the comments of the participants instead of trying to shape those claims into a coherent goal or policy agenda. Yet the project illustrated the difficulty the coalitions faced in articulating the diverse opinions of the public while also trying to influence the outcomes. The LMDC and the Port Authority essentially ignored Imagine New York's first workshop.

Many of the other coalitions also conducted public forums in the first few months and tried to translate the ideas generated in these discussions into concrete principles and policy suggestions. New York New Visions members worked diligently to produce its *Principles for the Rebuilding of Lower Manhattan* (2002). These principles identified seven priorities for the rebuilding: an open memorial process, a flexible mixed-use community, better connections to lower Manhattan, coordinated and regional growth strategies, design excellence and sustainability, an effective and inclusive planning process, and immediate (if temporary) action on all components of the project.

Producing a Site Plan

The LMDC solicited little public participation before releasing its first set of site plans (Neuman and Haberman 2002), though LMDC staff did benefit from the hard work of NYNV members. When the LMDC ultimately released its principles in May 2002, many reiterated themes that had been identified by New York New Visions. In April 2002, without public consultation or approval by the Port Authority, as Sagalyn (this volume) has detailed, the LMDC released a request for proposals (RFP) for urban planning consulting services. This signaled that the LMDC did not want public input, despite its stated commitment to a "transparent planning process in which the public has a central role in shaping the future of Lower Manhattan."[1] Port Authority officials were unhappy that the LMDC had issued the RFP on its own, and the LMDC quickly retracted it. The two agencies soon issued a nearly identical joint RFP.

Although the LMDC's *Principles and Preliminary Blueprint for the Future of Lower Manhattan* was well received by the architecture and planning community and held the potential for good planning, the Authority's program requirements constrained what could be done on the site and concentrated on developments that would generate revenues. It required that all twelve million square feet of commercial space be restored. Silverstein acknowledged the importance of public participation but saw its role as primarily input in creating a suitable memorial (Silverstein 2001). The LMDC had already attracted public ire over its business and residential retention programs. When the LMDC released six alternative site plans rendered by Beyer Blinder Belle that mainly reflected the interests of the Port Authority and Silverstein Properties, considerable indignation arose from the public, the coalitions, and the press. The plans were derided as six unimaginative and uninspiring variations on the same theme that failed to deliver on the high expectations for the site.

Herbert Muschamp (2002), the architecture critic for the *New York Times*, was especially critical of Beyer Blinder Belle's plans: "Mediocrity, the choice of this firm reminds us, is not a default mode. It is a carefully constructed reality, erected at vast public expense. Ignorance is the brick from which this wretched edifice is built. Secrecy is the mortar holding it together." Muschamp's attack resonated with members of the public who wanted to see something spectacular on the site, a sentiment common among Imagine New York participants.

Not everyone agreed. An NYNV member, Ernest Hutton (2002), argued:

[Muschamp] would seemingly have us renounce rational urban planning in favor of an unrealistic approach to city design in which an architecture of narcissism trumps all other considerations of program, use, context and public interest. The firm Beyer Blinder Belle has been properly charged with defining a plan that incorporates complex and often contradictory considerations of memorialization, underground and surface transportation, flexibility for yet-to-be-determined users and tenants, and its relationship to the waterfront, the fabric of Lower Manhattan and the skyline of the city. The firm has enough on its plate without demands for a premature architectural solution bearing no resemblance to reality—a bold risk, perhaps, but with no potential for return, a true waste of public time and money.

Hutton's remarks reflect the understanding among his colleagues at Beyer Blinder Belle and other professional planners and architects that a land use plan is not an architectural design. Yet LMDC officials failed to convey this fundamental distinction to the public.

Others felt that the six plans reflected the LMDC's and Port Authority's lack of sensitivity to a public that wanted to participate and expected something spectacular. The Civic Alliance provided a forum through which they could articulate their frustration. With financial support from the LMDC, the Civic Alliance convened 4,500 people at the Jacob K. Javits Convention Center in midtown New York to discuss their vision of the future of New York City and the region. This event, entitled "Listening to the City," sought to involve a broad public in the complex technical issues surrounding the project and to enable them to express their disdain for the six original site plans. "Listening to the City" was a turning point in the rebuilding process—and, some say, in the CA's relationship with the LMDC (Kallick 2004). In a July 16, 2002, LCAN meeting prior to the event, one Civic Alliance member sought to convince

LCAN members that it would enable them to criticize the process because LMDC staff wanted to push back against the Port Authority's rigid program requirements. LMDC officials may have gotten more feedback, however, than they anticipated.

"Listening to the City" participants echoed the press and architecture critics by uniformly criticizing the six plans. Memorable comments included, "It looks like Albany," and, "Nothing here is truly monumental" (Civic Alliance 2002a, 10). The report on the event identified two major goals: creating a vibrant, mixed-use downtown community, including a balance of commercial, cultural, and residential uses; and creating a "serene and dignified memorial" (8).

Event organizers recruited a broad cross-section of participants, including members of the victims' families in New Jersey. Whites and Asians participated in rough proportion to their presence in the general public, 67 percent and 12 percent, respectively, but African Americans (7 percent) and Hispanics (10 percent) were underrepresented. (Each accounts for 20 percent of the metropolitan population.) Participants also tended to be higher-income than the population as a whole ("Listening to the City" 2002a, 7). Despite these limitations, participants identified priority issues relevant to low-income and minority communities: affordable housing, job training and development programs, and child care. About the six concept plans, 70 percent said that "improving the ability to cross West Street" was very important. West Street is a multi-lane highway that separates Battery Park City and the World Financial Center (WFC) from the rest of lower Manhattan. Prior to 9/11, a pedestrian bridge connected the WTC to the WFC, but the street was extremely dangerous to cross. More than 70 percent also identified restoring the Manhattan skyline to its pre-9/11 splendor as "very important." No effort was made to calculate the cost of such decisions.

"Listening to the City" had a critical impact on the aesthetic, if not substantive, elements of the site plan. The LMDC and the Port Authority reacted to the overwhelmingly negative response to the six plans by starting the process anew. The LMDC quickly released a Request for Qualifications (RFQ) to conduct an "Innovative Design Study." New York New Visions provided the LMDC with a list of firms they thought were good candidates to submit such designs.

Starting Over: The Search for Something Extraordinary

The design study resulted in nine new site plans from top American and international architects. Not only were these new designs considerably more inspiring, but the design teams gave compelling presentations, and many actively courted the public and the coalitions. Daniel Libeskind's plan appealed to the family members and the civic coalitions by solving the dilemma of how to locate a memorial in the center of a sixteen-acre commercial space. All of the coalitions had suggested planning the memorial and the site together instead of through parallel processes, and the Libeskind plan did just that by allocating the entire "bathtub" area for a memorial space seventy feet below grade. This created a buffer between the bustling city streets and the dignified and solemn memorial space. Libeskind's plan also reduced the office space from twelve to ten million square feet. This reduction was particularly important to the civic coalitions, which were concerned that the original plans would flood downtown with more office space than it could absorb and create too much density on the site. Because of this vision, and because Libeskind made it clear that he wanted their input by meeting with them, most of the coalitions endorsed his plan.[2]

The LMDC formed a committee of board members and local officials to select the final design team. The two finalists were Libeskind's "Memorial Foundations" and the THINK team's "Towers of Culture." Though the LMDC's site committee endorsed the THINK team, Governor Pataki selected Daniel Libeskind as the master planner. The coalitions argued that the choice of Libeskind indicated that the public had had an impact. Their celebration was to prove short-lived.

Facts on the Ground

Between the governor's selection of Libeskind as the master planner in February 2003 and the independent jury's selection of a memorial design in January 2004, changes were made to the Libeskind plan that made it quite different from the one he initially presented. The Libeskind plan unraveled because it contravened the economic interests of the Port Authority, Silverstein Properties, and other downtown real estate owners like Brookfield Properties. It was also undermined by the development of the memorial planning process as a separate process, as well as by steps taken by Silverstein to assert his right to design his own buildings. Finally, it reflected a lack of consensus underneath the superficial support from family members and the civic coalitions.

The coalitions' decision to endorse the Libeskind plan had illuminated the difficulty they faced in balancing their twin goals of creating a forum for exchanging ideas and advocating particular outcomes. Members of the Civic Alliance viewed the Libeskind plan as the result of a public process that included their endorsement. The press had praised "Listening to the City" as an important democratic endeavor that gave legitimacy to the coalition's claim to speak for the public. When the governor selected the plan they had endorsed, the Civic Alliance and the other coalitions felt that the Libeskind plan was an important win for the public.

The Civic Alliance had been successful in part because it found ways to resolve, or obscure, differences within its broad membership base. Like the other coalitions, it could bring different member organizations together behind general principles because they were vague enough to be interpreted in various ways. The CA's working group system also made it possible for members with different ideological and professional approaches to work together. Environmental justice and affordable housing advocates, for example, could work alongside pro-growth members like the Real Estate Board of New York and the Alliance for Downtown New York. The coalition's endorsement of Libeskind's plan, however, aggravated the underlying tensions among its members. Some Battery Park City residents and businesses thought that the thirty-foot sunken plaza would isolate them from the rest of downtown. (The Port Authority had raised Libeskind's original plaza from seventy feet below grade to secure the bathtub and accommodate necessary mechanical equipment.) Some also thought that because one public official had overridden a committee recommendation the outcome was not democratic. As the Libeskind plan began to change, Civic Alliance members wrestled with how much to challenge those changes.

All of the coalitions were concerned that LMDC and Port Authority staff were rapidly changing the Libeskind master plan, increasing the square footage on the site. On June 11, 2003, the Civic Alliance held a press conference and released a rendering that showed how the site would look with the increased density. It pictured five towers and the four-acre memorial squeezed onto the space, a far cry from Libeskind's original vision. Civic Alliance members argued that although "not everyone agreed on the plan, it was the result of a historic public process" and that "Studio Libeskind's [original] master plan answered the public call for something truly special and remarkable, an innovation that would herald the revival of our city and draw visitors from around the world." On a practical level, critics were also concerned about flooding the area with more office space than it could absorb. They also had a problem with placing the retail space underground and suggested putting most of it at grade level to complement existing retail activities (Rebuild Downtown Our Town 2003).

Battery Park City residents and the large corporations housed in the World Financial Center also wanted to see a quick restoration of the area's amenities, services, and access. At a Civic Alliance steering committee meeting on July 2, 2003, a downtown resident warned coalition members that they were not recognizing the concerns of residents and the business community. "Historically, residents haven't worked with business, but many are in the rebuilding process and the Alliance really seemed to miss that. If you had lost sixteen acres, you would feel you were a stakeholder and . . . I don't think you get that." As a result of the Civic Alliance's strong backing for the Libeskind plan, the Alliance for Downtown New York, Community Board 1, and Wall Street

Rising withdrew from membership. This shift lessened the influence of business members and residents within the CA but increased its ability to advocate. Such tensions indicated that the consensus over Libeskind was delicately crafted, making it difficult to create a united front behind him.

The press conference signaled that the Civic Alliance was taking a more confrontational approach to the rebuilding process and the LMDC. Its early reports had generally been optimistic, claiming that the organization "played an important role in shaping the thinking and early actions of the LMDC, Port Authority and other agencies" (Civic Alliance 2002b, 3). It also regularly mentions "Listening to the City" as a turning point in the process and as an example of public participation in it. But the coalition's endorsement of the Libeskind plan created stresses between the organization and the LMDC, which the LMDC eased by hiring Holly Leicht, formerly of the Municipal Arts Society, Imagine New York, and the Civic Alliance, to work on the off-site lower Manhattan planning projects. Leicht reached out to the CA and NYNV.

New York New Visions members also worried about the amount of commercial space on the site. Arguing from a design perspective, they claimed that it was simply too dense. Though the Port Authority was initially unwilling to decrease the amount of office space, the LMDC provided a solution by purchasing the contaminated Deutsche Bank building south of the site as a place to build a "fifth" tower. This solution redistributed space off the original site but did not decrease the amount of planned space. When Westfield America sold its interest in the lease, which had entitled it to build one million square feet of new retail space, to the Port Authority, it said that doing so "will allow the public interest to take precedence" (Rogers 2003).

New York New Visions also faced difficulties in balancing information sharing with advocacy. Its actions on the memorial planning led the Architectural League to withdraw its membership. NYNV's search for independence from the LMDC also conflicted with its members' desire for access and influence. Several had professional relationships with Alexander Garvin, the then-vice president of planning at the LMDC. Garvin recognized the professional and political value of ongoing meetings with NYNV. When he left, two of his former students, Andrew Winters and Chris Glaisek, took his place and maintained these relationships. NYNV executive committee members met regularly with LMDC staff to give feedback on their work, and they produced several public analyses of LMDC and Port Authority proposals, helping them with issues of design feasibility, neighborhood connections, and sustainability.

This relationship gave NYNV members access to decisionmakers, and their participation gave the LMDC some legitimacy. However, when LMDC president Kevin Rampe suggested that NYNV was helping the LMDC produce guidelines for the site, the implication was that the coalition was responsible for guidelines that many NYNV members had not even seen yet. This dynamic made it difficult for NYNV to maintain that it was a neutral observer of the process. At the same time, it explains why the group rarely pursues outside confrontational strategies, although the NYNV did send an open letter to the LMDC criticizing its failure to release the guidelines to the public.

The Memorial Design Competition

The Port Authority and Larry Silverstein clearly did not want the public to have any say over the site plan. Instead, they suggested that the public concern itself with designing the memorial. Anita Contini, vice president for memorial, cultural, and civic programs at the LMDC, was also concerned that the public would want too much input in that process. She—and many other design professionals—were leery of design by committee, fearing the result would be inadequate. She also wanted to avoid the political tampering that seemed to plague the selection of the master plan. The public and stakeholders could discuss the mission statement and memorial program but would not partici-pate in the final decision. Instead, as James Young explains in his chapter, the memorial selection would be made by an independent jury.

The coalitions had mixed views on this issue. New York New Visions, the Civic Alliance, and Imagine New York actively participated in the memorial discussions. The CA and New York New Visions combined their memorial committee groups, and some of the members of that joint group served as informal consultants to Contini. They suggested names and recommended the ratio of professionals to nonprofessionals for the jury. They wanted family members, downtown residents, and others to be represented, but they also wanted design professionals to make up the majority of the jury. Some coali-tion members suggested that the LMDC hold a two-stage competition, with public feedback after the first round. By doing so, the jury would control the final selection, but the LMDC could also receive public feedback. When the LMDC balked at this idea, Imagine New York conducted memorial workshops to provide public input. Initially unresponsive to the workshops, the LMDC came to recognize that they would allow the public to voice concerns without jeopardizing the LMDC's professional competition.

As Young confirms, some jury members have since indicated that the jury was not entirely in favor of the existing Libeskind site plan, which proposed its own memorial setting. All eight semifinalists selected by the jury submitted designs that were inconsistent in some way with the Libeskind vision. In the end, Michael Arad's design, selected by the jury, truly seemed to reject the Libeskind plan. As a result, the Libeskind master plan seemed to be coming apart one component at a time. First Silverstein had his architect, David Childs, redesign the Freedom Tower. Then the jury chose a memorial design that eroded the heart of Libeskind's vision.

The memorial competition was difficult for the coalitions. The memorial process they had orchestrated yielded results that challenged the Libeskind plan, which most of them had supported. It was particularly awkward for New York New Visions, which reaffirmed its support of the jury process only the day before the result was announced. This situation underscored the ways in which the leadership had grown stronger as the constituent organizations had become further removed from the process, but also that a process did not always yield the desired outcome. In the first general meeting of New York New Visions after the memorial semifinalists were announced, many constituent members who had not been involved in the memorial discussions were vocal about their disappointment. Like the participants in "Listening to the City," they felt that the designs were simply not good enough or inspiring enough. Some suggested installing a new jury or having the jury select a broader spectrum of semifinalists. Libeskind himself did not attack the memorial design but indicated that he had begun working with Arad and his landscape architect collaborator, Peter Walker. Libeskind's unwillingness to fight for his own design ultimately convinced the coalitions to let the issue rest.

Beyond Sixteen Acres: Establishing Priorities for Lower Manhattan

Members of the public, the coalitions, and the press have sharply criticized the governor for his lack of leadership throughout the rebuilding project. The broader public had been most captivated by the design of the commercial space and the memorial on the sixteen-acre site. Libeskind's claim that the public was his client was weakened by the fact that final decisions about both issues undermined his original design plan. Although setting aside a four-acre memorial site roughly on the footprints of the original towers was a victory for the families, the Port Authority and Silverstein decided almost every other important aspect of the site. Compared to the Port Authority, the LMDC did make a considerable effort to solicit public input, but the final decisions did not reflect it.

The LMDC's other mandate was to develop and fund projects to revitalize lower Manhattan. Though the LMDC did seek public input on the site plan and memorial, it did not provide for public debate about its revitalization projects (Louis 2004). Most of those projects were funded with community development block grant (CDBG) money, but the Department of Housing and Urban Development (HUD) eliminated the standard public hearing requirement for this allocation. The LMDC's website states: "LMDC selects activities based on needs as articulated by the public including residents, businesses and workers, elected officials and government agencies, and community based organizations." The LMDC did so by meeting privately with stakeholders. It allowed the public a fifteen-day comment period on its proposed partial actions plans, but announced those plans only in local newspapers and on its website, leaving many members of the public and even the civic coalitions initially unaware of them. One LMDC staff member confirmed in September 2004 that these important initiatives, involving millions of dollars, rarely get public comments. LMDC spent CDBG money on business and residential retention grants, tourism and communications, cultural and community development, short-term capital projects, long-term planning, and memorial and cultural projects. Several projects, such as the Fulton Corridor and a transportation study in Chinatown, had not advanced past the "studies" stage in early 2005. Furthermore, the LMDC had not submitted partial action plan 6, which would create three hundred units of affordable housing to HUD, even though comments for the plan were due in January 2004.

LCAN members were especially critical of how the LMDC had allocated these funds and argued that the city of New York should make these decisions instead. As Mitchell Moss and Lynne Sagalyn indicate elsewhere in this volume, the city government's role in the rebuilding was quite limited, although Mayor Bloomberg had released his plan for lower Manhattan by January 2003. That announcement and the departure of LMDC executive director Louis Tomson galvanized the coalitions to push for a greater role for the city. As LCAN co-founder David Kallick (2003) argued:

> The time has come for the corporation to step aside and put the control where it belongs: with the elected government of New York City. LMDC was conceived by Pataki and Mayor Rudy Giuliani after 9/11 as a game of keep away from Mark Green, the mayoral candidate then leading in the polls. Now that the political show is over, the right place for city planning to be is in city government.

Other civic leaders were more cautious. In a January 30, 2003, statement, the Civic Alliance, New York New Visions, and Imagine New York jointly argued that "the Mayor and Governor should be equal partners in selecting the next executive director of the LMDC." In response to Kallick, Rick Bell (2003) of New York New Visions argued that it was "No Time to Get Rid of the LMDC." According to him, the agency was a good partner for the city because it provided balance, a commitment to design, and a commitment to the rest of lower Manhattan. The subsequent months produced no formal changes, but the LMDC and the city seemed to be working together on some projects, and the LMDC seemed to reach out to the downtown community. During the summer of 2003, the LMDC organized workshops based on the Imagine New York model to ask downtown residents and business owners how they wanted to spend the remaining $1.1 billion in CDBG funds. It also hired Holly Leicht, who had helped organize the Imagine New York workshops, as a MAS staff member.

Since the LMDC had neither issued its report on the workshops nor adopted the partial action plan for $50 million in affordable housing by the fall of 2003, the coalitions, except NYNV, decided to co-sponsor a series of public forums on the theme "Beyond Sixteen Acres" to explore the top priorities for programming to revitalize the downtown community. In November, R.Dot and the Pratt Institute held a "Neighborhood and Housing Roundtable," but the highlight of these forums was a March 2004 panel on "How Can $1.2 Billion Best Revitalize New York After 9/11," held after the LMDC finally released its workshops report.

Despite chilling winds and snow, the room was packed. Organizers gave each participant gold coins that represented $1.2 billion. David Kallick and Jeff Zupan of RPA opened by summarizing the CDBG situation, describing the alternatives, and asking participants to put their coins into transparent cylinders at the front of the room standing for different investment targets. Participants could put all of their money in one cylinder or divide it as they saw fit. All together, participants put 39 percent of their money into housing, 23 percent into local economic development, 17 percent into community services and facilities, 15 percent into arts and culture, and only 6 percent into the proposed JFK-LIRR link (Rebuild Downtown Our Town 2004). This clearly clashed with Governor Pataki's desire to use the CDBG money to provide a one-seat rail link from lower Manhattan to Kennedy Airport. Just as organizers had hoped, the participants had challenged the governor's anticipated endorsement of the new tunnel option. It was unclear what impact the event had, but it was well attended by the press and brought together transportation specialists, downtown residents, family members, and even homeless and jobless individuals from the Lower East Side to demonstrate how different their priorities were from the governor's.

At the time the MTA, Port Authority, LMDC, and ESDC were studying two basic options for the JFK Airport link. According to the LMDC's *Lower Manhattan Transportation Strategies Report* (2003), the option to use an existing subway tunnel would cost between $2 billion and $2.3 billion but would further strain overcrowded subway trains, while building a new tunnel would cost between $4.7 billion and $5.3 billion. Either would cost far more than the remaining $1.2 billion in CDBG money. Like the forum participants, many other observers criticized the governor's plan (Dunlap 2004). The Regional Plan Association and the NYPIRG Straphangers Campaign, an advocacy group for subway patrons, normally supporters of transportation investments, viewed the governor's proposal as siphoning money from far more important projects into one that would benefit only a few business travelers, Long Island commuters, and downtown land owners. Such a project should not, they felt, be financed with community development funds. By September 2004, three years after the attacks, the LMDC had allocated $2 billion of its $2.8 billion allocation on a piecemeal basis. At this point, the governor finally promised a framework for spending the remaining funds by March 2005.

CONCLUSION

The WTC rebuilding and revitalization project illustrates the acute governance problems often created by public-private development projects in the United States. In public-private collaborations, developers build newer, bigger, and better private investments with some symbolic or substantive improvement to the public—usually quite limited—in return for tax incentives, zoning bonuses, or the exercise of eminent domain. Typically, these deals are not subject to much public review, funnel increased tax revenues into paying for public improvements to the site, and benefit the developer far more than the public, at least in any direct and immediate sense. In the WTC site case, the public was far more interested in the public-private collaboration, wanted far more influence over the outcome, and wanted the developer to make important concessions to the public interest.

For a series of institutional and political reasons outlined here as well as in the chapters by Sagalyn, Fainstein, and Moss, this did not happen. Even when government and private decisionmakers did not especially welcome public input, the five civic coalitions described here invented a variety of ways to enable members of the public to articulate their views, gathered and developed these expressions into coherent positions, and used a variety of channels to convey these positions to decisionmakers. Decisionmakers, in turn, became obliged to listen to these views and consider them. Only one decisionmaking body, the LMDC, responded with any great enthusiasm, however, mainly because harnessing the process of public involvement served its institutional ends. It "listened" primarily to criticism of the initial site plan favored by the Port Authority and responded by gaining more influence over the process of coming up with the subsequent plan. It was far less attentive to the civic coalitions on other matters, but even so, it paid more attention than the other two key decisionmakers, the Port Authority and Silverstein Properties.

Coalition members went into the process of planning for the rebuilding of the WTC site and the revitalization of lower Manhattan cautiously sharing the public's high expectations for what should be built on the site, and they played a powerful role in concretizing and articulating these expectations. They facilitated a robust participatory process by organizing myriad public forums. The Civic Alliance and Imagine New York were especially effective in organizing large-scale events that gave a broad cross-section of the public an opportunity to have a meaningful and substantive debate about the planning and design surrounding the site. Along with New York New Visions, R.Dot, and LCAN, they also educated the public about many of the technical complexities of the process, often through smaller-scale presentations and forums. Each coalition built a significant constituency during the year after the attacks, when public emotions continued to run high. Finally, by undertaking these organizing efforts, many of these coalitions' member organizations, such as the Regional Plan Association and the Municipal Arts Society, moved beyond their elite status and engaged more closely with the public, albeit usually with professional members of the public. All of these must be considered quite positive achievements.

As the LMDC and the Port Authority made decisions about the site over time, some schisms developed within the coalitions. The Civic Alliance's strong advocacy of the Libeskind plan and its criticism of the new transit link with JFK Airport reflected an evolution of its ideological goals away from the interests of its business-oriented members. At the same time, some members, especially Battery Park City residents, felt that the Civic Alliance would have been more attentive to their interests and more aggressive about advocating them. At least one member felt that the Civic Alliance talked a better game about local participation than it actually played (Epstein 2004).

New York New Visions tried to play inside games compared to the outside games of the Civic Alliance, Imagine New York, and LCAN. Since New York New Visions coalition members relied on their professional expertise to gain influence with decisionmakers, they were initially less interested in holding public events and attracting large audiences. Although all five member organizations are still active, these coalitions have held fewer events and attracted fewer participants than they did previously. After three years, R.Dot held its final public meeting in the autumn of 2004, though some members have continued to meet in smaller committees. In February 2005, it formally withdrew as a member of the Civic Alliance, stating that R.Dot was refashioning its mission and focus. New York New Visions revived itself several times with large-scale meetings, but it became increasingly hierarchical over time, in part because of membership fatigue. Member organizations that had been asked to renew their participation were reported at one executive committee meeting (September 3, 2003) to have said that they would continue to offer their names as members but did not have time to get more involved. As the emotional impact and immediacy of the attacks faded over time, and as more of the basic decisions were made, the breadth of participation declined in all of the coalitions, and each came to rely more on a committed core of activists. These leaders in each coalition retained a camaraderie and certainly developed considerable knowledge about the technical details of the main rebuilding issues.

More generally, participants who maintained their membership in these five coalitions received an important validation of their commitment, increased their knowledge of rebuilding issues, and gained access to decisionmakers. With this learning and maturing came new focal interests for each coalition. With the exception of LCAN, few people of color had participated in any of the coalitions, which tended to draw from professional constituencies. Over time, however, the Civic Alliance and R.Dot gave more attention to issues of equity and environmental justice. As the participation of business-oriented members of the Civic Alliance faded, the influence of labor- and advocacy-oriented members waxed. LCAN co-chair David Kallick, for example, took a more prominent role, while other advocacy-oriented members joined the Civic Alliance steering committee. This led the Civic Alliance to give more emphasis to such issues as affordable housing. For its part, LCAN members also acquired a more nuanced understanding of planning and architecture issues by partici-pating in the Civic Alliance and through conversations with Rick Bell, which helped LCAN develop its position on these issues (Kallick 2004).

Although these achievements certainly validate the immense amount of time and energy that participants contributed to these five civic coalitions, it is also important to ask whether their efforts had an impact on key decisions about the rebuilding process. Perhaps the best way to characterize the answer is to say that these organizations had more access than influence, and more influ-ence than impact on the outcomes. The coalitions used both inside strate-gies—working with the rebuilding agencies—and outside strategies—mobi-lizing public opinion, directing reports and open letters to the agencies, and even (in LCAN's case) organizing protests—to influence the rebuilding deci-sions. They clearly scored some successes. The "Listening to the City" event enabled the Civic Alliance to push certain issues onto the agenda of the LMDC and the Port Authority. The event gave 4,500 people the chance to challenge the first public plans of these entities and led the LMDC and the Port Author-ity to launch a second phase of planning, the "Innovative Design Study," which led to eight new finalists (though the governor did not, in the end, select the winner recommended by that process). The memorial workshops conducted by Imagine New York allowed decisionmakers to listen to public comment without compromising their commitment to hold a professional design compe-tition. Finally, the "Beyond Sixteen Acres" events may have been a factor in shifting the governor's attention away from the CDBG funds as a major source of financing for his new rail link to JFK Airport. Instead, the LMDC again reached out to the Civic Alliance for help in developing its priorities. With support from LCAN and NYNV, the Civic Alliance steering committee devel-oped a process for thinking about how the remaining funds should be spent. On May 12, 2005, the governor announced allocations that reflected many of the coalition's priorities, including $190 million for community projects, $220 million for waterfront development, and $300 million for the WTC Memorial Foundation.

These accomplishments were significant, and they certainly provided robust opportunities for public deliberation. In this sense, the coalitions could be said to be doing a good job of providing a voice for the larger public. "Listening to the City" participants were highly critical of how much commercial space the Port Authority had proposed to build. Yet the Port Authority has steadfastly maintained the square footage it will build. Civic coalition members strongly coalesced around Daniel Libeskind's site plan, yet the LMDC, the Port Authority, and Silverstein Properties have made numerous decisions about the design and construction of the initial office buildings, the layout of the underground infrastructure, the design of the memorial, and other matters that have undermined key elements of the Libeskind plan.

Members of New York New Visions keenly felt the ambiguity of wanting to influence outcomes by developing close ties with decisionmakers without being used by them to legitimate decisions with which they did not agree. This coalition had the most homogeneous professional membership and was generous in helping decisionmakers understand how their proposals would be received and evaluated on technical grounds. To maintain this access, the coalition often kept its criticisms private. As a result, the LMDC sometimes relied on its relationship with New York New Visions to legitimate its decisions even when the coalition had not approved of them, as in the case of the WTC site guidelines.

The coalitions played a critical role in the rebuilding project by filling the void created when rebuilding officials failed to provide venues for consultation with the public. They reached out to involve a broad cross-section of New Yorkers and recruited a core of participants with strong professional credentials and a long history of involvement in community issues in New York City. Although there is always a risk that professionals will substitute their own ideas for those of the broader publics whom they claim to represent, in this case professional expertise probably helped members of the public gain greater access, express their ideas more effectively, and present more coherent alternatives than they might have been able to do as individuals. But the members of these coalitions could not sustain their initial levels of enthusiasm and commitment, and as time passed the sting of the attacks faded, foundation money dried up, and membership fatigue set in. Nor could they alter the fundamental parameters of what key decisionmakers were determined to do. Instead, rebuilding officials often used the existence of the public forums organized by the civic coalitions as evidence that the public had had an adequate chance to have its say, even when they did not actually adopt any of the suggestions the public made. The civic coalitions could not convert their success in generating and focusing public interest into actual leverage over the decisionmakers, nor could they persuade these decisionmakers to embrace their visions. Although by May 2005, the decision-makers publically acknowledged problems the co-

alitions had raised years earlier about lack of market demand and design problems with the Freedom Tower. Overall, their main legacy will be new networks of dedicated civic actors who will continue to contribute to New York
City long after the current mayor and governor have left office.

The author thanks John Mollenkopf, the Center for Urban Research at the CUNY Graduate Center, and the Russell Sage Foundation's working group on the political effects of September 11 for
advice and support.

NOTES

1. See mission statement at Lower Manhattan Development Corporation website,
    "About Us," www.renewnyc.com.
2. Libeskind began a January 13, 2003, meeting with LCAN members by saying: "I'm
    here to listen to you. I believe in a public process." He also indicated that he would
    be receptive to their subsequent input.

REFERENCES

Bachrach, Peter, and Morton S. Baratz. 1962. "Two Faces of Power." *American Political
Science Review* 56(4, December): 947–52.

Bell, Rick. 2003. "No Time to Get Rid of the LMDC." Unpublished letter to the editor.
November 29.

———. 2004. Interview with the author. November 2.

Civic Alliance to Rebuild Downtown New York. 2002a. *Listening to the City: Report of
Proceedings*. New York: Civic Alliance.

———. 2002b. *A Planning Framework to Rebuild New York*. New York: Civic Alliance.
September.

Doig, Jameson. 2001. *Empire on the Hudson: Entrepreneurial Vision and Political Power at the
Port of New York Authority*. New York: Columbia University Press.

Dunlap, David. 2004. "Grants and Rails, and the Debate in Between." *New York Times*,
March 21.

Epstein, Paul. 2004. Interview with the author. October 28.

Gittell, Marilyn. 1980. *Limits to Citizen Participation: The Decline of Community Organizations*.
Thousand Oaks, Calif.: Sage Publications.

Goldberger, Paul. 2004. *Up from Zero: Politics, Architecture, and the Rebuilding of New York*.
New York: Random House.

Hutton, Ernest W. 2002. "Visions of Downtown" (letter to the editor). *New York Times*,
May 29.

Imagine New York. 2002. *Imagine New York: The People's Vision: Summary Report*. New
York: Imagine NY.

Kallick, David. 2003. "Time to Get Rid of the LMDC" (letter to the editor). *New York Daily News*, January 27.

———. 2004. Interview with the author. October 21.

Kesner, Marcie. 2005. Interview with the author. March 4.

Leicht, Holly. 2005. Interview with the author. January 10.

Louis, Errol. 2004. "The 9/11 Black Hole" (op-ed). *New York Daily News*, July 6.

Lower Manhattan Development Corporation (LMDC). 2002. *Principles and Preliminary Blueprint for the Future of Lower Manhattan*. New York: LMDC.

———. 2003. *Lower Manhattan Transportation Strategies Report*. New York: LMDC (April 24).

Muschamp, Herbert. 2002. "An Appraisal: Marginal Role for Architiecture at Ground Zero." *New York Times*, May 23.

Neuman, William, and Maggie Haberman. 2002. "Panel Ignoring Families." *New York Daily News*, June 14.

New York New Visions (NYNV). 2002. *Principles for the Rebuilding of Lower Manhattan*. New York: NYNV (February 25).

Peterson, Paul E. 1981. *City Limits*. Chicago: University of Chicago Press.

Polletta, Francesca, and Lesley Wood. 2005. "Public Deliberations After 9/11." In *Wounded City: The Social Effects of 9/11*, edited by Nancy Foner. New York: Russell Sage.

Putnam, Robert. 1993. *Making Democracy Work: Civic Traditions in Modern Italy*. Princeton, N.J.: Princeton University Press.

Rebuild Downtown Our Town (R.Dot). 2003. *Strategies for Revitalizing Lower Manhattan*. New York: R.Dot (January 16).

———. 2004. *Beyond Sixteen Acres*. New York: R.Dot and Pratt Institute Center for Community Development.

Reed, Adolph, Jr. 1999. *Stirrings in the Jug*. Minneapolis: University of Minnesota Press.

Rogers, Josh. 2003. "Port Looks to Buy WTC Retail." *Downtown Express*, September 16–22.

Schattschneider, E. E. 1960. *The Semi-Sovereign People*. New York: Holt, Rinehart and Winston.

Silverstein, Lawrence. 2001. "At Ground Zero, Rebuild and Honor." (letter to the editor). *New York Times*, October 25.

Skocpol, Theda. 2003. *Diminished Democracy: From Membership to Management in American Civic Life*. Norman: University of Oklahoma Press.

Tocqueville, Alexis de. 1835/1988. *Democracy in America*. Reprint, New York: HarperPerennial.

Walsh, AnneMarie. 1978. *The Public's Business: The Politics and Practices of Government Corporations*. Cambridge, Mass.: MIT Press.

Yaro, Robert (president of the Regional Plan Association). 2004. Interview with the author. November 18.

CHAPTER 6

The Memorial Process: A Juror's Report from Ground Zero

James E. Young

THE FIRST memorials for the victims of the 9/11 attacks appeared within hours of the collapse of the World Trade Center towers: these were the posted flyers of the missing and the candlelight vigils at Union Square, on the Esplanade in Brooklyn Heights, and elsewhere around the city. These photos and descriptions of loved ones were the spontaneous commemorations of loss and grief. With their photographs and descriptions of loving fathers, mothers, sons, and daughters, the flyers read almost as epitaphs on paper instead of stone, as perishable and transitory as the hope that inspired them. These families' missing loved ones were, in turn, remembered and mourned by all who came across these "found memorials." In this view, the "WTC memorial" had already begun.

The memory of the attack and its victims would unfold in stages. Further stages of this process included the ever-changing landscape of destruction at Ground Zero. Where the seven-story mountain of tangled and jutting ruins had stood as a literal remnant of the ferocity of the attacks and a symbol of mass death, the gigantic hole in the ground now stands for the immeasurable void left in our lives and hearts, an open wound in the cityscape. The feverish pace of the attempted rescue and cleanup leading to this moment bespoke the need of all to remember this terrible breach by repairing it.

At every stage of the process, passionate voices advocated freezing memory in media res as its own best possible memorial icon, from preserving the smoking pile of debris to leaving emblematic parts of the ruins in place, such as the facade or crossed steel beams. Still others would have preserved only the void of the entire sixteen-acre site, emptied of everything but memory of what was lost. Some, like Mayor Rudolph Giuliani, argued for only a soaring memorial where the towers had stood. Others lobbied for rebuilding the towers exactly as they had stood before as the surest way to defeat the terrorists. The question was never whether there would be a memorial or not, but always what kind of memorial would finally rise—or sink—at Ground Zero.

What has also become clear is that the memorialization of the 9/11 attacks and its victims must be seen as a process, one that is in many ways the life-blood of memory itself. For as a process, every memorial demands its own space and time, its own debate and negotiated result. As a process, the memorial is animated and sustained by the public give-and-take, the constant working through, as it takes on a life of its own in the public mind.

In this view, the advent of off-site memorials to the victims of the 9/11 attack in every borough of the city, as well as in nearly every neighboring suburb, is perfectly understandable. From New York City to Westchester to Long Island and New Jersey, every community deserves its own memorial, one that reflects its particular losses, ways of mourning, and understanding of these events. Memory is necessarily repetitive, but these memorials are anything but redundant. Each deserves its own process, one that is allowed to be as messy and noisy as the next. Some communities have conducted full-scale competitions, and others have invited native artists to help them articulate their grief. But if all see their memorials as processes, each a part of an overarching process larger than themselves, all will give themselves the space to remember as they see fit.

PERSONAL VERSUS CIVIC MEMORY

We have long asked our memorials to do many different, often paradoxical, things. We ask them to help us mourn and grieve lost loved ones and also to help us heal and get on with life. We ask them to recall both the richness of lives lost and the loss itself, even as we demand that they also recall heroism and hope. We ask them to console us in our grief and to instruct us in the meaning of our loss, even as we ask them to express our disconsolate anger. Sometimes we ask them to redeem destruction with beauty, and sometimes we ask them to recall horror in all of its ugliness. Over time, we also ask our memorials to assign historical meaning to events that we cannot always comprehend in our temporal proximity to them.

Even now, three years later, and with the benefit of an eloquent and comprehensive report from the 9/11 Commission (convened to establish exactly what happened on that day and in its immediate aftermath), we are still struggling with the larger meanings of the events of September 11, 2001. Without public consensus on the overarching meaning of 9/11, it is almost impossible to fix the memory of this day in stone. In fact, only two groups could be said to agree absolutely on what the attacks have meant to them: for the families of the victims and the residents of lower Manhattan, the meaning of this event is the terrible loss they suffered, as individual families and as distinct neighborhood communities. The loss of 2,749 loved ones can never be adequately measured, despite the actuarial accounting offered by the Victims' Compensation Fund. Neither will the loss of the World Trade Center complex and its sixteen million square feet of office space ever be completely compensated. These losses may also never be adequately represented in their collective memorialization, despite the best public attempts to commemorate them. From the outset, therefore, the process has included a necessary tension between the private grieving of families and the communities of rescue workers and nearby residents for their personal losses and the larger public mourning for the loss of security and safety. The families of victims came to know the meaning of their loss almost immediately, while the larger public still struggles to know the meaning of the 9/11 attacks on collective, national, and political levels.

As a result, commemoration of the attacks has necessarily proceeded on two tracks, which at times intersect: the personal and the civic. For the victims' families, Ground Zero was turned into a mass grave, a de facto cemetery, seemingly sanctified by the blood and remains of their loved ones. At the civic level, however, the loss of some sixteen million square feet of office space and the destruction of the twin towers of the World Trade Center demanded both symbolic and practical redress. At first, this tension between personal and public memory was as unnerving for the politicians as it was disturbing for the families of victims. Public debate was loud and often rancorous. At their extreme poles, the needs of these two groups are virtually irreconcilable: the families' need to preserve the site's sanctity by protecting it from commercial development, on the one hand, and the civic need to compensate for the destruction by rebuilding, on the other. This tension has played itself out in almost every stage of redevelopment and commemoration, finding its most succinct expression in the uneasily yoked together triadic motto adopted by the Lower Manhattan Development Corporation (LMDC), the public entity charged with overseeing the complete redevelopment of the entire sixteen-acre site: "Remember, Renew, Rebuild."

It seems that never before have we asked a memorial to do so much, for so many people, so soon after such a catastrophe. On the one hand, we know that the entire sixteen-acre site of the World Trade Center, with a new complex of cultural and commercial buildings, will necessarily serve as a "living" memorial to the terrible destruction and loss of life that took place there on September 11, 2001. But as Governor George Pataki, Mayor Michael Bloomberg, the LMDC, and the families of victims have all agreed, the centerpiece of the new

World Trade Center complex will be the 4.7-acre memorial site itself. Although we recognize that, only three years after the attacks, memory itself has barely accrued, we also appreciate that, as the centerpiece of the new complex, a memorial must be chosen before the rest of the site plans can proceed—especially if memory and rebuilding are to be integrated, as all parties believe they must be. It may be too early to remember, but it is also clear that the financial capital of the world can ill afford to delay reconstruction. By dint of its placement at the center of redevelopment, the memorial must be initiated before rebuilding can commence, whether or not memory itself can be agreed upon.

FROM SITE DESIGN TO MEMORIAL AND BACK AGAIN

Within a year of the attacks, galleries, museums, and media outlets had begun to take upon themselves the task of inviting and arbitrating public memory. As early as January 2002, the Max Protech Gallery in SoHo invited some 125 artists and architects to propose memorial designs. More than half of the invitees responded with designs, which were then exhibited in the gallery for several months. By early summer of 2002, the *New Yorker* magazine had similarly invited a handful of artists and architects to propose memorial designs for Ground Zero, which were featured in the July 15, 2002, issue (Tomkins 2002). For the first anniversary of the attacks, Herbert Muschamp, then architecture critic of the *New York Times*, invited several artists and architects to propose designs for redevelopment, which then ran in the *Times* magazine in the week of September 11, 2002. Still preoccupied with the site's overall redevelopment, the LMDC had yet to hold its first meeting on the memorial by that summer, yet dozens of unsolicited designs had already begun to pour into LMDC offices.

In fact, the most memorable memorial installation in the immediate aftermath of the attacks was shown on the cover of the *New York Times* magazine only two weeks after 9/11. The downtown public arts organization and foundation Creative Time had recommended a project then called "Phantom Towers" (conceived and designed by Julian LaVerdiere and Paul Myoda) to the editors of the *Times*, who were looking for an image to accompany a story on memorialization and redevelopment for the September 23, 2001, issue of the magazine. When it appeared, two other architects, from the Proun Space Studio, revealed that they too had been independently developing an installation of two great light beams for the downtown sky. For the six-month anniversary of the attacks, in March 2002, the city agreed to install for several days a remarkable collaboration of the two teams, a light installation originally entitled "Towers of Light," which concentrated two clusters of high-intensity beams of light shining into the night (Ebony 2001). Diplomatically renamed "Tribute in Light," so as to commemorate the victims as well as the towers, the installation could be seen (depending on cloud conditions) for miles around and proved immensely popular with a public that needed some place—however ephemeral—to mourn collectively the loss of the towers and lives on that day.

Discussion about a memorial remained a hot topic during the LMDC's public forums on finding a site design for the entire sixteen acres. Some argued that the best memorial would be the immediate reconstruction of the towers; others (including many family members) believed that the best memorial would be to leave the entire site empty, as a sacred space. One of the more prominent representatives of the victims' families, Monica Iken, adamantly argued that the entire sixteen-acre site should be regarded as a burial ground, as sacred and therefore off-limits to any and all redevelopment. The site, she insisted, must remain empty and be visited only by the families coming to mourn their loved ones lost in the attacks there. Other representatives of the families argued just as insistently that their loved ones should be commemorated by rebuilding the WTC even bigger than it was before, right in the same place, and that to do otherwise would be to capitulate to the killers. As traders and bankers, the victims would have wanted to be remembered, these family members argued, by the icons of commerce they helped build. The families of firefighters and police officers tended to favor setting aside the footprints of the towers for a memorial place that would recall the heroism of their deaths.

Meanwhile, the Lower Manhattan Development Corporation was trying to balance the needs of the Port Authority, the developers, and the financial community against the needs of mourners. Moreover, the city was juggling its civic duty to commemorate the dead with its own need for renewal and economic recovery. Hence, the redevelopment and memorial processes seemed to unfold at an almost unseemly pace.

The first casualty of the resulting gridlock of competing agendas was the set of six designs commissioned by the LMDC from the architectural firm Beyer Blinder Belle. These were shown and discussed in a large public forum, "Listening to the City," in July 2002. In trying to please everyone—with a design that offered twelve million square feet of generic office space housed in a generic-looking cluster of mid-high-rise buildings, laced with spaces for proposed memorials and gardens—the designers pleased no one. Recognizing this on the day he unveiled the designs, LMDC chairman John Whitehead proposed a seventh alternative: none of the above. This was the only proposal universally applauded.

Thus rebuked by a public process they had hoped would affirm their initial commission of Beyer Blinder Belle, the LMDC issued a request for proposals (RFP) from a pool of over three hundred architectural teams. Six finalist teams were eventually selected, all of them now invoking their designs as memorials, if not in their formal elements then in name and spirit. Indeed, by the end of the summer of 2002 it had become clear to the LMDC that it could not proceed with the redevelopment of the devastated sixteen-acre World Trade Center site without a memorial component. In August 2002, Whitehead announced the appointment of Anita Contini to head a memorial design process for the WTC site.

As the founder of Creative Time and a former executive vice president at Merrill Lynch, Contini enjoyed broad support in both the financial and art worlds downtown. Within weeks she had begun to tap other civic organizations, such as the Civic Alliance to Rebuild Downtown New York and New York New Visions (NYNV), for their accumulated expertise and wisdom. Within months Contini had begun to organize forums for the family and residential councils, bringing in speakers like Museum of Modern Art director Kirk Varnedoe, *New Yorker* architecture critic Paul Goldberger, Queens Art Museum director Tom Finkelpearl, and the present author to open up the idea of the memorial and its function as public and commemorative art—its very process.

Meanwhile, on December 19, 2002, the LMDC announced that it had selected six finalist teams from the three hundred proposals received and put them on public display at the Winter Garden in an exhibition entitled "Plans in Progress," which ran for several months. The six finalist teams were Studio Daniel Libeskind; the THINK team, comprising Rafael Viñoly, Frederic Schwartz, and their colleagues; Norman Foster and Partners; Richard Meier, Peter Eisenman, and their colleagues; Peterson/Littenberg Architecture and Urban Design; and United Architects. Public commentary was invited and accepted until February 2, 2003, and a massive public hearing was held on January 13, 2003, in lower Manhattan, sponsored by the LMDC and the Port Authority of New York and New Jersey (PANYNJ). Between its opening on December 19 and February 2, over one hundred thousand people visited the exhibition, and more than eight thousand comment cards were collected, analyzed, and turned into pie charts to gauge the public's response to these designs. On February 3, 2003, the LMDC announced that it had narrowed the selection of a master site design plan to two finalists: Studio Libeskind and the THINK team.

From that day to the announcement of a final winning design on February 26, 2003, the media and public airwaves were filled with an intense and heated lobbying effort on the part of both teams and their advocates. The battle of the plans grew increasingly contentious, with public statements from both teams deriding aspects of the other and each team seeking to mobilize public opinion. The joint committee of the LMDC and the Port Authority, charged with choosing the winning design, was reported by the *New York Times* to be leaning toward the THINK team design. But in final presentations by the two teams to Governor Pataki and Mayor Bloomberg, it became clear that the governor in particular was uneasy with what he regarded as the THINK team's skeletal design of two towers. Though this design had in fact been recommended by the LMDC-Port Authority selection committee, the governor felt that it would offend the sensibilities of the victims' families, who were looking for a hopeful sign of renewal, not a ghost of the towers. Pataki preferred Libeskind's "Memory Foundations," with its soaring Freedom Tower and preserved "bathtub" that memorialized both a void and the slurry walls that withstood the attacks and held the waters of the Hudson River at bay. The governor made his choice clear to the committee, which in the end acceded to it, if somewhat reluctantly. The LMDC-Port Authority press release on February 27 announcing the selection of Libeskind's design was headlined, "Design Remembers Loss and Celebrates Life."

THE WORLD TRADE CENTER SITE
MEMORIAL COMPETITION

Amid the noisy, if healthy, tumult of discussion surrounding the announcement of the two site design finalists in February 2003 and their audacious designs for rebuilding at Ground Zero, debate about an actual memorial to the 9/11 attacks almost fell by the wayside. Because the designs by finalists Daniel Libeskind and the THINK Team included prominent memorial elements, some suggested that "the whole thing was a memorial" and that a separate memorial competition long planned by the Lower Manhattan Development Corporation as part of its renewal of Ground Zero would be redundant. But in fact, despite the suggestive commemorative dimensions to both designs, neither the architects nor the LMDC ever conceived of "the whole thing" as the only memorial to the 9/11 attacks.

Indeed, a separate design competition for a memorial was always part of the LMDC's original plan for the redevelopment of downtown—and for good reasons. From the outset, the LMDC seemed to recognize that as tempting as it might be to allow the new building complex to serve as a de facto memorial, the conflation of rebuilding and commemoration would also foreclose the crucial process of memorialization, a process they had also come to regard as essential to both memory and redevelopment. Rather than prescribing a particular aesthetic form or architectural approach for the memorial, the LMDC wisely chose to open up the question of the memorial, hammer out a mission and program statement outlining the various kinds of memory to be preserved, and then initiate an open, blind, international competition for a design that would, they hoped, return responsibility for the memorial to the public for whom it was intended (for a discussion of these issues, see Princenthal 2004).

Between November 2002 and March 2003, the Families Advisory Council of the LMDC (which included families of the victims, local residents and businesspeople, and other groups affected by the attacks) appointed a committee of various advisory council members and handpicked professionals and experts in public art to formulate a "Memorial Mission Statement," which was to serve as a guiding mandate for the memorial and its process.[1] In its final version the Memorial Mission Statement read:

- Remember and honor the thousands of innocent men, women, and children murdered by terrorists in the horrific attacks of February 26, 1993, and September 11, 2001.

- Respect this place made sacred through tragic loss.

- Recognize the endurance of those who survived, the courage of those who risked their lives to save others, and the compassion of all who supported us in our darkest hours.

- May the lives remembered, the deeds recognized, and the spirit reawakened be eternal beacons, which reaffirm respect for life, strengthen our resolve to preserve freedom, and inspire an end to hatred, ignorance, and intolerance.

In addition to the Memorial Mission Statement, the LMDC wanted a two-part Memorial Program that would lay out both programmatic guidelines and specific program elements for the memorial.[2] The LMDC Memorial Program drafting committee proposed two sets of concrete guidelines, which they called "guiding principles" and "program elements." "The Guiding Principles are the aspirations that must be embodied within and conveyed through the memorial," the committee wrote, "regardless of the various interpretations to which it will ultimately be subject." By contrast, the "Program Elements" were intended to "provide memorial designers with a list of specific elements that should be physically included in the memorial, without prescribing how or inhibiting creativity."

In its two parts, the Memorial Program asked that the memorial: embody the goals and spirit of the Memorial Mission Statement; convey the magnitude of personal and physical loss at this location; acknowledge all those who aided in rescue, recovery, and healing; respect and enhance the sacred quality of the overall site and the space designated for the memorial; encourage reflection and contemplation; evoke the historical significance and worldwide impact of September 11, 2001; and inspire people to learn more about the events and impact of September 11, 2001, and February 26, 1993. The program elements were to include: recognition of each individual who was a victim of the attacks on 9/11 and in February 1993; provision of space for contemplation; and sepa-

rate, accessible space to serve as a final resting place for the unidentified remains from the World Trade Center site. Program elements also mandated
that the memorial be distinct from other memorial structures like museums or
visitor centers; that it make visible the footprints of the original WTC towers,
that it include appropriate transitions and approaches to, or within, the memorial; and that it convey historic authenticity.

The Memorial Mission Statement and the Memorial Program were nothing
if not thorough, collating and then codifying and trying to balance the needs
and aspirations of all representatives of the victims' families, local residents,
and civic groups. Included as part of the announcement for an open, international competition for a World Trade Center Site Memorial, it would also
prove to be a very tall and complicated order to fill, in all of its parts, especially
when combined with what appeared to be the enclosed and sunken 4.7-acre
site designated for the memorial in Daniel Libeskind's "Memory Foundations"
site plan.

Meanwhile, during the spring of 2003, as the Memorial Mission Statement
and Memorial Program drafting committees polished their memorial précis,
the LMDC quietly began putting together an international design competition.
In consultation with the governor's and mayor's offices, and with the advice
of scholars and other experts in design competitions, Anita Contini began
assembling what the LMDC hoped would be an unassailable jury for the competition. Chosen from all walks of life, but with very particular credentials,
they were (the LMDC hoped) both representative enough and revered enough
in their professional worlds to bring an unimpeachable authority to whatever
design they would finally choose.

On April 10, 2004, the LMDC announced the members of the World Trade
Center Site Memorial jury: Paula Grant Berry, Susan Freedman, Vartan Gregorian, Patricia Harris, Maya Lin, Michael McKeon, Julie Menin, Enrique Norten,
Martin Puryear, Nancy Rosen, Lowery Stokes Sims, Michael Van Valkenburgh,
and this author. In honor of his "accomplishments and devotion to New York
City," David Rockefeller was also appointed to serve as an honorary member
of the jury. Though the precise details of how the LMDC arrived at this particular jury may never be made public, it was clear to all that the composition of
the jury had been carefully calibrated to achieve a representative balance of
design architects and artists (Norten, Van Valkenburgh, Lin, and Puryear), arts
community professionals (Freedman, Rosen, and Sims), academic and cultural
historians (Gregorian and Young), political liaisons (Harris and McKeon), a
family member (Berry), and a local resident and business community leader
(Menin).

Several of the jurors had already been approached to advise the LMDC in
its memorial process in both formal and informal capacities, and as it turned
out, most of the jurors already knew or knew of each other. The public re-

sponse to the jury's composition was generally positive, even as many continued to voice the fear that it was still too early for such an undertaking, sterling jury or not.

Soon after our appointment as jurors, we received by overnight mail a provisional and highly confidential set of "World Trade Center Site Memorial Competition Guidelines," which included a meticulously assembled competition outline, memorial mission and program statements, guidelines, background readings, confidentiality statement, public perspectives, and a schedule of dates for submissions, review, and selection.[3] In reading over the competition "boundaries," it became clear almost immediately to the design professionals on the jury that the combination of mandatory program elements, Libeskind's site design, and the actual state of the site itself (a pit some seventy feet deep, part of which would be filled in with necessary transportation, power, and water infrastructure) would pose a daunting challenge to even the most experienced artists and architects. We feared that once they realized just how overdetermined the 4.7-acre memorial site was by the site design and multiple layers of program elements, many potential designers would throw up their hands and walk away from the competition. With permission from the other jurors, several of us began working to expand what we considered the most constraining of the guidelines, especially as described in the competition boundaries, in order to open up the site to the widest possible number of memorial designs.

The resulting final set of competition guidelines that was issued to competitors worldwide reflected our proposed changes, but we also realized that it would take a very close reading of the guidelines to appreciate how open we wanted these boundaries to be. Section 4.4 of the official World Trade Center Site Memorial Guidelines, entitled "Competition Boundaries," thus read:

- Competitors may locate or integrate the memorial anywhere within the memorial site limits and boundaries as shown in Illustrations 5, 6, and 7. The memorial site limit is indicated by a blue line on the site plan and sections and labeled as "site boundary."

- Competitors may, within the boundaries illustrated, create a memorial of any type, shape, height, or concept. Designs should consider the neighborhood context, including the connectivity of the surrounding residential and business communities. All designs should be sensitive to the spirit and vision of Studio Daniel Libeskind's master plan for the entire site.

- Design concepts that propose to exceed the illustrated memorial boundaries may be considered by the jury if, in collaboration with the LMDC, they are deemed feasible and consistent with site plan objectives.

Though satisfied with this explicit invitation to "go beyond" the boundaries of the site plan, we feared that competitors still might not feel that they had license to "violate" the site plan as illustrated in accompanying drawings and maps.

Thus, by the time the LMDC held its April 28, 2003, press conference at the Winter Garden announcing the International Competition for a World Trade Center Site Memorial Design, we jurors had already concluded that part of our announcement would include, unbeknownst to the LMDC, an invitation to potential designers to break the rules and challenge the site-plan design, just as all the great buildings and monuments of our era had had to break the rules of their day—including Libeskind's own Jewish Museum design in Berlin and Maya Lin's Vietnam Veterans' Memorial in Washington, D.C. We worried that even with a second or third close reading of the guidelines, without our explicit permission at the press conference, competitors might view "Memory Foundations" as the overall memorial, into which they would somehow have to fit their own memorial design—a kind of memorial within a memorial. Our remarks were widely reported (the *New York Times* headline declared, "Officials Invite 9/11 Memorial Designers to Break the Rules") and well received by the LMDC itself; LMDC president Kevin Rampe congratulated us on asserting exactly the kind of independence that the LMDC had hoped from us.

Competition rules and requirements invited anyone over the age of eighteen anywhere in the world to register for the competition, with a nonrefundable submission fee of $25. Designs were to be presented on single 30-by-40-inch rigid boards (preferably foam), vertically oriented, coded only with a registration number to ensure anonymity. All registrations had to be received by May 29, 2003. By that date, the LMDC had received some 13,800 registrations from 92 countries around the world. By the second-stage deadline date of June 30, 2003, the LMDC had received 5,201 actual submission boards from 63 countries, and submissions from every state in the Union except Alaska. In a secret location in midtown, the LMDC worked day and night for the month of July, determining eligibility, sorting submissions, recording bar codes and registration information, and organizing the viewing of the design boards for the jury, to begin the first of August 2003.

THE JURY DELIBERATES

During the two months between our appointment and our first viewing of the proposals, the LMDC organized several large public forums designed both to introduce the jury to the public and to introduce the needs of the public— especially those of the families of firefighters, police officers, and workers who had died in the attacks—to the jurors. At these meetings we sat up on a stage and introduced ourselves briefly, each with a short reflection on the daunting task ahead. And then we were invited simply to listen as members of the audience—numbering in the hundreds and composed overwhelmingly of family members of victims—took the floor one by one to express their sense of loss, their memorial needs, and their own visions for a memorial at Ground Zero. Members of firefighters' families were well organized and used these meetings to lobby vociferously for a memorial that would distinguish the heroic rescue workers from the victims they were trying to save. Some in the media suggested that these meetings served as venting sessions, whereby the LMDC could allow all groups to have their say without having to respond directly to their concerns. But in fact, as jurors, we were deeply affected by the hours of devastating stories the families of victims related to us. By the end of these meetings the question of who this public memorial would actually be for was all but settled in our minds: it would be first for the victims' families, then for the city, and then finally for the public at large.

Closed luncheon meetings between the jury and Governor Pataki, Mayor Bloomberg, former mayor Giuliani, the LMDC board, and its advisory councils followed. Again, we introduced ourselves and then listened to what this memorial meant to the political powers-that-be. In every case—from the governor to the mayor to the chair of the LMDC, John Whitehead—the jury was assured that it would be given complete and absolute autonomy and that any decision it made would be final and could not be overruled by anyone. Of course, most of the jurors were initially skeptical of these promises, remembering as they did how the governor had recently in effect chosen Libeskind's design over the recommendation of the LMDC's own committee. Before long, however, it became clear that the public affirmation by the governor, the mayor, and the LMDC of the jury's independence and sole authority for selecting a design was also the most politically sensible position for them to take. If our selection was a good one, all involved could take credit for a successful process; if we chose badly, they would not have to bear responsibility for our poor judgment and taste. But in fact, Governor Pataki's extemporaneous and impassioned defense of the memorial as its own process demanding whatever time and money it would take left an indelible impression on the jury, most of whom were moved deeply by the extraordinary command the governor had of both the aesthetic and political issues surrounding the memorial.

On August 2, the jury began two solid weeks of deliberations, spending some ten hours a day viewing six hundred designs a day, in groups of two hundred. At the end of the first day we called a meeting of the whole jury in order to address what exactly we as a group wanted in the memorial. Rather than waiting for our aesthetic and conceptual notions of the memorial to emerge piecemeal as we argued over particular proposals, we wanted to open the question of the memorial up from the outset and to establish a working candidness that we hoped would carry us through to the end.

We began by asking questions that none of us could definitively answer. How will the memorial remember the loss of human life, the murderous intent of the killers, and the destruction of lower Manhattan? Will it remember the 9/11 attacks as part of a larger attack on the United States, one that prompted what could be a thirty-year war on terrorism? Will it remember the lives of the victims or only mourn their deaths? Will it glorify the sacrifice of the firefighters and police officers who came to help the victims? Or will it remember them too only as victims who were just doing their jobs? What is to be remembered here and how? To what political, civic, and aesthetic ends?

By granting the memorial its own process, we believed, the LMDC allowed such questions to animate and sustain memory. Neither, I suggested, should we fret about the appearance of memorial disunity. (All memorial processes are exercises in disunity, even as they strive to unify memory.) For just as memory is a negotiation between past and present, the WTC site memorial is an ongoing negotiation among all the groups of people whose lives were affected by this event and those whose lives will be shaped by what is built at Ground Zero. How will the memorial needs of competing constituencies, all with profoundly legitimate concerns, be balanced against each other? If, as part of a well-defined process, the debates are conducted openly and publicly, we hope they will be as edifying as we know they will be painful. The firefighters and their families, the police officers and their families, the office workers, neighborhood residents, city officials, developers, architects, artists, tourists— all may want something a little different in this site. There must be room in both the process and the actual commemorative site for the memory of all these people and their families.

By August 2003, it was clear to all the jurors that memory at Ground Zero would not be a zero-sum project; instead, it would be an accumulation of all these disparate experiences, needs, and competing agendas. Just as we accommodate ourselves to the competing needs of others every day of our lives in this city, just as we live together but separately, come and go together but separately, we must build into both the process and this site the capacity to remember together, but separately. All of which, we believed, would be possible as long as the LMDC's memorial process continued to unfold in tandem with its rebuilding project. Thus, almost from the outset, the twin motifs of loss and renewal emerged as foundational to the WTC memorial.

As jurors, we were also acutely aware of the more implicit aesthetic requirements of the WTC memorial—its dual role as commemorative site and architectural centerpiece of lower Manhattan's redevelopment. Here we had to balance the needs of memory against the needs of art and architecture to find an equilibrium between art for the sake of memory and art for its own sake. In fact, some on the jury feared that the more spectacular the work of art or architecture, the more eye-absorbing and viscerally evocative it was, the less intrinsic its memorial logic seemed to be. Unlike many great and beautiful works of contemporary public architecture (think of Frank Gehry's Bilbao museum), this memorial could not be about itself or its form. In fact, in Santiago Calatrava's beautiful and soaring design for the new transit center, we have found just such self-possessed beauty, and we may find more in the new cultural centers being planned as well. But the memorial will have to take us back to events, into ourselves, to the memory of those lost, and the memory of the now missing towers.

By the beginning of September, we had spent two weeks together, often in twelve-hour days, in the company of 5,201 designs. The competition management team did an excellent job of organizing what could have been a logistical nightmare. The jury was broken into three groups of four each (five in one group), which walked through aisle upon aisle of boards mounted on easels, in groups of two hundred boards each. We took all the time we needed to see every single board in every group, discussing, free-associating, explaining, laughing, and crying with each other throughout the day. At the end of each day all of us had seen the same six hundred designs and recorded in our jury-books which of these designs we would bring forward to the next stage. On any given day we were allowed to go back and see the proposals from previous days to compare and continue discussions among ourselves. The competition management team took our votes at the end of every day and tabulated how many votes each proposal had for being advanced to the next round. At the beginning of each day we met to discuss how many votes each design would need to move forward and to cast "passion votes" to bring forward a particular work, even if only one of us wanted it.

All of this was done in total secrecy, on the thirtieth floor of a building overlooking Ground Zero and only a couple of blocks away from the LMDC offices. No one but a handful of LMDC employees, the competition management team, Anita Contini, John Hatfield, and the senior officers of the LMDC were allowed into the space. We were fed there, housed in nearby hotels, and dined together at night to unwind. It was an exhausting and exhilarating period when none of us could be sure we would actually find a design we could agree on. Someone at the *New York Post* calculated that if all the members of the jury were to see every single one of the designs, it would take at least two weeks at twelve hours a day. This was one thing the *Post* got right.

Having culled some 250 designs from the 5,201 by the first of September, we then met for six further days, all day and into the night, to bring this list down to twenty or so. We continued to walk the floors of boards together, individually, in small groups, and occasionally as a whole jury, explaining to each other what we saw, what we were missing, trying to read all the small print on every design to make sure that nothing slipped through the cracks. We debated whether our final twenty should be a mix of different thematic kinds of memorials: whether, for example, we should include an equal number of landscape, water, sculptural, conceptual, and structural designs in the final mix. We debated what to do with the dozens of off-site proposals that we might like to see realized around the city over time, even if they could not be installed at Ground Zero. We debated what kind of exhibition there should be at the end, how to show the entire list of submissions, how to break them up thematically, how to generate a list of distinguished but unrealizable proposals.

Finally, we debated at length whether we would make our final choice before the public had a chance to see our list of finalists, or whether we would allow the public to respond to an exhibition of the finalists before we chose a winner from them. Of all the controversies on the jury, this one was probably the most contentious. I had advised the LMDC early on to exhibit the finalists publicly in order to make the public response part of our own deliberations at the end. But many on the jury, especially some of the architects, felt adamantly that this would corrupt our process, that the pressure and lobbying brought to bear by critics, advocates, and public relations firms had almost destroyed the site-design selection process. They argued, justifiably, that as professionals in the field, they would be subjected to enormous lobbying pressure by friends and colleagues and would thereby lose the independence we had been granted so completely until now. I argued that there had to be a way for us to distinguish between lobbying pressure and being informed by all we heard and that, in the end, I wanted to hear what all those out in the world thought of the finalists because, for better or worse, I would surely learn and see something in these designs that I had missed before they went public. In the end, over the strenuous objections of several jurors, the LMDC stuck by its initial plan to exhibit the finalists before we had chosen a winner. Having announced at the outset that this would be part of the public process, the LMDC felt that the integrity of the process as it had already described it was now at stake.

After intense deliberations, but without a clear sense of a dominant design, we arrived at a list of eight finalists in mid-October. By this time, it had also become clear to us that we were going to be an interventionist jury; because we could not recommend any of the designs without significant modifications, we would make specific recommendations to all the teams, subjecting each to what amounted to the kind of "critique" architecture students receive during their training. The LMDC approached each of these teams, still unidentified to the jury, and provided them with our detailed critiques and funds for developing their boards into three-dimensional models and animating their designs with a short computer-generated walk-through. We then met with each of the teams over the course of two days the second week of November 2003, exploring their models with them and hearing their own conceptual descriptions of their designs. In fact, until the morning we met them, we did not know their names or where they were from. On November 19, 2003, we announced the list of eight finalists. Their designs, models, and animations were revealed to the public in an exhibition at the newly reconstructed Winter Garden of the World Financial Center. They were:

- "Reflecting Absence" by Michael Arad

- "Passages of Light: The Memorial Cloud" by Gisela Baurmann, Sawad Brooks, and Jonas Coersmeier

- "Lower Waters" by Bradley Campbell and Matthias Neumann

- "Garden of Lights" by Pierre David with Sean Corriel and Jessica Kmetovic

- "Suspending Memory" by Joseph Karadin with Hsin-Yi Wu

- "Votives in Suspension" by Norman Lee and Michael Lewis

- "Inversion of Light" by Toshio Sasaki

- "Dual Memory" by Brian Strawn and Karla Sierralta

That most of the finalists were young but professionally well regarded was a source of both comfort and unease; we were left wondering where the big names had been. After meeting with all eight finalist teams and making several further recommendations we felt would enhance all their designs, as well as bringing them closer to the elements required by the Memorial Mission Statement, we issued our own jury statement. This was intended both to provide a rationale for our choices and to make public for the first time the kinds of issues that we felt had driven the memorial process to this moment.

Specifically, after introducing the structure of the competition itself, we made clear that the eight finalists shared a number of design characteristics. "They strive neither to overwhelm the visitor nor their immediate surroundings," we wrote in our jury statement. "They aspire to soar—not by competing with the soaring skyline of New York but rather by creating spaces that strive to reconcile vertical and horizontal, green and concrete, contemplation and inspiration. They allow for the change of seasons, passage of years and evolution over time." We concluded our statement by trying to reassure the public that the designs continued to evolve in the give-and-take of discussions between the jury and the architects and that the final design would be very different from what was then on display at the World Financial Center.

As we issued this statement we were perfectly aware that we would also be shaping memorial policies that had not been worked out yet. Specifically, we wanted to emphasize that not only would the memorial necessarily evolve in discussions between the jury and the designers but that whatever required elements seemed to be missing would in the end be incorporated somehow. We also realized that we now faced a diplomatic challenge: throughout our deliberations we were excruciatingly aware of the changes that Daniel Libeskind's master plan was undergoing as it ran up against the realities of New York City planning and politics. Though designed initially as a placeholder for the cultural buildings, one feature of Libeskind's design in particular seemed to be incompatible with all of the eight memorial designs we chose: the cultural building cantilevered over the top of the north footprint. The jury was unanimous in its judgment that it would have to be removed if the footprints themselves were to remain accessible and unencumbered, as the Memorial Mission Statement required.

It also seemed crucial to us that this memorial be enlarged in the minds of the public to include not only the design we chose but also the thousands of unbuilt designs proposed for this and other sites around the city. With the exhibit of all 5,201 designs, in fact, we wanted to suggest that these too were part of the memorial being built, that we were recognizing the millions of human hours spent on these thousands of designs as part of the massive work of memory already accomplished by this open and democratic competition.

In seeking a design that was both a great memorial and a great work of art, we took pains to choose among the eight final designs forms and environments that would neither diminish the essential role that visitors will play in the memorial nor overwhelm or dominate visitors with inhuman scale or spectacle. We sought a strong yet hospitable design, one that would allow for human reflection and contemplation.

This said, it is also true that we learned an enormous amount about memory while working with all eight teams of finalists. In the weeks after the November 19 announcement of the eight finalists, the jury met several times in an attempt to come up with a winner. On the one hand, we wanted to take the time we needed to decide, but on the other hand, all of us were anxious about taking so much time that the public might begin to arrive at its own consensus favorite, making our job that much harder. As it turned out, this was an unfounded fear, in that despite a large (if not altogether enthusiastic) following of the finalists' designs, none garnered anything approaching public acclamation. We struggled desperately to whittle the number of finalists down to three by the end of the year, and finally did so only with great difficulty. Even here, it was not clear whether we would be able to rally around only one with anything approaching the fervor and excitement we were all looking for.

By the time we came together again in January 2004, we had requested detailed elaborations and relatively extensive changes from three designs only: "Garden of Lights" by Pierre David with Sean Corriel and Jessica Kmetovic; "Passages of Light: The Memorial Cloud" by Giesela Baurmann, Sawad Brooks, and Jonas Coersmeier; and "Reflecting Absence" by Michael Arad. In fact, we had asked all the teams in November to add various experts to their teams to shore up deficiencies in lighting, stonework, and landscape. All three teams had responded very cooperatively to our requests, with the most significant addition being the world-renowned landscape architect Peter Walker joining Michael Arad's design team.

As it turned out, the additions each of the three final teams had made to their teams and their incorporation of the jury's critiques over the last several months had by January elevated these designs well above the others. We were also aware that the designs we now contemplated were in all three cases much further evolved than what the public was still viewing at the Winter Garden. After meeting with each of the now-expanded final three teams in two-hour-long presentations at Gracie Mansion at the beginning of January, the jury gave itself a week's deadline.

Of the final three memorial conceptions, "The Garden of Lights" by the Pierre David team—really an orchard and two gigantic squares of wildflowers in the footprints—seemed the most audacious and the surest to remind people that something unimaginable had happened here. Its predominant motif was the counterpointing of a densely built urban space with nearly five acres of trees and flowers. Unlike redevelopment in most cities, which bury such events beneath layers of new civilization, this design had chosen to let nature mark the site with its own cycles of rebirth, blossoms, blooms, death, and dormancy. This would be a living and dying form to mark living and dying human beings. It would be a place to nurture and to be reminded that without our tending memory it too would die. But in its overly complex subterranean layers and the designers' inability to simplify the scheme of lights planted in the orchard, combined with their unwillingness to open the site year-round so that it would remain completely integrated and accessible to the surrounding neighborhood, we finally found this design untenable.

In contrast to the garden, the "Memorial Cloud" design by the Giesela Baurmann team presented itself as a fascinating and engaging piece of architecture. As design, it was by far the most spectacular, and in the end that may have compromised its function as a memorial. For as spectacle, it absorbed all our visual and visceral attention into its amazing surfaces. Man-made materials like glass or translucent plastic seem impervious to memory. They are hard, brittle, repellent, not resilient, show no trace of visitors, are not interactive. Our discussion on the penultimate day of deliberations was completely absorbed in this design's materiality, its surfaces, its buildability, but there was almost no mention of its capacity for memory. Aside from its abstract reference to the smoking cloud of debris immediately after the attacks, we could not find its memorial logic. The debate about the cloud among jurors was easily the most animated and, in the end, the most wrenching. It was the clear favorite of nearly half the jury, with the other half favoring Michael Arad and Peter Walk-er's "Reflecting Absence."

In the end, arguments came down not to which of the two designs was more beautiful and moving, but which of the two made the better memorial. In the words of Michael Arad and Peter Walker in their own descriptive state-ment:

> This memorial proposes a space that resonates with the feelings of loss and absence that were generated by the destruction of the World Trade Center and the taking of the lives of thousands of people. It is located in a field of trees that is interrupted by two large voids containing re-cessed pools. The pools and ramps that surround them mark the general location of the footprints of the twin towers. A cascade of water that describes the perimeter of each square feeds the pools with a continuous stream. They are large voids, open and visible reminders of absence.
>
> The surface of the memorial plaza is punctuated by the linear rhythms of rows of Sycamore trees, forming informal clusters, clearings and groves. This surface consists of a composition of stone pavers, plantings and low ground cover. Through its annual cycle of rebirth, the living park extends and deepens the experience of the memorial.
>
> Bordering each pool is a pair of ramps that lead down to the memorial spaces. Descending into the memorial, visitors are removed from the sights and sounds of the city and immersed in a cool darkness. As they proceed, the sound of water falling grows louder, and more daylight fil-ters in from below. At the bottom of their descent, they find themselves behind a thin curtain of water, staring out on an enormous pool. Sur-rounding this pool is a continuous ribbon of names. The great size of this space and the multitude of names that form this endless ribbon underscore the vast scope of the destruction. Standing there at the wa-ter's edge, looking at a pool of water that is flowing away into an abyss, a visitor to the site can sense that what is beyond this curtain of water and ribbon of names is inaccessible.

The statement goes on to describe how the upper and lower levels are linked, how the slurry wall will be revealed as part of the design, and where the unidentified remains of victims will be contained at bedrock. It concludes with:

> The memorial plaza is designed to be a mediating space; it belongs both to the city and to the memorial. Located at street level to allow for its integration into the fabric of the city, the plaza encourages the use of this space by New Yorkers on a daily basis. The memorial grounds will not be isolated from the rest of the city; they will be a living part of it.

After two days of heated debate, much wine and dinner consumed, and a dozen different votes, at nearly midnight on January 7 we finally reached the ten-to-three plurality for a winner that we had set for ourselves, choosing Michael Arad and Peter Walker's "Reflecting Absence." In its minimalist conception, the memorial logic of the voids, and the essential incorporation of Peter Walker's groves of trees, "Reflecting Absence" seemed to capture most succinctly the twin motifs of loss and renewal already articulated so powerfully in Daniel Libeskind's "Memory Foundations." It also brought the memorial site to grade, thus weaving it completely back into the urban fabric.

In our jury statement issued on January 13, 2004, we asked how any memorial could ever collect all the disparate memories of the mourners into one space. After briefly reiterating the memorial's mission and required elements, we suggested that of all the 5,201 designs received, we found that "Reflecting Absence" by Michael Arad, in concert with landscape architect Peter Walker, came closest to achieving the daunting—but absolutely necessary—demands of this memorial. "In its powerful, yet simple articulation of the footprints of the Twin Towers," we wrote,

"Reflecting Absence" has made the voids left by the destruction the primary symbols of our loss. By allowing absence to speak for itself, the designers have made the power of these empty footprints the memorial. At its core, this memorial is thus anchored deeply in the actual events it commemorates—connecting us to the towers, to their destruction, and to all the lives lost on that day.

In our descent to the level below the street, down into the outlines left by the lost towers, we find that absence is made palpable in the sight and sound of thin sheets of water falling into reflecting pools, each with a further void at its center. We view the sky, now sharply outlined by the perimeter of the voids, through this veil of falling water. At bedrock of the north tower's footprints, loved ones will be able to mourn privately, in a chamber with a vault containing unidentified remains of victims that will rest at the base of the void, directly beneath an opening to the sky above.

While the footprints remain empty, however, the surrounding plaza's design has evolved to include beautiful groves of trees, traditional affirmations of life and rebirth. These trees, like memory itself, demand the care and nurturing of those who visit and tend them. They remember life with living forms, and serve as living representations of the destruction and renewal of life in their own annual cycles. The result is a memorial that expresses both the incalculable loss of life and its consoling regeneration. Not only does this memorial creatively address its mandate to preserve the footprints, recognize individual victims, and provide access to bedrock, it also seamlessly reconnects this site to the fabric of its urban community.

At the end of our statement, we recommended that provisions be made to accommodate the annual showing of Myoda and LaVerdiere's "Tribute in Light," which was accepted by the LMDC, as well as our suggestion that all 5,201 designs be exhibited online until a space (or spaces) could be found to exhibit the boards themselves.

CODA

On January 14, 2004, the winning design and its architects were introduced to the public at Federal Hall by Governor Pataki, Mayor Bloomberg, and Vartan Gregorian, who read the jury statement (Collins and Dunlap 2004). The public, the media, and the critical responses to "Reflecting Absence" were generally warm and supportive, with most echoing the New York Times opinion that this would be "A Memorial Worth Preserving." Like any memorial, it had been a negotiated process, and like any memorial, it is still being negotiated, now between the architects, the master planners, and the LMDC. A foundation has since been established, bringing together an amalgam of family members, cultural elites, and major figures in the financial world to create a $500 million endowment for the memorial and its cultural institutions.

Of course, some critics questioned the efficacy of an open and blind competition for finding a great work of public memorial art. Like democracy itself, such competitions are notoriously inefficient, and as one of the jurors reminded us, they are about as reliable as democracy in picking the best candidate for president. To those who say that such an open process discouraged the best artists and architects from entering this competition by neutralizing their fame and notoriety on a level playing field, we would ask, where was the civic-mindedness of our generation's greatest artists and architects? Why don't we ask them why they declined the open invitation to take the time so many others took to contemplate how to memorialize the devastating attacks of 9/11? Ask them whether they declined that invitation because they had nothing to say or whether the investment in such memory-work without a guaranteed payoff in a commission was just not worth their while. And what of the jurors, all of them at the top of their fields, who gave hundreds and hundreds of hours to the process without compensation? Is the time of elite artists and architects any more valuable than that of Maya Lin, Michael Van Valkenburg, Enrique Norten, Martin Puryear, or Vartan Gregorian?

Would a process that invited only fifty of the world's greatest artists and architects and excluded the thousands of people and teams who collectively spent millions of human hours on their designs really have been preferable to an open, democratic competition? What was more important? A great piece of art for our time—a new ornament for the city of New York—or a process in which everyone could participate to find a memorial for these specific events? The LMDC courageously chose the latter priority.

While some commentators believed we should abandon the open process and start again with a list of elite artists and architects, others complained that none of the designs had enough horror in them. As we have learned from other memorials, however, particularly those to the Holocaust, to commemorate the horror of people's deaths, making how they died more important than how they lived, is to lose sight of life itself and what makes it so precious. It is to reduce the richness of lives as they were lived to the terrible moment of death. In this memorial, the jury believed that we would come to mourn the loss of life, not just the manner in which the victims of the attack had died. The meanings of how the victims died, and the horror of their deaths, will certainly be conveyed in the site's underground Memorial Center, illustrated by the relics of destruction recovered from the massive ruins. But to reduce the victims' lives to the terrible moment of their death is a travesty of memory, despite the vicarious thrill it may give to some commentators calling for a memorial to the horror alone. Instead of terror, we chose to recall the terrible absence left behind by the buildings' footprints, the hopeful renewal of life as found in the groves of trees, and the individual lives of the victims, many of whom died trying to save the lives of others.

In the end, none of us believed that any single memorial could ever adequately express the overwhelming sense of loss experienced by the city and by the victims' families that day. What single design could ever capture the richness of lives lost, the courage of rescuers, the terrible suffering that the victims, the survivors, and their families have had to endure? What garden, building, or monument could reflect the mental transformations that took place that day, the disintegration of trust and the release of demons in us and around us? What single space can recall the blow to our psychic girders?

Of course, people want a memorial response that is proportionate to the events being commemorated. But short of repeating the event, no memory is ever proportionate—nor should it be. Instead, we need to understand how this memorial integrates memory into our lives and does not allow it to exist outside of life, however prosaic a symbol that may seem to be. To the extent to which we can fold the events of 9/11 back into our lives and live with their memory, we have defeated the terrorists' attempt to stop our lives in their tracks. But to the extent that we leave this site as a festering wound in our cityscape or concentrate only on the destruction, we invite memory to disable life in this city, not to nourish it. If a memorial is disproportionately smaller than the event in our consciousness and thereby allows us to remember enough to go on with life, then it succeeds by letting us live day by day, generation by generation, with the memory of these events.

NOTES

1. Members of the LMDC Memorial Mission Statement drafting committee included Kathy Ashton, Lt. Frank Dwyer, Tom Eccles, Capt. Steve Geraghty, Meredith Kane, Michael Kuo, Julie Menin, Antonio Perez, Nikki Stern, and Liz Thompson.
2. The LMDC Memorial Program drafting committee included Diana Balmori, Frederic Bell, Paula Grant Berry, Max Bond, Albert Capsuoto, Christy Ferer, Monica Iken, the Rev. Alex Karloutsos, Richard Kennedy, Tom Roger, Jane Rosenthal, and Christopher Trucillo.
3. All competition guidelines, press releases, jury statements, and a virtual exhibition of all submitted designs may be found at the Lower Manhattan Development Corporation's website, www.renewnyc.com.

REFERENCES

Collins, Glenn, and David W. Dunlap. 2004. "The 9/11 Memorial: How Pluribus Became Unum." *New York Times*, January 19.

Ebony, David. 2001. "Towers of Light for New York City." *Art in America* (November): 35.

Princenthal, Nancy. 2004. "Absence Visible." *Art in America* (April): 39–45.

Tomkins, Calvin. 2002. "After the Towers: Nine Artists Imagine a Memorial." *The New Yorker* (July 15): 59–67.

PART III

The Larger Political Dynamics

CHAPTER 7

Outside the Circle: The Impact of Post-9/11 Responses on Immigrant Communities in New York City

Lorraine C. Minnite

THE NATIONAL search for greater security against the terrorist threat evidenced by the September 11 attacks has had a strong and negative effect on New York City's immigrant communities, particularly those whose faith is Islam. In contrast to the local reaction to the attacks, the nation experienced a rise in patriotism, nativism, and even xenophobia as the United States plunged into war. These sentiments provided support for the federal government's hunt for terrorists in Muslim immigrant neighborhoods across the country, particularly among the growing Muslim immigrant populations from Pakistan, Bangladesh, India, and elsewhere in metropolitan New York. Like the attacks themselves, the federal presence has torn at the social and political fabric of the city.

At the same time, members of those communities and their advocates have responded to increased surveillance and the other law enforcement measures directed against them by developing new doctrines regarding their rights and new political alliances to back them up. This political development seeks to reinterpret and expand the basis for civil liberties protection to the human rights enjoyed by all residents, whatever their legal status. Since many immigrants typically lack political rights because they are not citizens, they have no other choice but to claim civil rights as human rights. The dynamic interplay of increased federal pressure on vulnerable immigrant communities and the local mobilization to defend immigrant rights is the focus of this chapter.

The September 11 attacks and their aftermath were a setback for immigrant rights. The terrifying and distorting impact of the attacks prompted the Bush administration to turn to the nation's immigration laws as a tool for fighting terrorism. In so doing, it accelerated a trend that had begun with the Republican-controlled Congress of the Clinton years, which adopted several measures in 1996 denying benefits previously extended to immigrants, broadening the grounds under which immigrants could be deported, and streamlining that process. These changes were incorporated into anticrime, welfare reform, and antiterrorism legislation passed in response to the first World Trade Center and Oklahoma City bombings. At the time, their far-reaching consequences for immigrants were not publicized, and they were little understood by the public at-large. After the 9/11 attacks, the Bush administration combined the Clinton-era immigrant-related collection of disparate laws, administrative rules, and bureaucratic practices into a powerful new regulatory regime for immigrants. The Clinton administration had been slow to implement the new laws; 9/11 strengthened the Bush administration's political will to further transform immigration regulation by subordinating it to terrorism policy. As David Cole (2003) has pointed out, the incursions into civil liberties adopted in the name of national security are aimed mostly at immigrants. In New York, as elsewhere, the result was a sharp, deep, and severe impact on the Arab, Muslim, and South Asian immigrant communities profiled by the federal government's crackdown. The newcomer status of these Muslim groups, including their deficient connections with the city's political elites, makes them particularly vulnerable to the repressive dimension of the domestic antiterror effort. Gradually, however, immigrants and their advocates are developing new strategies to cope with the punitive new regulatory regime.

HYPERDIVERSITY AND THE RISE OF NEW IMMIGRANT POLITICS IN NEW YORK

Changing patterns of migration in the 1990s altered New York's already complex demography and contributed to the formation of new immigrant identities. The newest migration is "globalized" because it represents more diversified migratory streams from all regions of the globe. In particular, recent population flows from South Asia, the Middle East, and Africa, nontraditional sources of migration to New York, are fostering a more complex "hyperdiversity" of social differences based on national origin, language, culture, and religion. This hyperdiversity is superimposed on an older framework of diversity defined by "racial" distinctions between whites, blacks, Latinos, and Asians and in some ways undermines it. The older patterns still determine broad community and neighborhood differences, but communities and neighborhoods are less ethnically homogeneous and change more rapidly than before. Moreover, global migration is fraying the traditional social boundaries between groups and destabilizing political identities based on race and ethnicity. Where these distinctions were once sharp and stable, they are now blurred and fluid.

The 1990s was a decade of high immigration to New York City from a bewildering number of foreign countries. During this period more than 1.2 million new, legally admitted immigrants settled in New York (see table 7.1). By most estimates, another half-million undocumented immigrants resided in the city, driving a decade-long increase in the foreign-born population from about 2 million to nearly 3 million people by 2000 (New York City Department of Planning 2004). The census reports that 43 percent of the adults living in New York are foreign-born. This huge immigrant population contains both longtime residents and very recent newcomers. Two of every five immigrants in the city arrived in the United States after 1990, confirming New York's continuing attraction as a pole of migration to this country.

Most of this immigrant flow came from the same countries that sent people in the 1980s, reflecting the priority that U.S. immigration law gives to family relations and the history of prior flows to New York, or what demographers call "chain migration."[1] The size and composition of the city's different immigrant communities are products of the different migration trajectories that have characterized those communities over time. Since 1970, the heavy flow of migrants to New York has led to the formation of large immigrant enclaves of people from China, the Dominican Republic, and the West Indies. Table 7.2 shows that during the 1990s immigrants came from many of these same places, with the Dominican Republic, China, Jamaica, Guyana, and Haiti remaining the five largest sending countries, accounting for 58 percent of new arrivals from the top twenty sending countries. Mature migration from China and the Caribbean therefore is reinforcing and stabilizing neighborhood settlement patterns for these immigrant groups while also contributing to the creation of "daughter" communities outside the zones of first settlement.

For the city's changing political environment, the most significant development in the global flow of people and workers to New York is the new migration from South Asia—specifically, the countries of the Indian subcontinent, Bangladesh, India, and Pakistan.[2] For the first time these countries were among the top ten sending countries for migrants to New York City. As table 7.3 details, there are over 163,000 South Asian immigrants in New York, and South Asians are among the most rapidly growing groups. Since 1990, the Bangladeshi population has increased by 374 percent, the Pakistani population by 180 percent, and the Indian population by 65 percent—well above the 38 percent growth of the overall foreign-born population over the decade. As a consequence, new South Asian neighborhoods have emerged along the number 7 subway line in Jackson Heights, Elmhurst-Corona, Jamaica Estates, and Floral Park, as well as in Midwood, Brooklyn. These groups have found ethnic niche

TABLE 7.1 YEAR OF ENTRY FOR THE FOREIGN-BORN POPULATION OF NEW YORK CITY, 2000

| | Total | Total Foreign-born | Recently Arrived, 1990 to 2000 | | | 1980 to 1989 | 1970 to 1979 | 1965 to 1969 | Before 1965 |
			Total	1995 to March 2000	1990 to 1994				
New York City	8,008,278	2,871,032	1,224,524	616,769	607,755	831,758	417,348	157,856	239,546
Bronx	1,332,650	385,827	167,666	80,917	86,749	119,950	48,760	20,349	29,102
Brooklyn	2,465,326	931,769	411,103	197,205	213,898	270,382	135,656	46,485	68,133
Manhattan	1,537,195	452,440	190,381	106,356	84,025	112,302	72,170	28,662	48,925
Queens	2,229,379	1,028,339	429,294	219,492	209,802	310,722	148,138	57,213	82,972
Staten Island	443,728	72,657	26,080	12,799	13,281	18,402	12,624	5,147	10,404

Source: U.S. Dept. of Commerce (2002).

TABLE 7.2   Top Twenty Sending Countries of Legally Admitted Immigrants to the New York City PMSA, Fiscal Years 1992 to 2002

Rank	Sending Countries	Number of Immigrants	Rank	New Arrivals	Number of Immigrants	Rank	Adjustments	Number of Immigrants
1	Dominican Republic	179,596	1	Dominican Republic	156,922	1	Former Soviet Union	121,705
2	Former Soviet Union	140,016	2	China	71,043	2	China	31,261
3	China	102,304	3	Jamaica	51,000	3	Dominican Republic	22,674
4	Jamaica	68,070	4	Guyana	45,283	4	Jamaica	17,070
5	Guyana	54,488	5	Haiti	29,693	5	Trinidad and Tobago	14,992
6	India	39,382	6	Bangladesh	29,122	6	Philippines	14,099
7	Haiti	38,885	7	India	28,663	7	India	10,719
8	Ecuador	38,064	8	Ecuador	28,627	8	Korea	9,640
9	Poland	32,981	9	Poland	24,786	9	Ecuador	9,437
10	Bangladesh	32,828	10	Pakistan	23,106	10	Colombia	9,260
11	Trinidad and Tobago	32,173	11	Colombia	18,497	11	Guyana	9,205
12	Philippines	29,047	12	Former Soviet Union	18,311	12	Haiti	9,192
13	Pakistan	27,849	13	Trinidad and Tobago	17,181	13	Poland	8,195
14	Colombia	27,757	14	Philippines	14,943	14	Mexico	8,342
15	Korea	16,606	15	Ireland	13,875	15	Former Yugoslavia	6,820
16	Mexico	15,570	16	Peru	11,307	16	United Kingdom	5,360
17	Peru	15,509	17	Ghana	9,185	17	El Salvador	5,185
18	Ireland	14,897	18	El Salvador	8,246	18	Pakistan	4,743
19	El Salvador	13,431	19	Honduras	8,112	19	Israel	4,442
20	Ghana	12,519	20	Mexico	7,228	20	Peru	4,202
Total		931,972			615,130			326,543

Source: U.S. Immigration and Naturalization Service (1993, 1997, 1998, 2000a, 2000b, 2002a, 2002b); U.S. Department of Homeland Security (2004a, 2004b); author's calculations.

Note: The INS legal immigrant standard public use files measure the "flow" of legal immigrants in a single fiscal year. They contain records for newly arriving immigrants who, while living abroad, obtained visas for legal permanent residence from the U.S. Department of State and immigrants already living in the United States who have adjusted their status to legal permanent residency. These files record the intended place of residence of new legal immigrants. Beginning with the fiscal year 2000 file, the Department of Homeland Security stopped releasing the data by zip code, making this and subsequent files incompatible with previous files (available through the Inter-University Consortium for Political and Social Research [ICPSR] until 2000). Instead, at the lowest level the data are now aggregated by primary metropolitan statistical areas (PMSAs). The New York City PMSA includes the five counties of New York City and neighboring suburban Westchester, Putnam, and Rockland Counties. Immigrants from the top twenty sending countries represent 78 percent of all legally admitted immigrants for the fiscal years 1992 to 2002. The federal government no longer releases this data series to the public.

TABLE 7.3 PLACE OF BIRTH FOR THE FOREIGN-BORN POPULATION OF NEW YORK CITY, 1990 TO 2000

	1990	2000	Percentage Change
South Asia			
Bangladesh	8,748	41,428	373.6
India	42,674	70,598	65.4
Pakistan	14,450	40,496	180.3
Other South Asia	11,015	10,588	−3.9
Arab Middle East/North Africa	29,009	43,155	52.6
Caribbean			
Dominican Republic	226,560	375,420	65.7
Guyana	73,846	130,496	76.7
Haiti	70,987	97,847	37.8
Jamaica	116,100	176,906	52.4
Other Caribbean	192,548	226,704	17.8
Central and South America			
Mexico	34,856	126,115	261.8
Other Central America	88,420	112,734	27.5
Colombia	68,787	84,491	22.8
Ecuador	60,119	112,661	87.4
Other South America	65,041	84,016	29.2
Africa	28,750	71,361	148.2
China and Southeast Asia			
China and Hong Kong	145,361	241,929	66.4
Taiwan	19,842	22,458	13.2
Korea	57,555	74,731	29.8
Philippines	37,307	48,507	30.0
Other Southeast Asia	38,151	68,481	79.5
Europe			
Former Soviet Union	80,333	207,209	157.9
Other Europe	432,967	416,057	−3.9
Canada	15,974	19,588	22.6
Other	171,546	58,032	−66.2
Total	2,130,946	2,932,992	37.7

Source: U.S. Department of Commerce (1995, 2002); author's calculations.
Note: The "Arab Middle East/North Africa" category includes Algeria, Egypt, and Morocco in North Africa and Iraq, Jordan, Kuwait, Lebanon, Saudi Arabia, Syria, Yemen, and "other" in the Middle East. Israel is included in the "other" category at the bottom of the table. "Africa" excludes Algeria, Egypt, and Morocco. The countries included in the "former Soviet Union" category are Russia, Ukraine, Uzbekistan, Belarus, Moldova, Azerbaijan, Georgia, and Armenia. Guyana, which is in South America, is included in the "Caribbean" category because of Guyana's British colonial past and the identification of Guyanese immigrants with their Caribbean rather than South American Spanish-speaking co-ethnics.

employment in computer programming, newsstands, restaurants, and other small businesses, in health care, and especially in the taxi industry (Mohammed-Arif 2002; Das Gupta 2005). New York has also experienced a substantial rise in migration from Africa (by 148 percent), the Muslim countries of the Middle East (by 53 percent), Mexico (by 262 percent), and Latin America (by 40 percent). One of the most important consequences is the impact of this new hyperdiversity on the city's politics (Logan and Mollenkopf 2002).

A PORTRAIT OF THE IMMIGRANT ELECTORATE IN NEW YORK

It is generally not well recognized that immigrants make up a substantial segment of the voting electorate in New York City, perhaps as high as 30 percent. This lack of recognition may partly result from the fact that the diversity of national origins among New York's immigrants and a political culture shaped historically by successive waves of migration have deterred the newest immigrants from forming a collective political identity of their own. Although many immigrants have not naturalized, naturalized citizens who vote nevertheless reflect the immigrant population of the city as a whole in a number of ways. For example, they are less white and more Latino and Asian than native-born voters, but about equally black. Similarly, immigrant voters are linguistically diverse and much less likely than native-born voting-age citizens to speak English at home. They are largely from working-class families, while the native-born electorate is distinctly more upper-class. Just under three-quarters of foreign-born voters earn annual family incomes of less than $50,000 a year, while almost half the native-born voters live in families with incomes exceeding that figure. Native-born voters have higher education rates, while foreign-born voters are more likely to be married with children under the age of eighteen living at home (see table 7.4).

Table 7.5 compares the voting profiles for native- and foreign-born electorates in the 2000, 2002, and 2004 state and federal elections. Noteworthy is the weaker connection to partisanship among immigrants compared to native-born voters. In 2000 immigrant voters were more likely than the native-born to identify themselves as Democrats, but more likely than native-born voters to identify as Republicans in 2002 and 2004. They gave substantially more of their votes to Democratic presidential candidate Al Gore in 2000 than did native-born voters, but they also gave more of their votes to Republican gubernatorial candidate George Pataki in 2002 and Republican presidential candidate George W. Bush in 2004 than did native-born voters in those elections.

Immigrant voters are also more likely to be new voters and less likely to be embedded in the traditional networks of party organizations and other groups

(Text continues on p. 176.)

TABLE 7.4 DEMOGRAPHIC PROFILE OF THE NEW YORK CITY ELECTORATE, 2000, 2002, AND 2004, STATE AND FEDERAL ELECTIONS

	2000 Presidential			2002 State and Federal			2004 Presidential		
	Total	Native-born	Foreign-born	Total	Native-born	Foreign-born	Total	Native-born	Foreign-born
Race									
White	39.1%	49.4%	22.4%	38.2%	48.3%	22.2%	34.6%	43.4%	20.4%
Black	28.0	28.6	27.0	25.1	25.2	24.6	27.1	29.5	22.9
Latino	20.3	16.5	26.5	24.6	20.9	30.6	25.0	19.9	33.4
Asian	7.2	1.9	15.8	8.7	2.5	18.5	8.5	2.8	17.3
Other	5.4	3.7	8.3	3.5	3.1	4.2	4.9	4.3	5.7
Education									
Less than high school	6.9	4.1	11.5	8.1	4.6	13.3	7.0	4.3	11.2
High school graduate	17.4	15.3	20.8	17.8	15.9	20.4	18.8	17.7	20.5
Some college	21.5	22.8	19.5	21.4	23.0	20.3	22.6	22.8	22.6
College graduate	33.6	32.1	35.9	30.1	27.5	34.0	33.3	32.1	35.0
Postgraduate	20.6	25.6	12.4	22.1	29.1	12.0	18.4	23.1	10.6

Annual family income									
Less than $15,000	14.7	10.5	21.8	14.9	9.1	23.9	15.4	9.9	24.7
$15,000 to $29,999	18.2	16.3	21.5	17.1	14.5	21.1	19.0	18.0	20.9
$30,000 to $49,999	24.2	25.7	21.6	26.6	27.5	25.1	24.9	24.6	25.4
$50,000 to $74,999	22.3	23.3	20.5	18.8	20.8	15.7	20.4	22.8	16.3
$75,000 to $99,999	10.3	11.4	8.6	10.8	13.0	7.4	8.9	10.5	6.0
$100,000 or more	10.3	12.8	6.1	12.0	15.2	6.9	11.5	14.3	6.8
Family composition									
Married	46.5	37.7	60.8	49.3	40.4	61.7	42.6	35.7	54.2
Child under eighteen	37.1	33.1	43.9	33.0	26.6	43.2	30.3	26.1	37.8
Gender									
Male	44.7	44.6	44.8	46.2	45.9	46.7	43.5	45.5	40.3
Female	55.3	55.4	55.2	53.8	54.1	53.3	56.5	54.5	59.7
Age									
Eighteen to twenty-four	9.4	12.0	5.0	7.1	9.8	3.1	15.0	18.4	9.2
Twenty-five to thirty-nine	37.3	42.0	29.2	31.0	33.9	26.3	37.1	42.4	28.2
Forty to forty-nine	20.4	19.0	22.8	21.6	20.4	23.7	18.2	15.9	22.2
Fifty to sixty-five	24.3	19.8	32.1	25.8	23.1	30.1	19.8	16.9	24.7
Over sixty-five	8.6	7.2	10.9	13.4	12.8	16.9	9.8	6.4	15.7

Source: New Americans Exit Polls (2001, 2003, 2005).

TABLE 7.5 VOTING PROFILE OF THE NEW YORK CITY ELECTORATE, 2000, 2002, AND 2004, STATE AND FEDERAL ELECTIONS

	2000 Presidential			2002 State and Federal			2004 Presidential		
	Total	Native-born	Foreign-born	Total	Native-born	Foreign-born	Total	Native-born	Foreign-born
Voter registration									
Democrat	77.1%	75.3%	80.0%	73.0%	74.4%	69.6%	74.1%	74.3%	73.5%
Republican	8.4	8.4	8.4	12.6	11.2	14.7	10.5	9.5	12.1
Other party	4.1	5.5	1.9	3.1	4.4	2.0	3.0	3.6	1.9
No party	10.4	10.8	9.7	11.3	10.0	13.6	12.5	12.6	12.5
First-time voter	19.6	10.8	34.4	8.1	4.2	14.6	21.8	17.2	29.8
Vote for president									
Al Gore/John Kerry	82.1	78.0	88.8	n.a.	n.a.	n.a.	81.7	82.8	79.9
George W. Bush	11.1	12.4	9.0	n.a.	n.a.	n.a.	16.3	15.0	18.3
Other	6.5	9.3	2.2	n.a.	n.a.	n.a.	1.7	1.9	1.3
Vote for governor									
George Pataki	n.a.	n.a.	n.a.	37.9	31.8	46.7	n.a.	n.a.	n.a.
Carl McCall	n.a.	n.a.	n.a.	51.0	55.1	44.9	n.a.	n.a.	n.a.

Stanley Aronowitz	n.a.	n.a.	n.a.	2.5	3.6	.9	n.a.	n.a.	n.a.
Thomas Golisano	n.a.	n.a.	n.a.	5.5	6.4	4.3	n.a.	n.a.	n.a.
Someone else	n.a.	n.a.	n.a.	1.6	2.0	1.1	n.a.	n.a.	n.a.
Vote for U.S. House									
Democrat	84.8	82.7	88.2	73.8	74.8	72.2	81.8	83.2	79.1
Republican	10.0	10.4	9.2	17.8	16.5	20.1	12.6	10.8	15.6
Someone else	2.5	3.2	1.5	4.5	4.6	4.3	2.0	1.8	2.3
Problems at the polls									
Required to show ID	n.a.	n.a.	n.a.	24.9	18.8	34.6	2.0	1.3	3.2
Name not in book	n.a.	n.a.	n.a.	7.3	3.5	13.2	8.4	5.4	13.7
Machine broken	n.a.	n.a.	n.a.	1.2	1.0	1.7	1.6	2.2	.6
Needed language help	n.a.	n.a.	n.a.	.6	.4	1.0	.5	.3	.9
Other problem	n.a.	n.a.	n.a.	5.0	6.5	2.7	3.8	4.4	2.7
Support Bush on Iraq	n.a.	n.a.	n.a.	29.2	26.1	34.7	13.6	12.3	15.6

Source: New Americans Exit Polls (2001, 2003, 2005).
Note: See appendix for question wordings. n.a. = no data available.

that mobilize the vote (see table 7.6). Fluid partisanship, weaker connections to mobilizing networks, and linguistic isolation all contribute to the fragile integration of immigrants into the city's politics, despite their size and routine participation in elections. Immigrants do not yet represent a cohesive force in the city's politics, a disadvantage that left their more vulnerable community members exposed when the federal government cracked down on immigration status violators following the 9/11 attacks.

THE NATIONAL DOMESTIC POLICY RESPONSE TO 9/11

The terrorists who on September 11, 2001, commandeered four American commercial aircraft and flew them into the World Trade Center, the Pentagon, and a field in southwestern Pennsylvania had been living quietly in the United States on legal non-immigrant visas for months before the attacks (National Commission on Terrorist Attacks Upon the United States 2004b).[3] After September 11, the federal government swiftly expanded its police powers to hunt for clues about what had happened. Through executive orders and decrees, administrative rule changes, and legislation, the Bush administration aimed a sweeping new set of policies at enabling federal, state, and local law enforcement agencies to investigate, detain, surveille, and prosecute people they believed had any links to terrorism (Acer et al. 2003; American Civil Liberties Union 2002a, 2002b, 2004a, 2004b; American Immigration Lawyers Association 2003a; Baker 2003; Brown 2003; Cole 2003; Doherty et al. 2002, 2003; Human Rights Watch 2002; Leone and Anrig 2003; Stanley and Steinhardt 2003). Because the terrorists were foreigners, immigrants were easy targets of government surveillance and have suffered more in the ensuing civil liberties crackdown. In the three years after the 9/11 attacks, the administration's dragnet for terrorists swept up thousands of immigrants, none of whom had anything to do with the 9/11 attacks. Underlying these policies is an unstated assumption that the nation's immigration laws were responsible for terrorism directed against the United States—an unfortunate conclusion because it would ultimately be proven wrong (National Commission on Terrorist Attacks Upon the United States 2004a; Stock and Johnson 2003; U.S. Congress 2002).[4] The administration's policies have had a disproportionate impact on Muslim Arab and South Asian immigrants, notwithstanding the public pledge to protect the civil liberties of Muslims residing in the United States (Murray 2004).[5] Despite the best efforts of many diligent government employees, the Department of Justice's domestic antiterrorism effort targeting these groups has failed to result in a single significant conviction for crimes related to 9/11 or terrorism (Cole 2003, 2004; Janofsky 2004).

The administration expanded its domestic antiterrorism policy in three

TABLE 7.6 MOBILIZATION PROFILE OF THE NEW YORK CITY ELECTORATE, 2000, 2002, AND 2004, STATE AND FEDERAL ELECTIONS

	2000 Presidential			2002 State and Federal			2004 Presidential		
	Total	Native-born	Foreign-born	Total	Native-born	Foreign-born	Total	Native-born	Foreign-born
Finances compared to four years ago									
Better today	57.8%	56.5%	59.9%	25.2%	26.8%	22.9%	20.0%	21.1%	18.1%
Worse today	6.4	7.2	5.2	28.1	27.6	28.7	38.4	36.9	41.1
About the same	35.8	36.3	34.9	46.6	45.6	48.3	41.6	42.0	40.8
Labor union household	40.3	39.8	41.1	44.2	46.1	41.0	37.6	41.0	32.7
Internet access	73.1	80.1	61.8	72.6	79.7	62.2	n.a.	n.a.	n.a.
Contacted to vote in last month	49.0	52.1	43.9	41.8	48.5	31.8	37.7	40.7	33.3
Attended meeting on voting in last year	16.0	15.7	16.3	13.2	13.8	12.0	13.4	14.4	11.9
Membership									
Political club	n.a.	n.a.	n.a.	6.3	6.4	5.9	4.8	6.7	1.7
Neighborhood group	n.a.	n.a.	n.a.	13.0	15.5	8.8	10.3	12.4	7.2
Tenants association	n.a.	n.a.	n.a.	6.2	7.8	3.8	4.6	5.9	2.5
Parent-Teacher Association	n.a.	n.a.	n.a.	8.6	10.2	6.1	7.3	8.0	6.2
Church, synagogue, mosque, or temple	n.a.	n.a.	n.a.	36.5	39.8	31.2	26.5	27.1	25.9

Source: New Americans Exit Polls (2001, 2003, 2005).
Note: See appendix for question wordings. n.a. = no data available.

loosely overlapping phases distinguished by the addition of new approaches to fighting terrorism on U.S. soil. According to one prominent New York Muslim attorney and civil rights activist, "First they [the federal government] went after the illegals, then the people who were here temporarily, and now they are going after [foreign-born] citizens" (Mohammedi 2004). The first phase involved mass arrests and detentions of people without charge, surveillance of private communications without legal basis, widespread ethnic and racial profiling, and the use of secret judicial proceedings over previously public immigration matters (Chang 2002). Federal law enforcement agencies and the Immigration and Naturalization Service focused many of these activities on New York City.

The second phase began in the summer of 2002 with the introduction of the National Security Exit-Entry Registration System (NSEERS), also known as the Special Registration Program. NSEERS, which would be phased in over the coming months, required that immigrant men between the ages of sixteen and sixty-four entering the United States on non-immigrant visas from any one of twenty-five foreign countries—all but one (North Korea) predominantly Muslim or Arab—to register with the federal government (Ashcroft 2002c; U.S. Department of Justice 2002). With NSEERS fully implemented by early 2003, the FBI/INS raids began to abate, but the deportations continued and increased (Sada-e-Pakistan 2003). The third phase institutionalized changes in homeland security policy by implementing new tracking systems for all foreigners entering the country, transforming civil immigration law into criminal enforcement, and breaking up and transferring most INS functions to the new Department of Homeland Security (DHS).

The September 11 Detainees

Within days of the attacks, the Attorney General reported that he had directed federal law enforcement officials to use "every legal means at our disposal to prevent further terrorist activity by taking people into custody who have violated the law and who may pose a threat to America" (Ashcroft 2001a; Shenon and Toner 2001). The FBI launched a massive investigation into the attacks known as the Pentagon-World Trade Towers Bombing investigation, or PENTTBOM.[6] A linchpin of PENTTBOM was the use of the nation's civil and administrative immigration laws to detain thousands of people suspected of having ties to terrorism, despite the weak evidence for conducting such sweeps and the failure of mass arrests to produce any actual terrorists. Those held in detention facilities became known as the September 11 detainees, and although the federal government has refused to release information about them, the majority most likely were arrested in New York City.[7]

The U.S. Department of Justice Voluntary Interview Project

Shortly after 9/11, the attorney general authorized the creation of joint terrorism task forces (JTTFs) comprising federal, state, and local law enforcement officials, under the direction of U.S. attorneys, and charged them with carrying out Justice's antiterrorism plans.[8] A November 9, 2001, memorandum to U.S. attorneys from the attorney general directed them to begin a "voluntary" interview project that in the end, after two rounds of interviews, resulted in the interrogation of at least 3,200 people the government believed were likely to be knowledgeable about or involved in terrorism (U.S. Government Accounting Office 2003). JTTF members were responsible for conducting the interviews and participating in follow-up investigations when necessary. The GAO studied the initiative and concluded that it was hastily created, haphazardly conducted, and ultimately produced inconclusive results.

The National Security Entry-Exit Registration Program

One of the "illegals" about whom Omar Mohammedi, the Muslim civil rights lawyer, spoke "Ismael," is a Pakistani immigrant who has resided in the United States for many years and has six American-born children. When the government announced the NSEERS program requiring men on non-immigrant visas to register their presence with the INS, Ismael did so, fearing that he would be deported if he was caught failing to comply. One cold winter day in November 2003, Ismael explained his experience with the Special Registration Program to a group of people protesting at the federal office building in downtown Manhattan. Pointing at the tenth floor of the Javits Federal Building at 26 Federal Plaza, where INS investigations officers interrogated registrants, he said he had not known how horrendous the conditions would be there. He was detained for over twenty-four hours and deprived of food and water. He saw people around him who were shackled and handcuffed. He was terrified. The authorities questioned him about whether he had relations with terrorist organizations, how many times he went to prayer, and so many other stupid questions, he said, that he realized that he had walked into a trap. His command of English was not strong. The INS agents made him sign papers he did not understand, and they did not tell him that he could have legal assistance; nor did the officials provide a translation so that Ismael could understand what was going on. "I did not know my crime or what I did," Ismael said through an interpreter as he started to weep. He signed the papers because he wanted so badly to leave; he was afraid and weak and felt as if he might have a heart attack. But the papers he signed will help the government deport him; indeed, he may already be gone.

Stories like Ismael's are very common. New York's large ethnic and community press contains countless stories of immigrants whose lives have been destroyed and families shattered by federal law enforcement strategies. Arab and South Asian community newspapers such as *Weekly Thikana*, *Akhon Samoy*, *Aramica*, *Sada-e-Pakistan*, *Bangla Patrika*, the *Pakistan Post*, and *Weekly Bangalee*, as well as newspapers in other immigrant communities, have reported on many individual cases of immigrants caught up in the dragnet for terrorists. The American Immigration Lawyers Association (AILA) has also documented reports of the conditions inside the New York INS office, corroborating stories like Ismael's. According to the AILA, the New York office permitted lawyers to be present at special registration interviews but mostly kept them out of a second round of interviews held with people deemed to be out-of-status. Attorneys reported that they routinely observed registrants handcuffed and shackled to the floor as they sat in their seats. The initial interviews took place inside one big room with bank teller–style booths and INS clerks sitting behind Plexiglas. While the men waited for their names to be called, they were all photographed and fingerprinted. Most were questioned without counsel or interpreters present (American Immigration Lawyers Association 2003b).[9]

Just two weeks after the protest in front of the federal building, and after only one year of operation, the federal government suspended the NSEERS program. What was gained by implementing it? Not one of the over 83,000 men who came forward to register with the government turned out to be a terrorist or to have connections to terrorism or terrorist organizations.[10] Nearly 14,000 of them, immigrants like Ismael, men with jobs and families and American-born children or American-born wives, were identified as undocumented or in violation of their visas and now face deportation (Swarns 2003).[11] Many of those visa violators did not realize that they were out-of-status.

An example is provided by an immigrant community organizer in Queens who reports that he has seen the Special Registration Program destroy "thousands and thousands of families." He describes a Bangladeshi man he calls Mr. H. who came to the United States legally in 1997 to seek medical treatment for his four-year-old daughter. Employed as a baker, Mr. H. applied for an employer-sponsored labor certificate in April 2001 to adjust his status to legal permanent residency. Nearly three years later, the federal government was still processing Mr. H.'s application.[12] Meanwhile, in the fall of 2003, Mr. H. complied with the Special Registration Program and presented himself to federal authorities. Because his labor certification was still pending, he was technically out-of-status, and the government began deportation proceedings against him. He was ill advised by an immigration attorney to take voluntary departure. The attorney never told him about the appeals process open to him, nor did Mr. H. fully understand what was happening to him because he does not speak English well. He was scheduled to leave the country in February 2004 for

Bangladesh with his wife and now eleven-year-old daughter. The community organizer reports that Mr. H.'s daughter, who was born in South Africa, has never been to Bangladesh, does not speak Bangla, and was depressed and crying constantly at the thought of leaving behind the only country she has known and her friends and schoolmates (Banerjee 2004). If forced to leave the United States, many of those complying with the Special Registration Program will leave behind devastated wives, children, and other relatives. Deprived of their principal breadwinner, their economically marginal families will face untold hardship.[13]

Immigrant rights and civil rights organizations and leaders of religious and ethnic organizations fiercely criticized the Special Registration Program from its inception. Over two hundred organizations signed on to a letter to the U.S. attorney general that shared the sentiment of the New York Immigration's Coalition executive director, who called the program "a monumental failure," adding: "The Special Registration program has devastated the lives of tens of thousands of innocent immigrants and their families, squandered untold millions in immigration and law enforcement resources, made a mockery of our democratic values, and brought immigration processing to a virtual standstill for all other immigrants. How much more wrong can one program be?" (New York Immigration Coalition 2003). In December 2003, DHS suspended the program. Critics of the Special Registration Program have blamed it for contributing to immigrant benefit backlogs because it diverted scarce staff and resources to the fingerprinting, photographing, and interrogating of tens of thousands of Arabs and Muslims (Bernstein 2004b).[14] DHS estimates that ending the Special Registration Program will allow it to reallocate to the provision of more homeland security 62,000 work-hours—or a year's worth of time for a thirty-person staff.

IMMIGRANT RESPONSES TO FEDERAL COUNTERTERRORISM POLICIES

How have immigrants and their advocates responded to these new federal counterterrorism efforts? South Asian, Muslim, and Arab immigrants have adopted a variety of strategies that draw on different individual and collective capacities to cope with the harsh treatment of their communities at the hands of government authorities. Individual strategies were a response to terrifying fear, confusion, and isolation; in the first months after the attacks, many Muslim immigrants saw only two options: flee New York or remain and cope in silence. Individual strategies, however, never produce more than individual solutions. Collective action, on the other hand, has prompted the search for a collective political identity among Muslims and immigrants; it is taking the form of new organizing and coalition-building efforts between immigrant advocates and more traditional civil liberties organizations in the city. Sustained and strengthened, these efforts could reshape New York's political landscape.

It is difficult to ascertain the number of immigrants who fled New York City in the immediate aftermath of 9/11. The Pakistani embassy has claimed that between ten thousand and fifteen thousand Pakistani nationals left, a number that conforms with advocates' estimates (Powell 2003; Solomon 2003; Khan 2004a). South Asian community leaders interviewed for this study agree that the U.S. government has a right to patrol its borders and safeguard its people, but they are confounded about why their communities are being profiled for harassment and abusive treatment, especially given the cooperation of the Pakistan government with the war on terrorism (Alam 2004; Banerjee 2004; Bhuyan 2004; Khan 2004a). These community leaders note that none of the hijackers were Pakistani, that Pakistani immigrants died in the World Trade Center attacks, that only a handful of the hundreds of Pakistanis deported since 9/11 have had criminal records, and that none of them have been linked to terrorism (see also Powell 2003). Nonetheless, one of the architects of the Special Registration initiative, Kris Kobach, a Department of Justice counsel to the U.S. attorney general, defended the profiling of South Asian immigrants when he told reporters at a January 17, 2003 press conference: "The United States recognizes that Pakistan has been a great ally in the war against terrorism ... [but] the unfortunate reality [is] that some of our greatest allies ... their citizens are involved in this" (Sarkar 2003a).

Immigrant activists describe what is happening to their communities as a kind of state-sponsored terrorism. Activists consistently told me that their communities were terrified of the federal government. They described many cases of immigrants who were victims of police raids on their homes and businesses. In the weeks and months immediately following the attacks, FBI agents, sometimes accompanied by INS agents and local law enforcement officers, engaged in blatant profiling to conduct mass street arrests of people they suspected of having links to terrorism. They based their suspicions on the fact that those arrested were living in immigrant neighborhoods and appeared to be Arab, South Asian, or Muslim. When the authorities discovered that arrestees also were in violation of immigration laws, they frequently detained them for months before notifying their families about their whereabouts. (Although being "out-of-status" or undocumented is a violation of *civil* immigration law, it is not a crime.) Before 9/11, getting caught by the INS for being undocumented usually resulted in administrative deportation proceedings. Indeed, over the past forty years the United States has expelled more immigrants than it has legally admitted (see figure 7.1). Most of those expelled had entered illegally, used fraudulent documentation to obtain visas, or violated the terms of their visas. Most were given the opportunity to leave the United States on their own (known as "voluntary departure"), with no penalties on legal reentry.

FIGURE 7.1   LEGAL MIGRATION FLOWS IN AND OUT OF THE UNITED STATES:
TOTAL ALIENS ADMITTED AND EXPELLED, 1965 TO 2002

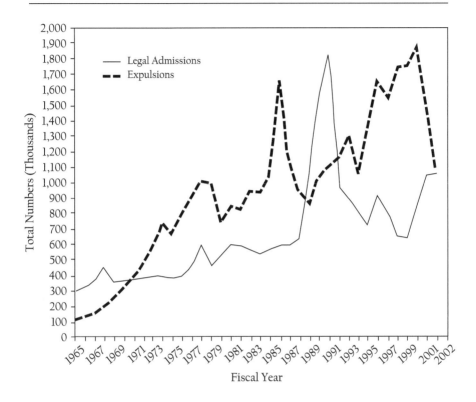

Source: U.S. Department of Homeland Security, Office of Immigration Statistics, *Yearbook of Immigration Statistics, 2002*, Tables 1 and 43.
Note: The sharp increase in legal admissions at the end of the 1980s is anomalous: it reflects the onetime legalization features of the 1986 Immigration Reform and Control Act, which legalized certain agricultural workers and undocumented aliens who had been continuously present unlawfully in the Untied States since 1982.

An *alien* is any person not a citizen or a national of the United States. *Legal admissions* refers to aliens admitted as legal permanent residents (LPRs). LPRs are legally accorded the privilege of residing permanently in the United States. They may be issued immigrant visas by the Department of State overseas or adjusted to permanent resident status by the Bureau of Citizenship and Immigration Services (BCIS), formerly the Immigration and Naturalization Service. Adjustments are allowed for aliens who are already in the United States on non-immigrant visas (tourist, temporary worker, and student visas) or were admitted as refugees or parolees. *Parolees* are aliens who appear to be inadmissible to the inspecting officer but are allowed into the United States for urgent

(*Figure continues on p. 184*)

After 9/11, undocumented and out-of-status immigrants swept up in the antiterrorist dragnet were treated like hardened criminals, kept without charge in detention centers and local jails with murderers, rapists, and thieves, denied proper legal counsel, and denied bond (U.S. Department of Justice 2003; American Civil Liberties Union 2004a). Many of those arrested in the New York area were shipped to a federal detention center in Oakdale, Louisiana, where the cost of housing them is lower (Bahree and Feldman 2003; Etheridge 2004). Their families were often not notified of this transfer, which sometimes took place in the middle of the night. Other detainees, some with standing deportation orders, were summarily put on charter flights back to Pakistan.[15] Still

---

Figure 7.1 (*Continued*)

humanitarian reasons or when his or her entry is determined to be of significant public benefit. Parolees are not considered formally admitted to the United States, and they are given temporary status only; they are required to leave when the conditions supporting their parole cease to exist. Examples include parents in search of urgent medical care for a child, aliens who enter to take part in legal proceedings, and people who arrive at a port of entry with papers but for whom questions about their admissibility still remain. Non-immigrant aliens may change their status to legal permanent resident if they are eligible to receive an immigrant visa and one is immediately available. Under certain circumstances, undocumented immigrants, otherwise known as aliens entering without inspection (EWIs), may also adjust their status to LPR.

Expulsions take two basic forms, voluntary departure and formal removal. *Voluntary departure* is the departure of an alien from the United States without an order of removal. It may or may not have been preceded by a hearing before an immigration judge. An alien allowed to voluntarily depart concedes removability but is not barred from seeking admission at a port of entry at any time. Failure to leave within the time granted results in a fine and a ten-year bar to several forms of relief from deportation. *Formal removal* is otherwise known as deportation. Aliens who are found to have violated the immigration laws may be formally removed. Deportation is ordered by an immigration judge without any punishment being imposed or contemplated. Before 1997 and the passage of the Illegal Immigration Reform and Immigrant Responsibility Act (IIRIRA), there was a distinction in the law between deportation and exclusion, or inadmissibility at the point of entry. The decision to exclude an alien was made by an immigration judge after an exclusion hearing. IIRIRA consolidated these procedures to allow for "expedited removal" authorizing the INS to quickly remove certain inadmissible aliens from the United States. The authority covers aliens who are inadmissible because they have no entry documents or because they have used counterfeit, altered, or otherwise fraudulent or improper documents. In the majority of cases, expedited removal removes the immigration judge from the process of reviewing the removal or deportation of undocumented aliens, except where the alien makes a claim to lawful permanent residence or can demonstrate a "credible fear" of persecution if returned to the home country. "Administrative reasons for (formal) removal" applies to aliens deemed in violation of the immigration laws who are apprehended at the border or in the interior. By far the largest operation is border patrol. Interior apprehensions occur through the BCIS, which investigates criminal cases, usually fraud investigations (most often the misrepresentation of one's status). Mexican nationals dominate formal removals, over 100,000 Mexicans were deported in 2002. The next largest national group were Guatemalans, at 4,790.

others who fled to Canada have been vigorously pursued by federal agents (*Bangla Patrika* 2003; Sachs 2003). In the first quarter of 2003 alone, more than 2,200 Pakistani U.S. residents sought refuge in Canada (Solomon 2003). Asylum and refugee policies there are more liberal than in the United States, but applications can take up to a year to process, and it has been routine to return refugees coming across the U.S. border until their cases can be heard. The Geneva Convention stipulates that refugees waiting for the resolution of their appeals who have been returned to countries from which they have fled must be accorded protection until their cases can be settled. Reports from the U.S.-Canadian border on the flood of Pakistani immigrants from the United States suggest that U.S. authorities have sometimes violated the protected status of immigrants seeking asylum in Canada by taking them into custody as they waited for their claims to be processed (Khan 2004a; New York Advisory Committee to the U.S. Commission on Civil Rights 2004).

When thousands of Pakistani nationals fled New York, they sometimes left behind not only their children and wives but businesses built up over a generation. No community suffered more than the working-class Pakistani community in Midwood, Brooklyn, known as "Little Pakistan" (Elliott 2003; Sarkar 2003b; Solomon 2003). INS raids, detentions, deportations, and harsh treatment by the Special Registration Program took their toll. Reports by local Muslim business owners of fall-offs in business in Midwood for the first year after 9/11 are estimated at between 40 and 60 percent (Powell 2003), though there are signs of recovery today. Pakistani-owned construction companies, auto shops, and garages are sometimes employers of undocumented Pakistanis. The closure of a ten-year-old Midwood construction company when the owner was deported, despite his pending sponsor application and an appeal for asylum, resulted in the loss of twenty-five well-paying jobs (Solomon 2003). "In Little Pakistan, on Coney Island Avenue in Brooklyn," wrote the *Pakistan Post* in early 2003, "the grocery stores, money changers, restaurants, insurance offices, clothing and jewelry stores look deserted. It's not just a lack of customers; many of the shop owners themselves have fled to Canada."

Across the city, Muslim immigrant families went into hiding, afraid of being picked up off the street by the authorities or targeted for abuse and anti-Muslim harassment. Parents kept their children out of school. Arab American and immigrant services organizations coordinated ad hoc safety patrols to walk children to school or women and the elderly to doctor's appointments (Samara 2004). Interviews with principals of Islamic day schools in Brooklyn and Queens confirmed anecdotal evidence of the disappearance of students from Islamic schools in the months after 9/11. At one K-12 school of about three hundred students, the principal related that one-third of the students vanished after 9/11, though about half of those students have since returned (Abuasi 2004; Ali 2004).

New Organizing and Coalition Building

The crisis of 9/11 exposed weaknesses in the communal institutions of immigrant communities. Immigrant services organizations were overwhelmed by the needs of their constituents, some of whom were immigrants who had suffered directly from the attacks and collapse of the World Trade Center, and others of whom had been targeted and caught up in the post-9/11 antiterror sweeps (Samara 2004; The New York Immigration Coalition 2002). Fragile families saw their fathers and sons deported for overstaying their visas. Breadwinners watched their low-wage jobs cleaning offices, making restaurant deliveries, driving trucks, and busing tables evaporate in a cloud of toxic dust. Undocumented workers were ineligible for most government aid, and the families of those killed in the catastrophe were invisible to the authorities because their loved ones were not officially there.

In response, Muslim and immigrant communities began to organize themselves in new ways and with political purpose. Across the United States, the confusion and fear spread by the ad hoc implementation of the Special Registration Program brought diverse immigrant groups—Asian, South Asian, Arab, and North African—together to develop shared resources, forging a sense of commonality among them. "We are now more convinced of the need to get together and put our differences aside," said one Muslim immigrant attorney. He gave as an example a meeting of many different national and local Muslim groups to plan a unified response to comments made by Representative Peter King (R-N.Y.) on the nationally syndicated Sean Hannity radio program. On the February 9, 2004, broadcast, King complained that "no [American] Muslims are cooperating" with law enforcement officials to combat terrorism. He added: "I would say, you could say that 80 to 85 percent of mosques in this country are controlled by Islamic fundamentalists [and that] this is an enemy living amongst us" (*American Muslim Perspective* 2004). The Muslim community, explained the attorney, is similar to the United States: it encompasses many differences and many different nationalities. "People were not prepared," he said, for the blow of 9/11 (Mohammedi 2004).

Referring to Muslim immigrants, the attorney continued: "They had worked very hard for years to build lives here, and then it was over. A lot of people were in shock; they saw everything they worked for go down like the buildings." Now, he said, his community is trying to figure out how to respond to what has happened to them and deal with lives that have changed beyond recognition. The communal response is beginning to take on an activist orientation. In this respect, "we are becoming more American," he said. Muslim groups used to work on political and civic engagement activities on their own. If they did voter registration, they did it on their own, with their own members and within their own communities. Now it is more common to see groups reaching out to one another before engaging in these kinds of activities so that they can plan them together. Muslims are trying to better understand the American political system and how to make it work for them. "And we are learning from the historical experiences of other groups who have faced discrimination and adversity" in the United States, said the attorney, referring mainly to African Americans and Jews (Mohammedi 2004).

Collective political strategies are being channeled through a combination of established and new organizations and through traditional non-electoral means, such as lawsuits, lobbying, advocacy, protest, and activist campaigns aimed at bringing new actors into the political process. At the local level, innovative forms of collective action are emerging. First, issues pertaining to immigrant rights have rapidly taken on higher priority among established civil liberties groups. In the immediate aftermath of 9/11, these groups worked more closely with immigrant advocates and organizers than they had before to respond to the crackdown on immigrants in New York. Organizations such as the American Civil Liberties Union (ACLU) and its local chapter organization, the New York Civil Liberties Union, and the Center for Constitutional Rights (CCR) are pursuing high-profile legal interventions to protect the rights of immigrants. In legal filings and publications, these organizations are striving to expand prevailing notions of immigrant rights by recasting them as human rights and to find a basis for traditional civil liberties claims in international law. For example, in October 2003, the ACLU convened what it claimed was the first national conference ever held on using international human rights law in the American justice system. "Our goal," said ACLU associate legal director and conference organizer Ann Beeson, "is nothing less than to forge a new era of social justice where the principles of the United Nations' Universal Declaration of Human Rights are recognized and enforced in the United States" (American Civil Liberties Union 2004a). On behalf of thirteen of the September 11 detainees, nearly all of them swept up and held in detention by federal authorities in New York, the ACLU filed its first-ever petition with the United Nations High Commissioner on Human Rights, claiming the detentions were arbitrary under international law. The petition sought recognition from the UN Working Group on Arbitrary Detentions that the United States could not abrogate the human rights of violators of U.S. civil immigration laws when those rights are guaranteed to them through international agreements like the International Covenant on Civil and Political Rights, to which the United States is a signatory.

The Center for Constitutional Rights, a New York–based civil rights legal organization, has long championed the human rights of noncitizens, pioneering the use of the formerly obscure Alien Tort Claims Act (ATCA) as an instrument for rights claims by noncitizens in U.S. courts.[16] In *Filártiga v. Peña-Irala* (630 F.2d 876 [2d Cir. 1980]), a lawsuit brought in 1979 by surviving family members of a Paraguayan youth tortured and murdered by Paraguayan police in retaliation for his father's dissident political views, CCR lawyers filed a claim under ATCA and won a landmark case recognizing the rights of foreign nationals to seek redress in U.S. courts for human rights violations anywhere in the world. In cases that have followed, ACTA has been used primarily by foreign nationals seeking justice in U.S. courts for human rights abuses suffered abroad. As counsel of record in *Turkmen v. Ashcroft* (E.D.N.Y. [02 CV 2307 (Gleeson, J.)]), CCR has brought a class action by several of the September 11 detainees in which ATCA violations again figure prominently. In this case, however, the human rights abuses of foreign nationals are alleged to have been committed on U.S. soil, in Brooklyn's Metropolitan Detention Center and the Passaic County Jail in Hudson County, New Jersey, following the 9/11 attacks.

Second, the post-9/11 crackdown on immigrants in New York stimulated self-organizing campaigns among immigrants that have resulted in the formation of new groups that are struggling to protect and expand immigrant rights. These new organizations are small, with only a handful of paid staff and tiny budgets, but they are making a place for themselves in New York's otherwise disorganized local politics. For example, about the time of the 9/11 attacks, the New York Civic Participation Project (NYCPP) was created as an experiment in social unionism. The NYCPP is an unusual collaboration of three union locals with large immigrant memberships; a Brooklyn-based, grassroots anti-poverty and social justice organization that works mainly with low-income African American and Latino neighborhood residents; and a thirty-year-old public policy organization that advocates for low-wage workers, the poor, and the unemployed. The unions donate office space for the NYCPP's small staff but do not direct the organization's work, which is focused on three or four neighborhoods in the Bronx, Brooklyn, and Queens where many immigrant union members live (Sadhwani 2004). NYCPP's neighborhood organizers work with other community-based organizations and community residents, many of whom are undocumented immigrants, on developing community campaigns to press for issues of concern to community members.

The signature campaign of the NYCPP is a defensive mobilization against New York State's post-9/11 initiative to revoke the licenses of drivers who fail to provide a valid Social Security number to the state's Department of Motor Vehicles (DMV). New York is one of only a handful of states that do not officially restrict driver's licenses to legal residents. In early 2004, the DMV ran its database of 11.2 million drivers against records from the federal Social Security Administration and found nearly 600,000 people whose Social Security numbers did not match. The first of several batches of warning letters informing drivers about problems with their Social Security numbers went out in March 2004 (Bernstein 2004a); at risk of having their licenses revoked unless they can provide a valid Social Security number are some 300,000 people, most of them likely to be immigrants. Immigrant advocacy organizations like NYCPP, the New York Immigration Coalition, and the National Employment Law Project argue that the policy is not required under New York law and will have a devastating impact on New York's economy, which depends on immigrant labor, as well as on immigrant families who depend on the bread-winner's ability to drive to work. These groups have organized rallies, brought a lawsuit (*Cubas v. Pataki*, no. 04112371 [N.Y. Sup. Ct.]), and urged the issue on the State Assembly, which held a hearing in August 2004 before the Standing Committee on Transportation to gather information about the DMV's process for verifying driver Social Security numbers and its impact on communities across the state (New York State Assembly 2004). The driver's license initiative and the immigrant-organized campaign against it exemplify how immigrant politics in New York have changed since 9/11. New York's laissez-faire approach to immigration has tightened up, and immigrants who were once unwilling to come out of the shadows are finding their voice.

Another example of new organizing is New Immigrant Community Empowerment (NICE), a small, Queens-based immigrant rights group best known for its earlier campaigns against anti-immigrant billboards that began appearing in Queens in the 1990s and its work on hate crimes in Jackson Heights and other heavily immigrant neighborhoods in the district of then longtime councilwoman Julia Harrison. In the late 1990s, with hate crimes against immigrants on the rise in Jackson Heights, NICE claimed that Harrison was openly hostile toward the needs of new immigrant groups and out of touch with the vast demographic changes under way among her constituents. NICE sees itself as a good government group as well as an immigrant rights group and stresses that government accountability is at the core of its mission. With only four full-time paid staff, NICE organized community meetings, collected information on bias crimes by holding hearings and eliciting testimony from alleged victims, and organized a small army of dedicated volunteers to push for more government accountability. The organization believes in lifting the bar against voting by noncitizens, many of whom, as longtime members of the local community, pay taxes and make other positive contributions to the community. To NICE, the bar on voting undermines accountability, especially when noncitizens make up a substantial portion of the community, as they do in Jackson Heights and Elmhurst-Corona (Sanjek 1998).

After 9/11, one NICE staff member devoted all his time to uncovering and publicizing hate crimes against South Asian, Arab, and Muslim New Yorkers and working with immigrant families caught up in the antiterror sweeps and detention nightmare experienced by so many immigrant residents of New York (Banerjee 2004). His work with victims of post-9/11 hate crimes and exposure to the ferocity of government profiling in the months after 9/11 was decisive. NICE became a principal advocate of noncitizen voting rights and joined a fledgling campaign to push the idea with its constituents, the city's immigrant advocacy community, and liberal political elites.[17] NICE expects to play an important role in the drafting of legislation, to be introduced in the New York City Council in the near future, permitting noncitizen voting in local elections.

CONCLUSION

Studies of immigrant political incorporation often neglect the critical role of the state in setting the conditions for incorporation, assimilation, and the like. Immigrant status does not reflect innate human qualities or even changing social relations, but rather marks a changing relation to nation-states. In making people who relocate across national borders immigrants, states exercise an awesome power. They diminish immigrants by making them live in a parallel legal world of unique rules and reduced rights. Politics then determines the policies that make immigrants citizens.

Politics unfolds in civil society, and civil society entails membership in a community of one sort or another. Citizenship is a particular form of membership in the political community of civil society. With this recognition, the state confers on the individual civil rights to participate in the political system and civil liberties for protection against the arbitrary and overbearing power of the state. American citizenship also applies a principle of equality before the law (Shklar 1991). Whether membership is assumed through birthright or acquired by other means, the individual citizen is positioned equally in relation to all other citizens with respect to the law. The noncitizen is distinguished by his or her exclusion from the doctrine of equality under the law.

Immigrant status reveals a contradiction at the heart of this notion of citizenship. Immigrant status is not essential, but it is permanent. The immigrant and the citizen are both made by the state—they are both political subjects. They stand, however, in different relations to the state's borders, which bound the political community to which the citizen belongs. Borders also mark the migrant as an immigrant, as one born outside the political community to which the citizen belongs. Immigrants can become citizens, but birthright citizens cannot become immigrants in their own country. Thus, citizenship, which is not exchanged but acquired, can never erase the mark of the immigrant. The permanent root of immigrant status is foreign birth. The permanent quality of this status, however, is a wholly political and structurally determined condition.

This said, the formation of a collective immigrant identity has proven elusive in New York and elsewhere, despite the permanence of immigrant status and despite the large numbers of immigrants residing in the city. Citizenship contributes to this by transforming foreign birth into an ethnic category, a hyphenated identity that signifies only partial belonging. Moreover, this partiality is meant to fade away in a generation. Under American law, immigrants, like the native-born, can pass birthright membership in the political community to their children as long as the children are born within its borders. If an immigrant stays an immigrant by not returning home, the immigrant status of his or her family disappears over time.

The tenuousness of immigrant identity—here now, then gone over time—reduces its power as a political resource for collective action (Polletta and Jasper 2001). Immigrant status is plastic. Because this status is so tightly tethered to the nation-state's legal power to name who is an immigrant, the state holds the balance of power in defining immigrant identity. The story of immigrant politics thus becomes the struggle of immigrants to define themselves and their interests against the powerful actions of the state. This is how immigrant politics in New York has been unfolding since 9/11. Immigrants are struggling to define themselves through politics. Immigrants who are not citizens are further disadvantaged in claiming an immigrant identity for themselves by their legal and political marginalization. They inhabit a parallel legal world of rules, courts, and procedures reserved for adjudication of claims made solely on the basis of a status that the state itself controls.[18] The power of the state to interfere in the search for a collective identity, an identity that originates with the state and is therefore doubly vulnerable, is a major obstacle to the ability of that community to engage in politics.

This often makes relations between immigrants and the state crude, leading new immigrant groups to exploit soft areas of the immigration system to shield nonconforming community members from harsh laws that would require them to return to their home country. Many immigrants live lives of quiet desperation, unnoticed, overlooked, and invisible in the shadows of public life. They take advantage of their invisibility to work hard, stay out of trouble, avoid politics and confrontation, and establish better material conditions for themselves, more often for their children. Historical accounts suggest that all new immigrant groups begin their sojourn in America this way, with a mix of "legal" and "illegal" members living together, often in the same families, tied to one another by their common origins and aspirations. Indeed, data from the 2000 census suggest that one in every five American families includes people of mixed immigration status (American Bar Association Commission on Immigration 2004). Their exclusion from politics is part of the price noncitizens pay for their invisibility.

Those lacking citizenship have no formal means of seeking redress of their condition. As one immigrant rights activist said, noncitizen immigrants "are the new slaves," exploited for their labor, lacking in political rights and a political voice. The 9/11 aftermath makes clear the deep contradictions between immigrant status and citizenship in the American constitutional order. It reveals the vulnerability of a political identity rooted in a status determined by the nation-state. The assault on the civil liberties of immigrants thought to share ties of ethnicity, religion, or national origin with the 9/11 hijackers shows how the state can overwhelm civil society and use the resources of civil society against itself. Yet these resources have also provided some basis for action to reclaim an identity for the immigrant from the grip of the state. The politics that immigrants make, therefore, is often a politics in confrontation with state action that targets immigrants to reduce their freedom. Critical to the success of an immigrant political project is the construction of a new immigrant identity that moves beyond ethnicity to lay claim to basic human rights.

In their response to the post-9/11 assault on civil liberties, immigrant activists are trying to construct a new doctrine of civil liberties that will place them more squarely in the realm of human rights. Immigrant politics could invigorate the democratic claims of politics on civil society. This potential is based on the fact that immigrant politics is the politics of extremely marginalized groups, excluded from formal politics, whose relatively small size and lack of other resources for collective action put them in a weakened position to make claims. That they are able to do so despite these limitations is significant for the expansion of democratic politics.

Because social elements of civil society like religion, ethnicity, and national origin rather than political ideology are the rationale for state action against immigrants today, those elements themselves are insufficient as a basis for countermobilization. Immigrants must transcend them, both because they need allies and, more importantly, because they cannot trump state power that ties them to a subordinate political identity and status. What is needed is a more universal political claim against the state, a claim for democratic rights and for human dignity.

The crisis provoked by the federal government's assault on civil liberties has thus stimulated new organizing and unorthodox coalition-building efforts among new partners. In New York City, immigrant advocacy organizations have forged a new alliance with the civil liberties legal establishment. If these relationships mature, the new alliances between the immigrant advocates and the civil liberties groups may prove to be the most important development in grassroots politics of the post-9/11 period. The rise of an immigrant rights movement outside both organized labor and the city's multiracial political order suggests the degree to which the traditional power of these institutions to organize working-class politics in New York has eroded over the last decade. Were these institutions to embrace this new immigrant rights–civil and human rights political formation, it would represent a significant shift in local politics. It is too early, however, to know how deeply immigrant politics is changing local politics in New York and whether, as something new, immigrant politics will displace the city's traditional ethnic political dynamic.

APPENDIX

The New Americans Exit Poll (NAEP) Project is aimed at improving our understanding of the size and influence of the immigrant electorate in New York City. Begun in 2000, the project has collected data from over eight thousand voters exiting their polling places in the past three federal elections. Surveys were made available to voters in English, Chinese, Spanish, and Russian translations and administered by a trained, multilingual survey staff recruited from the city's ethnic and immigrant neighborhoods. Survey supervision on election day was generously provided by the staff of the New York Immigration Coalition.

The sampling strategy was originally developed by Dr. John Mollenkopf, director of the Center for Urban Research at the City University of New York Graduate Center. It involves stratifying the city's election districts by the proportion of foreign-born residents (drawn from the 1990 U.S. census for the 2000 exit poll and adjusted with 2000 U.S. census data for the 2002 and 2004 exit polls) and randomly sampling within three strata, with the lowest stratum set at 25 percent foreign-born (or less), the election district average for the percentage of foreign-born in the population. Foreign-born voters are oversampled in the NAEP in order to build up a large enough representative sample for finer statistical analysis. Across the three surveys, approximately 38 percent of the respondents are immigrant voters. Thus, according to estimates from the U.S. Census Bureau's November 2000 Current Population Survey (CPS) and the 2001 Edison Survey Research exit poll, which identified but did not oversample immigrants, the foreign-born are overrepresented in the NAEP by about ten to fifteen percentage points.

The data in tables 7.4 through 7.6 are weighted to the actual turnout in the election districts assigned to the polling sites sampled for the survey. The sample size for the 2000 exit poll is 2,805 respondents; for the 2002 exit poll, the sample size is 2,607 respondents; and 2,760 voters were interviewed in 2004. Data are reported for the total sample and various subpopulations and should be read down the table columns. Copies of all survey instruments are available upon request.

Selected Questions from the New Americans Exit Poll

"No matter how you voted today, are you registered to vote as a: (1) Democrat; (2) Republican; (3) other party; (4) no party?"

"Is this the first time you have ever voted? (1) yes; (2) no."

"Did you experience any of the following problems at the polls today? (check *all* that apply): (1) name wasn't in the poll book; (2) voting machine was broken; (3) needed language assistance and didn't get it; (4)

was asked for ID when it wasn't required; (5) other problem (write in); (6) no problem."

"Do you approve or disapprove of the way President Bush is handling the situation in Iraq? (1) approve; (2) disapprove; (3) don't know."

"Compared to four years ago, is your family's financial situation: (1) better today; (2) worse today; (3) about the same?"

"Over the last month, did anyone personally contact you to urge you to vote? (1) yes; (2) no."

"Over the last year, did you attend a meeting or forum about voting and the elections? (1) yes; (2) no."

I would like to thank Abed Aladien for critical assistance with the interviews conducted for this study. I am especially grateful to the many activists, advocates, and community leaders I have met over the past three years for their generosity in making time to share with me their perspectives and their experiences in those difficult months following the 9/11 tragedy. I have benefited enormously from ongoing discussions with members of the Civil Rights Civil Liberties Working Group, a New York–based group of immigrant and civil liberties activists initially convened to monitor the NSEERS program and coordinate support for detainees and their families. The New Americans Exit Poll (NAEP) Project, a collaboration between me and the New York Immigration Coalition, has received financial and other assistance over the years from the New York Foundation, the Russell Sage Foundation, Barnard College, and Dr. John Mollenkopf, director of the Center for Urban Research at the City University of New York. I thank Dr. Mollenkopf for inviting me to write this chapter. Early drafts were read by him, Herbert Gans, David Kettler, Immanuel Ness, and Frances Fox Piven, and I thank them for their helpful comments. All errors, of course, are my own.

NOTES

1. Other causal factors initiating migratory flows to the United States include the sending countries' proximity to the United States and the extent of U.S. involvement in the economies of those countries.
2. Equally significant overall, but not dealt with in this chapter, is the skyrocketing surge in Mexican migration to New York, from an official count of 32,689 in

1990 to 122,550 a decade later, making Mexicans the city's fifth-largest immigrant group (New York City Department of City Planning 2004; Smith 2005). Experts believe that the official counts made by the U.S. Bureau of the Census widely underestimate the presence of Mexicans in New York. The Mexican Consulate in New York estimates that three-quarters of a million Mexicans live in the New York metropolitan area (Deibert 2004).

3. "Non-immigrant" visas are issued to foreign nationals for temporary sojourns in the United States to study or travel, for pleasure, and for certain types of work. While the 9/11 hijackers all entered the United States legally, there is evidence that some of them used fraudulent documents to obtain visas abroad and that several were out of compliance with the terms of their visas at the time they hijacked the planes.

4. This assumption underlies the administration's effort to criminalize immigration law in response to 9/11 and is clearly evident in the two most significant legal and bureaucratic post-9/11 reforms of the immigration system, namely, the new alien detention authorities of the U.S.A. Patriot Act and the separation of the service and law enforcement functions of the Immigration and Naturalization Service, with the transfer of most of the agency to the new Department of Homeland Security. The notion that the nation's immigration laws were responsible, at least in part, for the 9/11 attacks is also an underlying assumption of many of Attorney General John Ashcroft's post-9/11 speeches and statements made in defense of the administration's domestic antiterrorism policies (Ashcroft 2001b, 2001c, 2002a, 2002b).

5. At a September 13, 2001, press conference, Attorney General John Ashcroft urged Americans not to "descend to the level of those who perpetrated Tuesday's violence by targeting individuals based on race, religion or national origin" (Simpson, McRoberts, and Sly 2003). For the administration's public statements on preserving the civil liberties of Arab Americans, Muslims, and South Asians, see Boyd (2001) and U.S. Department of Justice (2001). There is, however, substantial documentation of profiling and the impact of the administration's immigration-focused policies on Arab Americans and South Asian Americans and other Muslims (Chishti et al. 2003; American Civil Liberties Union 2004b; New York Advisory Committee to the U.S. Commission on Civil Rights 2004). Steven Brill (2003, 116) put the matter succinctly: the Bush administration's evolving arrest and detention policy "was all part of a dragnet that if it had had a code name fitting its focus, or lack thereof, would have been called 'Operation Find and Hold the Muslims.' There was little other rhyme or reason to it."

6. In his testimony before the Senate Committee on the Judiciary on December 6, 2001, the attorney general called PENTTBOM "the largest, most comprehensive criminal investigation in world history" (Ashcroft 2001d).

7. The September 11 detainees included people labeled by the attorney general to be of "special interest," a newly invented term that has no basis in law (Association of the Bar of the City of New York 2004). The "special interest" designation was used by the attorney general to keep secret the arrest, detention, and deportation of hundreds of Muslim immigrants in the months following the 9/11 attacks.

On chief immigration judge Michael Creppy's (2001) order barring the press and the public from attending immigration hearings of "special interest" detainees (the "Creppy Directive"), see *Detroit Free Press v. Ashcroft*, 303 F.3d 681 (6th Cir. 2002), *Haddad v. Ashcroft*, 221 F. Supp. 2d 799 (E.D. Mich. 2002), and *North Jersey Media Group v. Ashcroft*, 205 F. Supp. 2d 288 (D.N.J. 2002); on the Department of Justice's refusal to comply with a Freedom of Information Act request filed in October 2001 seeking the names of the detainees, see *Center for National Security Studies v. U.S. Department of Justice*, 215 F. Supp. 2d 94, 103 (D.D.C. 2002) and 331 F. 3d 918 (D.C. Cir. 2003) (Chang and Kabat 2004). The inspector general of the Department of Justice found that 475 of 762 detainees arrested between September 11, 2001, and August 2, 2002, were housed in just two facilities, a federal detention center in Brooklyn and a local jail in Paterson, New Jersey, where the overflow of detainees arrested in New York were sent (U.S. Department of Justice 2003).

8. Each of the FBI's fifty-six domestic field offices leads a joint terrorism task force. The New York office's JTTF was created in 1980, the first time federal, state, and local law enforcement agencies were brought together to focus their efforts directed against terrorism. In addition to the FBI, JTTF's can include agents from the INS; the Secret Service; the Bureau of Alcohol, Tobacco, and Firearms (ATF); the Postal Inspection Service; the Internal Revenue Service (IRS); state police and local police department personnel; and other federal, state, and local agency representatives.

9. For more details on the special registration process at the INS's New York district office, see Anderson (2003).

10. The U.S. Immigration and Customs Enforcement Division of the Department of Homeland Security (2003) reports that as of September 30, 2003, the total number of "domestic" registrations was 83,519; an additional 93,741 people were registered at ports of entry upon their arrival in the United States. These numbers are challenged, however, by at least one critic who maintains that the actual number of persons registered is not known but is likely to be much higher (Cainkar 2003).

11. According to Karin Anderson (2004), policy associate at the New York Immigration Coalition, the federal government has never formally acknowledged the number of people deported or in deportation proceedings as a result of complying with the Special Registration Program. The widely cited number of 14,000 comes from a private meeting between immigration advocates and federal officials held in the summer of 2003. The number of people complying with special registration who have actually been deported is unknown.

12. Foreign workers on temporary work visas may apply for permanent U.S. residency through employer sponsorship. Employers must prove that there are no qualified U.S. citizen candidates for the job held or sought by the non-citizen green card applicant. New York State has the worst backlog of applications for labor certification of any state in the nation, with over fifty thousand applications pending by the end of 2002, leading to delays in the state of up to five years for a labor certificate (Fifield 2002). A January 2002 external review of the Department of Labor's permanent labor certification process found delays of up to forty-five

months at the New York State Workforce Agency's office, the first level of review for labor certificate applicants like Mr. H. (PriceWaterhouseCoopers 2002).

13. The *Chicago Tribune* tracked seventy-five men deported to Pakistan in July 2003 after complying with the Special Registration Program or being otherwise detained after September 11, 2001, on an immigration visa violation (McRoberts et al. 2003; Simpson, McRoberts, and Sly 2003). For an inside look at the impact of special registration–related deportations on immigrant youth in New York City, see *Whose Children Are These?*, an award-winning documentary directed by Theresa Thanjan (2004).

14. By January 2004, after twenty-eight straight months of increases, immigrant benefit backlogs were at an all-time high of 3.7 million cases out of a pending workload of 6.1 million cases (U.S. Department of Homeland Security Bureau of U.S. Citizenship and Immigration Services 2004). Processing times for naturalization and family-based petitions doubled, while they tripled for adjustments to status, from thirteen months to thirty-three months.

15. According to Ahsanuallah Bobby Khan (2004b), executive director of the Coney Island Avenue Project, as of April 2004, approximately six hundred New York–based Pakistani immigration detainees have been repatriated to Pakistan via seven U.S. government–chartered flights. See also Embassy of the Islamic Republic of Pakistan (2004).

16. ATCA's action for tort reads: "The district courts shall have original jurisdiction of any civil action by an alien for a tort only, committed in violation of the law of nations or a treaty of the United States."

17. For a summary of arguments for and against noncitizen voting and an account of several local campaigns to promote the idea, see Hayduk (2004).

18. The Supreme Court has long held that the individual rights applying to "persons" under the U.S. Constitution, such as the due process protections of the Fifth Amendment, apply to citizens and noncitizen residents of the United States alike. Moreover, prominent legal scholars have argued that the discrete and insular nature of immigrants as a group calls for special judicial attention to the treatment of noncitizens to ensure that they are not subject to illegitimate government discrimination. But the Court has also found that the plenary power of Congress to regulate immigration extends to legitimate forms of discrimination that have led to the creation of an immigration legal regime in which noncitizens may be subject to laws that would otherwise violate the constitutional rights of citizens. So, for example, Congress can make laws determining the qualifications for legal entry into the United States and also for deportation, as long as those laws respect procedural and due process protections (Tumlin 2004).

REFERENCES

Abuasi, Nidal (principal, Al Noor School). 2004. Interview with the author. February 19, Brooklyn, N.Y.

Abdul-Munim, Firdos (civil rights coordinator, Council on American-Islamic Relations/New York). 2004. Interview with the author. (April 21), Manhattan, N.Y.

Acer, Eleanor, Eric Biel, Deirdre Clancy, Erin Corcoran, Fiona Doherty, Kenneth Hurwitz, David Lisson, Elora Mukherjee, Deborah Pearlstein, Corey Smith, Rebecca Thornton, and Talia Townsend. 2003. *Assessing the New Normal: Liberty and Security for the Post–September 11 United States.* New York: Lawyers Committee for Human Rights.

Alam, Morshed. 2001. Interview with the author. July 24, Manhattan, N.Y.

———. 2004. Interview with the author. February 29, Jackson Heights, N.Y.

Ali, Shekh (principal, Razi School). 2004. Interview with the author. February 16, Woodside, N.Y.

American Bar Association. Commission on Immigration. 2004. *Immigration Detainee Pro Bono Opportunities Guide.* Chicago: American Bar Association. Available at: http://www.abanet.org/immigration/probonoguidefinal.pdf.

American Civil Liberties Union (ACLU). 2002a. *Civil Liberties After 9/11: The ACLU Defends Freedom.* New York: ACLU.

———. 2002b. *Insatiable Appetite: The Government's Demand for New and Unnecessary Powers After September 11.* New York: ACLU.

———. 2004a. *America's Disappeared: Seeking International Justice for Immigrants Detained After 9/11.* New York: ACLU.

———. 2004b. *Sanctioned Bias: Racial Profiling Since 9/11.* New York: ACLU.

American Immigration Lawyers Association. 2003a. *Executive Branch Actions Since September 11, 2001* (civil liberties issue packet). New York: AILA.

———. 2003b. "Office-by-Office Summary of How INS Is Handling Call-In Special Registration." February 20. Available at: http://www.aila.org/contentViewer.aspx?bc=16,4634,4973.

American Muslim Perspective. 2004. "President Bush Urged to Repudiate Anti-Muslim Statement of Rep. Congressman Peter King." *American Muslim Perspective* (February 12). Available at: http://www.amperspective.com/html/call_for_repudiation.html.

Anderson, Karin. 2003. Testimony before the U.S. Commission on Civil Rights regarding special call-in registration. May 21. Available at: http://www.thenyic.org/templates/documentFinder.asp?did=184.

———. 2004. Interview with the author. April 16, Manhattan, N.Y.

Ashcroft, John. 2001a. "Attorney General Remarks" (press briefing, FBI headquarters, September 18). Available at: http://www.usdoj.gov/archive/ag/speeches/2001/0918press briefing.htm.

———. 2001b. Testimony before the Senate Judiciary Committee (September 25). Available at: http://www.usdoj.gov/archive/ag/testimony/2001/0925AttorneyGeneral JohnAshcroftTestimonybeforetheSenateCommitteeontheJudiciary.htm.

———. 2001c. "Attorney General John Ashcroft and INS Commissioner Ziglar Announce INS Restructuring Plan" (November 14). Available at: http://www.usdoj.gov/archive/ag/speeches/2001/agcrisisremarks11_14.htm.

———. 2001d. Testimony before Senate Committee on the Judiciary (December 6). Available at: http://www.usdoj.gov/archive/ag/testimony/2001/1206transcriptsenate judiciarycommittee.htm.

———. 2002a. "Attorney General Transcript: Administrative Change to Board of Immigration Appeals" (news conference, DOJ Conference Center, February 6). Available at: http://www.usdoj.gov/archive/ag/speeches/2002/020602transcriptadministrative changetobia.htm.

———. 2002b. "Attorney General Transcript: SEVIS" (news conference, DOJ Conference Center, May 10). Available at: http://www.usdoj.gov/archive/ag/speeches/2002/051002newsconference-sevistranscript.htm.

———. 2002c. "Attorney General Prepared Remarks on the National Security Entry-Exit Registration System" (June 6). Available at: http://www.usdoj.gov/archive/ag/speeches/2002/060502agpreparedremarks.htm.

Association of the Bar of the City of New York. Committee on Immigration and Nationality Law and Committee on Communications and Media Law. 2004. "Dangerous Doctrine: The Attorney General's Unfounded Claim of Unlimited Authority to Arrest and Deport Aliens in Secret." *The Record* 59. New York: Association of the Bar of the City of New York.

Bahree, Megha, and Cassi Feldman. 2003. "Southern Discomfort: Local Deportees Sent Out of State." *City Limits*, December 8.

Baker, Nancy B. 2003. "National Security Versus Civil Liberties." *Presidential Studies Quarterly* 33(3): 547–67.

Banerjee, Partha. 2004. Interview with the author. March 11, Jackson Heights, N.Y.

Bangla Patrika. 2003. "Don't Go Out Without Making Appointment with Canada Immigration." Translated by Moinuddin Naser, Independent Press Association. Reprinted in *Voices That Must Be Heard* 56 (March 7). Available at: http://www.indypressny.org.

Bernstein, Nina. 2004a. "Albany Social Security ID Checks Threaten Driver's Licenses." *New York Times*, March 18.

———. 2004b. "A Longer Wait for Citizenship and the Ballot in New York." *New York Times*, June 11.

Bhuyan, Mohammed Wadud (president, Jamaica Muslim Center). 2004. Interview with the author. February 29, Jamaica Estates, N.Y.

Boyd, Ralph. 2001. "Statement Regarding the Treatment of Arab, Muslim Americans or Americans of South Asian Descent" (September 13). Available at: http://www.usdoj.gov/opa/pr/2001/September/468cr.htm.

Brill, Steven. 2003. *After: How America Confronted the September 12 Era*. New York: Simon & Schuster.

Brown, Cynthia, ed. 2003. *Lost Liberties: Ashcroft and the Assault on Personal Freedom*. New York: New Press.

Cainkar, Louis. 2003. "Special Registration: A Fervor for Muslims." *Journal of Islamic Law and Culture* 7(Fall–Winter): 73–101.

Chang, Nancy. 2002. *Silencing Political Dissent*. New York: Seven Stories Press.

Chang, Nancy, and Alan Kabat. 2004. *Summary of Recent Court Rulings on Terrorism-Related Matters Having Civil Liberties Implications*. New York: Center for Constitutional Rights (February 4).

Chishti, Muzaffar A., Doris Meissner, Demetrios G. Papademetriou, Jay Peterzell, Michael J. Wishnie, and Stephen W. Yale-Loehr. 2003. *America's Challenge: Domestic Security, Civil Liberties, and National Unity After September 11*. Washington: Migration Policy Institute.

Cole, David. 2003. *Enemy Aliens: Double Standards and Constitutional Freedoms in the War on Terrorism*. New York: New Press.

———. 2004. "Taking Liberties: Ashcroft 0 for 5,000." *The Nation*, October 4.

Creppy, Michael J. 2001. "Cases Requiring Special Procedures" (memo to all immigration judges and court administrators; the "Creppy Directive," August 21). Available at: http://news.findlaw.com/hdocs/docs/aclu/creppy092101memo.pdf.

Das Gupta, Monisha. 2005. "Of Hardship and Hostility: The Impact of 9/11 on New York City Taxi Drivers." In *Wounded City: The Social Impact of 9/11*, edited by Nancy Foner. New York: Russell Sage Foundation.

Deibert, Michael. 2004. "Mexico's Latest Wave Hits the City: A New Explosion of Immigrants Has Added Challenges on Jobs and Linguistic Fronts as City Groups Rush to Cope." *Newsday*, September 15.

Doherty, Fiona, Kenneth Hurwitz, Elisa Massimino, Michael McClintock, Raj Purohit, Corey Smith, and Rebecca Thornton. 2003. *Imbalance of Powers: How Changes to U.S. Law and Policy Since 9/11 Erode Human Rights and Civil Liberties*. New York: Lawyers Committee for Human Rights.

Doherty, Fiona, Kenneth Hurwitz, Elisa Massimino, Michael McClintock, Raj Purohit, Corey Smith, Rebecca Thornton, and Stephen Vladeck. 2002. *A Year of Loss: Reexamining Civil Liberties Since September 11*. New York: Lawyers Committee for Human Rights.

Elliott, Andrea. 2003. "In Brooklyn, 9/11 Damage Continues." *New York Times*, June 7.

Embassy of the Islamic Republic of Pakistan. 2004. "Sixty-five Detainees to Be Repatriated to Pakistan" (press release). April 13. Available at: http://www.embassyof pakistan.org/news68.php.

Etheridge, Frank. 2004. "Exile in Oakdale." *Gambit Weekly*, August 10. Available at: http://www.bestofneworleans.com/dispatch/2004-08-10/cover_story.html.

Fifield, Adam. 2002. "Stacked Cards." *City Limits Monthly* (December). Available at http://www.citylimits.org/content/articles/articleView.cfm?articlenumber=905.

Hayduk, Ronald. 2004. "Democracy for All: Restoring Immigrant Voting Rights in the U.S." *New Political Science* 26(December): 499–523.

Human Rights Watch. 2002. *Presumption of Guilt: Human Rights Abuses of Post-September 11 Detainees*. Report G1404. Washington, D.C.: Human Rights Watch (August 15).

Janofsky, Michael. 2004. "9/11 Panel Calls Policies on Immigration Ineffective." *New York Times*, April 17.

Khan, Ahsanuallah Bobby (executive director, Coney Island Avenue Project). 2004a. Interview with the author. February 16, Brooklyn, N.Y.

———. 2004b. E-mail communication with the author. April 14.

McHugh, Margie (executive director, New York Immigration Coalition). 2001. Interview with the author. (July 20), Manhattan, N.Y.

Leone, Richard C., and Greg Anrig Jr., eds. 2003. *The War on Our Freedoms: Civil Liberties in an Age of Terrorism*. New York: Century Foundation.

Logan, John, and John Mollenkopf. 2002. *People and Politics in America's Big Cities: A Critical Conversation About the Implications of the Profound Demographic Transformation Now Under Way in Our City*. New York: Drum Major Institute.

McRoberts, Flynn, et al. 2003. "Torn from Families and Jobs, Deportees Face Bleak Future." *Chicago Tribune*, November 17.

Mohammed-Arif, Aminah. 2002. *Salaam America: South Asian Muslims in New York*. London: Anthem Press.

Mohammedi, Omar. 2004. Interview with the author. February 19, Manhattan, N.Y.

Murray, Nancy. 2004. "Profiled: Arabs, Muslims, and the Post-9/11 Hunt for the 'Enemy Within.'" In *Civil Rights in Peril: The Targeting of Arabs and Muslims*, edited by Elaine C. Hagopian. Chicago: Haymarket Books.

National Commission on Terrorist Attacks Upon the United States. 2004a. *The 9/11 Commission Report*. Authorized edition. New York: W. W. Norton.

———. 2004b. "Entry of the 9/11 Hijackers into the United States" (staff statement no. 1, seventh public hearing, January 26–27). Washington: National Commission on Terrorist Attacks Upon the United States. Available at: http://www.9–11commission .gov/staff_statements/staff_statement_1.pdf.

New Americans Exit Poll. 2001. *The 2000 Presidential Election*. Computer file. Available from author.

———. 2003. *The 2002 New York State Gubernatorial Election*. Computer file. Available from author.

———. 2005. *The 2004 Presidential Election*. Computer file. Available from author.

New York Advisory Committee to the U.S. Commission on Civil Rights. 2004. *Civil Rights Implications of Post–September 11 Law Enforcement Practices in New York*. New York: New York Advisory Committee to the U.S. Commission on Civil Rights.

New York City Department of City Planning. Population Division. 2004. *The Newest New Yorkers 2000: Immigrant New York in the New Millennium*. NYCDCP 04–10. New York: NYCDCP.

New York Immigration Coalition. 2002. "Proposals to Address the Unmet Needs of Immigrant Victims of the September 11 Disaster." 100-Day FEMA Accountability Campaign. June 23.

———. 2003. "Protestors Tell Feds to REGISTER *THIS!* Community and Religious Leaders Condemn Arab and Muslim Registration Program as Discriminatory, Ineffective, and a Cause of Increasing Immigration Backlogs for All" (press release). November 17.

New York State Assembly. Standing Committee on Transportation. 2004. Public hearing on DMV licensing, driver's license issues. August 19, New York, N.Y.

Pakistan Post. 2003. "As Pakistanis Leave for Canada, Many Businesses Languish in Jackson Heights, Coney Island Avenue." Translated by Rehan Ansari, Independent Press Association. Reprinted in *Voices That Must Be Heard* 47. (January 8). Available at: http://www.indypressny.org.

Polletta, Francesca, and James M. Jasper. 2001. "Collective Identity and Social Movements." *Annual Review of Sociology* 27: 283–305.

Powell, Michael. 2003. "An Exodus Grows in Brooklyn; 9/11 Still Rippling Through Pakistani Neighborhood." *Washington Post*, May 29.

PriceWaterhouseCoopers. 2002. *U.S. Department of Labor Employment and Training Administration Permanent Labor Certification Process Management Review*. New York: PriceWaterhouseCoopers (January). Available at: http://www.doleta.gov/sga/rfp/ PwCFinalReport.doc.

Sachs, Susan. 2003. "Pakistanis Fleeing U.S. for Canada, Stopped; U.S. Crackdown Sets Off Unusual Rush to Canada." *New York Times*, February 25.

Sada-e-Pakistan. 2003. "Since the Registration Process Began, FBI-INS Raids Have Stopped." Translation by Independent Press Association. Reprinted in *Voices That Must Be Heard* 50 (January 30). Available at: http://www.indypressny.org.

Sadhwani, Gouri (executive director, New York Civic Participation Project). 2004. Interview with the author. June 14, Manhattan, N.Y.

Samara, Awali (program coordinator, Arab American Association of New York). 2004. Interview with the author. March 4, Brooklyn, N.Y.

Sanjek, Roger. 1998. *The Future of Us All: Race and Neighborhood Politics in New York City.* Ithaca, N.Y.: Cornell University Press.

Sarkar, Saurav. 2003a. "Taking Pakistan Out of Brooklyn." *The Next American City* ("The Changing Neighborhood" issue) (2, June). Available at: http://www.americancity .org/article.php?id_article=87.

———. 2003b. "We Are Not Terrorists: The Impact of INS Special Registration." *Samar: South Asian Magazine for Action and Reflection* 16(Fall–Winter). Available at: http:// www.samarmagazine.org/archive/article.php?id=132.

Shenon, Philip, and Robin Toner. 2001. "A Nation Challenged: Policy and Legislation; U.S. Widens Policy on Detaining Suspects; Troubled Airlines Get Federal Aid Pledge." *New York Times,* September 18.

Shklar, Judith. 1991. *American Citizenship: The Quest for Inclusion.* Cambridge, Mass.: Harvard University Press.

Simpson, Cam, Flynn McRoberts, and Liz Sly. 2003. "Immigration Crackdown Shatters Muslims' Lives." *Chicago Tribune,* November 16.

Smith, Robert C. 2005. *Mexican New York: Transnational Lives of New Immigrants.* Los Angeles: University of California Press.

Solomon, Alisa. 2003. "Fleeing America: Thousands of New York's Pakistanis Leave Under U.S. Pressure." *Village Voice,* September 10–16.

Stanley, Jay, and Barry Steinhardt. 2003. *Bigger Monster, Weaker Chains: The Growth of an American Surveillance Society.* New York: ACLU Technology and Liberty Program.

Stock, Margaret D., and Benjamin Johnson. 2003. "The Lessons of 9/11: A Failure of Intelligence, Not Immigration Law." *Immigration Policy Focus* (American Immigration Law Foundation, Immigration Policy Center) 2(3): 1–20. Available at http://www .ailf.org/ipc/icf121203.pdf.

Swarns, Rachel L. 2003. "More Than 13,000 May Face Deportation." *New York Times,* June 6.

Thanjan, Theresa, director. 2004. *Whose Children Are These?* (documentary film). New York: NYC Maharani Productions.

Tumlin, Karen C. 2004. "Comment: Suspect First: How Terrorism Policy Is Reshaping Immigration Policy." *California Law Review* 92(July): 1173–1238.

U.S. Congress. 2002. *Findings of the Final Report of the Senate Select Committee on Intelligence and the House Permanent Select Committee on Intelligence Joint Inquiry into the Terrorist Attacks of September 11, 2001.* Available at: http://intelligence.senate.gov/pubs107.htm.

U.S. Department of Commerce. Bureau of the Census. 1995. *Census of Population and Housing, 1990 (United States): Public Use Microdata Sample: 1/1,000 Sample* (computer file). Washington and Ann Arbor, Mich.: U.S. Bureau of the Census and Inter-University Consortium for Political and Social Research.

———. 2002. *Census of Population and Housing, 2000 (United States): Summary File 3, New York* (computer file). Washington and Ann Arbor, Mich.: U.S. Bureau of the Census and Inter-University Consortium for Political and Social Research.

———. 2003. *Census of Population and Housing, 2000 (United States): Public Use Microdata Sample: 5 Percent Sample* (computer file). Washington and Ann Arbor, Mich.: U.S. Bureau of the Census and Inter-University Consortium for Political and Social Research.

U. S. Department of Homeland Security (DHS). Bureau of U.S. Citizenship and Immigration Services. 2004. *Backlog Elimination Plan: Fiscal Year 2004, Third Quarter Update.* November 5. Available at: http://uscis.gov/graphics/aboutus/repsstudies/BEPQ3v2_1.pdf.

U.S. Department of Homeland Security. Office of Immigration Customs and Enforcement. 2003. "Changes to National Security Entry-Exit Registration System (NSEERS)" (fact sheet). December 1. Available at: http://www.ice.gov/graphics/news/factsheets/NSEERSfactsheet120103.pdf.

U.S. Department of Homeland Security. Office of Immigration Statistics. 2003. *Yearbook of Immigration Statistics, 2002.* Washington: U.S. Government Printing Office.

———. 2004a. *Immigrants Admitted to the United States, 2001* (computer file). Washington: DHS.

———. 2004b. *Immigrants Admitted to the United States, 2002* (computer file). Washington: DHS.

U.S. Department of Justice. 2002. "National Security Entry-Exit Registration System" (fact sheet). June 5. Available at: http://www.usdoj.gov/ag/speeches/2002/natlsecentryexittrackingsys.htm.

U.S. Department of Justice. Civil Rights Division. 2001. "Statements of Federal Agencies." Available at: http://www.usdoj.gov/crt/legalinfo/nordwg_statements.html.

U.S. Department of Justice. Office of the Inspector General. 2003. *The September 11 Detainees: A Review of the Treatment of Aliens Held on Immigration Charges in Connection with the Investigation of the September 11 Attacks.* Washington: Department of Justice (June). Available at: http://www.usdoj.gov/oig/special/0306.

U.S. Government Accounting Office. 2003. *Homeland Security: Justice Department's Project to Interview Aliens After September 11, 2001.* GAO-03-459. Washington: Government Accounting Office (April). Available at: http://www.gao.gov/new.items/d03459.pdf.

U.S. Immigration and Naturalization Service. 1993. *Immigrants Admitted to the United States, 1992* (computer file). Washington and Ann Arbor, Mich.: U.S. Department of Justice and Inter-University Consortium for Political and Social Research.

———. 1997. *Immigrants Admitted to the United States, 1993–1995* (computer file). Washington and Ann Arbor, Mich.: U.S. Department of Justice and Inter-University Consortium for Political and Social Research.

———. 1998. *Immigrants Admitted to the United States, 1996* (computer file). Washington and Ann Arbor, Mich.: U.S. Department of Justice and Inter-University Consortium for Political and Social Research.

———. 2000a. *Immigrants Admitted to the United States, 1997* (computer file). Washington and Ann Arbor, Mich.: U.S. Department of Justice and Inter-University Consortium for Political and Social Research.

———. 2000b. *Immigrants Admitted to the United States, 1998* (computer file). Washington and Ann Arbor, Mich.: U.S. Department of Justice and Inter-University Consortium for Political and Social Research.

———. 2002a. *Immigrants Admitted to the United States, 1999* (computer file). Washington and Ann Arbor, Mich.: U.S. Department of Justice and Inter-University Consortium for Political and Social Research.

———. 2002b. *Immigrants Admitted to the United States, 2000* (computer file). Washington and Ann Arbor, Mich.: U.S. Department of Justice and Inter-University Consortium for Political and Social Research.

CHAPTER 8

How 9/11 Reshaped the Political Environment in New York

John Mollenkopf

THE ATTACKS on the World Trade Center and the Pentagon created a disequilibrium in the politics of the city, state, and nation. These altered environments favored some candidates and worked against others. Despite expectations in many quarters, for example, New York City did not elect a Democratic mayor to succeed Mayor Rudolph W. Giuliani in November 2001, but took the unprecedented step of electing its third Republican in a row, Michael Bloomberg. Rudolph Giuliani did not leave office as a self-wounded, term-limited cancer patient whose wife had accused him of conducting an affair with one of his aides, but as a widely hailed hero, "America's Mayor," and *Time*'s "Person of the Year."

The attacks and their aftermath also gave New York governor George Pataki, whose second term was considered to be running out of gas, a new lease on political life; he too became widely admired for his fortitude in the face of the attacks and was handily reelected in November 2002. Finally, by mounting a War on Terror, attacking the Taliban regime in Afghanistan, and declaring war against Iraq, George Bush seized the chance to assert himself as commander in chief; he too was reelected in November 2004, by a small margin that was nonetheless convincingly larger than in 2000; in fact, a majority of the electorate voted for him. Instead of campaigning as a barely legitimate officeholder who had presided over a recession and a ballooning federal deficit, he was the man who deposed Saddam Hussein. Instead of being described as someone who had allegedly not met all his National Guard obligations, he put John Kerry on the defensive about his Vietnam War medals and his support for American troops.

September 11 provided these political actors with the chance to reframe the local, state, and national political debate in ways that favored Republican officeholders. Bloomberg, Giuliani, Pataki, and Bush and their strategists and supporters made effective use of these opportunities, while their Democratic opponents, who were more comfortable discussing how to share the fruits of prosperity with the middle and working classes, had much more difficulty navigating this environment. Although George Bush, George Pataki, and Michael Bloomberg might all have won their respective elections in the absence of 9/11, they would have had considerably more difficulty in doing so. Michael Bloomberg in particular probably would not have been elected mayor if the attacks had not taken place.

THE IMPACT ON THE 2001 MAYORAL ELECTION

It was ironic that the attack took place on the day of the Democratic and Republican primary elections for mayor. Owing to term limits, the mayoralty of Republican Rudolph W. Giuliani was coming to a troubled end in 2001. In his first attempt at higher office in 1989, Giuliani, a former federal prosecutor, had narrowly lost to New York City's first, and so far only, African American mayor, David W. Dinkins. Dinkins had succeeded the iconic Ed Koch, a once-liberal Democrat who veered away from his party's embrace of blacks, other minorities, and labor unions. Koch's term had ended amid political scandal and in the wake of a series of acts of violence by whites against blacks (Mollenkopf 1993). Racially polarizing events continued during the Dinkins administration, which faced a major racial clash between blacks and Jews in Crown Heights, a severe economic downturn, and a violent crime rate that seemed to many to be out of control. These factors contributed to Giuliani's narrow victory in his second attempt to become mayor in 1993.

In office, Giuliani consciously attempted to break the liberal tradition in New York City's government by directly attacking the crime problem, reducing the welfare caseload and reforming the welfare program, and lowering taxes. A combination of effective management, "tough love," and a rebounding economy yielded a substantial degree of success on all three of these fronts. (Progress with an additional plank in Giuliani's platform, achieving more control over and better results in the city school system, proved more illusive.) By cracking down on "quality of life" infractions, the Giuliani administration also greatly reduced the amount of panhandling, visible homelessness, and graffiti around the city, removing conditions that annoyed the city's middle-class taxpayers. This solid performance enabled Giuliani to win a lopsided victory over his

Democratic challenger, Manhattan borough president Ruth Messinger, in 1997. Owing to a term limits measure adopted in 1993, however, Giuliani thereafter became a lame duck.

As his second term progressed, the balance between the positive and negative aspects of the Giuliani administration seemed to shift toward the latter. Although the crime rate and welfare rolls continued to drop, the changes were more in the nature of incremental additions. More importantly, a series of incidents took place in which members of the police department inflicted injury or death on black males, who generally had not done anything wrong. These included the August 1997 brutalization of Abner Louima, a Haitian immigrant, in a Brooklyn precinct house, and the February 1999 killing of Amadou Diallo, an African immigrant, in a forty-one-shot fusillade fired by members of the Street Crime Unit, a key part of the Giuliani administration's full-court press against criminals. (The cops also killed an apparently deranged Hasidic Jewish man in Borough Park, Brooklyn, in August 1999.) These incidents led to a month-long series of demonstrations and acts of civil disobedience in front of police headquarters, across from City Hall, that involved the arrest of 1,200 protesters, including former mayor Dinkins, Congressman Charles Rangel, and Bronx borough president Fernando Ferrer in March 1999. At the end of the year, New York State attorney general Eliot Spitzer issued a report strongly criticizing the stop-and-frisk practices of the police department. In general, however, Mayor Giuliani consistently defended the practices of the police department, while highly publicized police killings of blacks continued to occur. In September 1999, the mayor picked a public fight with the Brooklyn Museum over an exhibition featuring what he considered to be sacrilegious art. Many observers thought he might be taking his battle against threats to "quality of life" a bit too far.

Compounding the growing public concern over whether these incidents meant that the mayor's emphasis on law enforcement also reflected a tolerance for police brutality was the deterioration of the mayor's health in 2000 and his marriage in 2001. A diagnosis of prostate cancer in early 2000 dissuaded him from undertaking a campaign for the U.S. Senate against the probable Democratic nominee, Hillary Clinton, whom many Republicans had urged Giuliani to take on. This was also the period in which the mayor was rumored to be having an affair, a rumor later publicly affirmed by his estranged wife, Donna Hanover. The breakdown of the marriage became increasingly acrimonious, with the mayor filing for divorce in October 2000 and moving out of Gracie Mansion in June 2001.

By the summer of 2001, therefore, with the Democratic and Republican mayoral races well under way, Mayor Giuliani's star was tarnished, if not setting. An August preelection poll by the *New York Times* indicated that the electorate had a positive mood about the future of the city, were not concerned that a change in administration would knock the city off its upward trajectory, would support any Democrat over the probable Republican nominee, Michael Bloomberg, and also gave all of them better marks against Giuliani than had been the case in 1997. Although the electorate was still not paying much attention, registered Democrats who were following the election gave public advocate Mark Green an edge over Bronx borough president Fernando Ferrer (Nagourney and Connelly 2001).

In the run-up to the September 11 primary, Ferrer consistently presented himself as the candidate of "the other New York," the largely working-class group of people who had not benefited from the late 1990s upsurge in the city's economy to the degree that white New Yorkers in management and the professions had done. Green continued to stress a series of discrete issues and his experience as a consumer advocate. The two other candidates, council speaker Peter Vallone and city comptroller Alan Hevesi, attracted less support, and Mayor Giuliani got into a spat with Hevesi over whether Hevesi had sought to help a campaign contributor. An important event was the endorsement of Ferrer by the Rev. Al Sharpton—perhaps the most prominent African American activist in New York and a person with demonstrated appeal to black Democrats—as well as a host of other black leaders. This gradually eroded one main source of support for Green's front-runner status. Green had previously won strong backing from black voters, had served as a commissioner in the Dinkins administration, and had Dinkins's endorsement. Most of the tracking polls conducted before the primary continued to show Green in the lead, but in a diminishing lead.

At 10:53 A.M. on September 11, twenty-five minutes after the collapse of the North Tower, Mayor Giuliani announced to the stunned and horrified residents of New York City that he was suspending the primary election and postponing it for two weeks. After making a brief announcement at 9:30 in Sarasota, Florida, President Bush disappeared from media presence as he flew first to Barksdale Air Force Base in Louisiana, where he made another statement at 1:00 P.M., and then to Offutt Air Force Base in Omaha; he would return to Washington by the early evening. Meanwhile, Mayor Giuliani, who had made a harrowing escape from the collapse earlier that morning and who lost several close colleagues in the attack, provided the main media presence informing the city and nation about the attack during the day.

There can be no doubt that Mayor Giuliani responded to the gravest challenge ever to face the city with courage, dignity, and resolve. He had arrived at the World Trade Center just as the second plane hit, headed for his newly constructed command center on the twenty-third floor of 7 World Trade Center across the street. As the collapse of the South Tower made it clear that this site was endangered, he evacuated northward on foot and set up a new command post at the Police Academy on Twenty-third Street. (The building with the command center caught fire and also collapsed later in the day.) During the day he ordered the evacuation of lower Manhattan, supervised the immediate response to the damage at Ground Zero, and set recovery operations in motion. In the following days the mayor helped to calm and guide a deeply troubled city.

In the weeks after the attack, New York City politics moved ahead despite the trauma. During the two-week postponement period, Ferrer's Hispanic-black coalition continued to pick up momentum, aided by the mobilization efforts of local 1199 of the Health Care Workers Union and support from the Bronx County Democratic organization. On September 25, the Democratic primary election finally took place, yielding an unexpected outcome: not only did some 780,000 voters turn out, but Freddy Ferrer came in first, with 35.8 percent of the vote. Mark Green trailed Ferrer by 36,000 votes, and the other two candidates received far fewer votes. (Bloomberg also soundly defeated Badillo for the Republican nomination.) This set the stage for a six-week runoff campaign culminating on October 11, just two months after the attack.

During the runoff campaign, Ferrer picked up a number of endorsements, and such odd bedfellows as former mayor Ed Koch, Senator Daniel Moynihan, and Peter Vallone joined Al Sharpton in backing Ferrer. (This reflected the deep distaste within the Democratic establishment for consumer advocate and reform critic Mark Green.) Green responded by criticizing Ferrer's ability to rebuild the city and saying he would have done as good a job at handling the attacks as Giuliani, whose poll ratings had soared into the 90 percent range (Cooper and Nagourney 2001). Mayor Giuliani also began to say that his term in office should be extended by ninety days. This became a hot topic in the runoff campaign: Green reluctantly agreed to support Giuliani's request, as did Bloomberg, while Ferrer did not. The race turned increasingly sharp as Green aired commercials saying New York "could not afford to take a chance" on electing Ferrer, which the Ferrer camp thought was unfairly designed to deepen racial polarization in a manner reminiscent of closing-day attacks on the Latino mayoral candidate in Los Angeles, Antonio Villaraigosa (Cooper and Archibold 2001).

The bitterly contested runoff election was highly polarized. Green edged Ferrer by only 16,000 votes out of 790,000 cast. The fallout from this contest continued to vex Green during the three-week run-up to the general election on November 6; Ferrer gave Green a lukewarm endorsement, and his supporters refused to do even that, sitting out the election (with some even tacitly supporting Michael Bloomberg). Meanwhile, Mayor Giuliani, at the height of his popularity, gave nominee Bloomberg a strong, if belated, endorsement, which the Bloomberg campaign deployed effectively in the most costly campaign ever to take place. (Bloomberg spent some $73 million of his own money on the campaign, breaking all records and outspending the Green campaign by a huge margin.)

When the final result became clear about midnight, Bloomberg had narrowly won. Out of nearly 1.5 million votes cast, Bloomberg received about 35,000 more than Green. Subsequent analysis of the precinct-level results showed that the distribution of Bloomberg's votes strongly resembled the pattern of support for Giuliani in his three races, and previously, that of Ed Koch in 1989 (Mollenkopf 2003). Ironically, Bloomberg's areas of support coincided with those that had provided the votes for Green to beat Ferrer in the runoff primary. Clearly, many "Giuliani Democrats" had voted first to help Green thwart Ferrer and then to help Bloomberg defeat Green. The tendency of white voters who normally support Democratic nominees for state or national office to vote for the Republican mayoral candidate in racially polarized races thus once more contributed to Bloomberg's victory. This was augmented by a slight defection of Ferrer supporters to Bloomberg over Green, as well as their tendency to sit out the election.[1]

Although the ethnic and racial tensions within the Democratic electorate contributed to this outcome, there can be little doubt that September 11 also played a primary role. It shifted voter attention away from the moral imperative of helping "the other New York" to the economic imperative of rebuilding a shattered city. Green relied on this theme to win the runoff primary, but the exit poll suggested that this issue worked strongly to Michael Bloomberg's advantage in the general election. (Thirty percent of those who voted said that 9/11 made them more likely to vote for Bloomberg, but only 14 percent said they were more likely to vote for Green, yielding a net shift of 16 percent of the electorate toward Bloomberg on this issue. This boost obviously helped Bloomberg win the hard-fought contest.) Giuliani's heightened approval in the wake of 9/11 and his strong endorsement of Bloomberg also clearly helped Bloomberg win. (Some 60 percent of those who approved of the way Giuliani was doing his job voted for Bloomberg.) Just as Mayor Giuliani owed his political rehabilitation and rebounding popularity to his actions on 9/11, so did Michael Bloomberg owe his ascent to the mayoralty to the attack.

THE IMPACT ON THE 2002 GUBERNATORIAL ELECTION

This "halo effect" also worked in favor of Republican Governor George Pataki's reelection in November 2002, a year after the attacks. The governor took on the mission of rebuilding lower Manhattan as the main focus of his administration after September 2001. In the weeks after 9/11, he worked with Mayor Giuliani to submit a $50 billion request for aid to the federal government. As

Lynne Sagalyn (this volume) has pointed out, President Bush responded with an aid package of more than $20 billion, which flowed primarily through entities controlled by the governor. As Sagalyn and Mitchell Moss (this volume) have shown, at the behest of business leaders, Governor Pataki designed this process not only to cut out the State Legislature, especially its Democratic speaker, Sheldon Silver, who represented a district in lower Manhattan, but to exclude any real influence by New York City government. As Moss points out, this design reflected a concern that Democrat Mark Green might become mayor of New York City. It also reflected the governor's desire to maintain control over the rebuilding process and the reality—described by Sagalyn and Susan Fainstein (this volume)—that the Port Authority, an entity controlled by Governor Pataki and the governor of New Jersey, owned the site, while the state possessed a development entity, the Empire State Development Corporation (ESDC), whose authority exceeded that of any local agency.

As Moss has indicated, with effective help from Democratic senators Charles Schumer and Hillary Clinton, the governor developed an aid package that gained the backing of the president, leading Congress to adopt three pieces of legislation in the period after the attacks.[2] The first, H.R. 2888, the Emergency Supplemental Appropriations Act for Recovery from and Response to Terrorist Attacks on the United States, became P.L. 107–38 on September 18, 2001. Besides authorizing $40 billion for the war in Afghanistan and homeland defense, it funded efforts to recover from September 11 and appropriated $20 billion immediately. It stated that "not less than one-half of the $40 billion shall be for disaster recovery activities and assistance related to such terrorist acts in New York, Virginia, and Pennsylvania." This money was to flow through federal agencies such as the Federal Emergency Management Agency (FEMA), which funded the immediate cleanup of the site, and the U.S. Departments of Housing and Urban Development and Transportation, which would provide funding to entities controlled by the state of New York.

A second bill, H.R. 3888, became P.L. 107–117 on January 10, 2002. This Department of Defense Appropriations Act of 2002 appropriated the second $20 billion authorized in the first, allotting $8.2 billion more to New York, Virginia, and Pennsylvania, bringing the total appropriated for these purposes to about $10.2 billion. A $2 billion community development block grant (CDBG) was specifically directed to the Lower Manhattan Development Corporation (LMDC). The relevant legislative language is as follows:

> $2,000,000,000 ... PROVIDED, That such funds shall be subject to the first through sixth provisos in section 434 of Public Law 107–73: PROVIDED FURTHER, That *the State of New York, in conjunction with the City of New York, shall, through the Lower Manhattan Redevelopment Corporation ("the corporation"): (1) distribute the funds ... (2) within 45 days of enactment of this*

Act, issue the initial criteria and requirements necessary to accept applications from individuals, nonprofits, and small businesses for economic losses…and (3) begin processing such applications: PROVIDED FURTHER, That *the corporation shall expeditiously respond to any application from an individual, nonprofit, or small business for economic losses under this heading:* PROVIDED FURTHER, That … *no less than $500,000,000 shall be made available for individuals, nonprofits, or small businesses* described in the prior three provisos, *with a limit of $500,000 per small business for economic losses:* PROVIDED FURTHER, That amounts … shall only be available for individuals, nonprofits, or small businesses … [in the] area *located on or south of West 14th Street (west of its intersection with 5th Avenue), or on or south of East 14th Street (east of its intersection with 5th Avenue):* PROVIDED FURTHER, That … $10,000,000 *shall be used for a program to aid the travel and tourism industry* in New York City. (emphasis added)

Other sections of the bill designated specific amounts for other entities, including, for example, $34 million for the Consortium for Worker Education to provide assistance to displaced workers.

Finally, on the eve of the six-month anniversary of the attack in March 2002, Congress passed and President Bush signed a supplemental appropriation containing another $5.5 billion in direct aid for New York City and an economic stimulus bill that contained a $5 billion "liberty zone" incentive package for lower Manhattan. The supplemental bill appropriated $1.8 billion to the Port Authority and Metropolitan Transportation Authority (MTA) to build an intermodal transit facility in lower Manhattan, $2.75 billion more to FEMA to reimburse city costs (bringing the total FEMA amount to $9.1 billion), $167 million more to rebuild the West Side Highway, and $750 million more in community development block grants to rebuild lower Manhattan's power and telecommunications distributions systems. The $5 billion tax package provided a $2,400 per employee tax credit for two years to every business south of Canal Street employing two hundred or fewer workers; provided for accelerated depreciation on an increased amount of business equipment; authorized the state to issue $8 billion in tax-exempt bonds to construct office space, rental housing, and public utilities ($2 billion of which may be used outside lower Manhattan); and allowed the city to refinance existing debt, easing annual interest costs. This package was adopted after some contention, including a charge by federal Office of Management and Budget (OMB) director Mitch Daniels that New York was "money grubbing," but it revealed a close link on this issue between the president and the governor and the deep investment both had in being identified with the rebuilding process (Hernandez 2002).

As Sagalyn, Fainstein, and Moss have detailed elsewhere in this volume, Governor George Pataki controlled all of the organizations that were pivotal to the rebuilding process and named close allies to run each of them. Chief among them was the Port Authority: Pataki appointed half the board members and the top executive (with the governor of New Jersey appointing the other half of the board, including the chairperson). The Port Authority owned the site, ran the PATH train, and had great technical expertise in the area of facilities design and management. The governor also controlled the boards and appointed the top executives of the MTA (which would build any new subway facilities), the Battery Park City Authority (which built and manages the commercial and residential complex just to the west of Ground Zero), and the LMDC. He appointed trusted senior staff members who had worked for him in many previous positions to head these organizations. For example, the president of LMDC, Louis R. Tomson, had been the governor's first deputy secretary in charge of overseeing the state's public authorities, chairman of the State Thruway Authority, and adviser on creating the Long Island Power Authority. The new executive director of the Port Authority, Joseph J. Seymour, had been city manager of Peekskill, New York, when the governor was mayor of that city; Seymour had also held senior positions in the State Department of Motor Vehicles, the Department of General Services, and the New York Power Authority.

When Governor Pataki formed the Lower Manhattan Development Corporation in November 2001 as a subsidiary of the Empire State Development Corporation, the state's economic development arm, he appointed seven of its board members, while then-mayor Giuliani named four. Because the ESDC had descended from the Rockefeller-era Urban Development Corporation (UDC), it had the right to override New York City's zoning and building code regulations, though not state and federal environmental regulations, and it could condemn land and issue construction bonds. (At that time, the ESDC had issued about $3.8 billion in bonded debt, much for constructing prisons.)

Then-candidate Michael Bloomberg had disagreed with the appointment of such a body before the election, and Assembly speaker Silver announced on October 30 that he favored a "Lower Manhattan Resurgence Authority" whose members would be appointed by the city and state legislatures as well as the governor. The governor obviously chose an institutional design that would deny New York City's new chief elected official, whoever that might be, direct influence over this entity. He appointed John C. Whitehead, a former investment banker, Reagan administration State Department official, and major Republican party contributor, to be LMDC chairman. He also appointed Roland Betts, the Chelsea Piers developer and a former Texas Rangers co-owner (with George W. Bush); Lewis Eisenberg, former chairman of the Port Authority board and a former Goldman Sachs partner; Ed Malloy, president of Building and Construction Trades Council; Frank Zarb, former CEO of NASDAQ as well as Smith Barney and a Reagan administration official; Community Board l chairperson Madelyn Wils; and Deborah Wright, Carver Federal Bank president and a former Giuliani administration housing official. Mayor Giuliani appointed Paul Crotty, his former corporation counsel; the chairman of the New York Stock Exchange, Richard Grasso; his deputy mayor for economic development, Robert Harding; and Howard Wilson, a corporate lawyer and chairman of the School Construction Authority.

As the *New York Times* noted shortly after the LMDC was formed, "Mr. Bloomberg has more authority to suspend alternate side of the street parking regulations than in determining the course of what happens" at the WTC site (Nagourney 2002). Recognizing this fact, the governor extended Mayor Bloomberg the courtesy of appointing three of his own members to the LMDC board in March 2002, while denying City Council speaker Gifford Miller's demand that the council be given the right to name two members. The mayor's appointees included his deputy mayor for economic development, Dan Doctoroff, and the LMDC also hired several staff people close to Doctoroff, including the urban designer Alex Garvin, who had worked on Doctoroff's plan for attracting the Olympics to New York in 2012. Still, the governor continued to dominate the process.

A year after the September 11 attacks, Governor Pataki was slated to stand for reelection. He made his role in the rebuilding process a central theme in this campaign. As Sagalyn (this volume) has noted, the rebuilding process gave the governor numerous opportunities to stand before the public on a matter of great interest to it. His two chief Democratic opponents were state comptroller Carl McCall, the first African American to hold statewide elected office, and former U.S. Department of Housing and Urban Development secretary Andrew Cuomo, son of the former governor. In the course of the Democratic primary campaign, Cuomo said of Pataki's role after 9/11: "[he] stood behind the leader. He held the leader's coat. He was a great assistant to the leader. But he was not a leader. Cream rises to the top, and Rudy Giuliani rose to the top" (Slackman 2004). This intemperate remark elicited a storm of criticism that contributed to Cuomo's withdrawal from the campaign, allowing McCall to become the nominee.

A senior political reporter for the *New York Times* observed that McCall fared no better in handling the issue. Michael Slackman (2004) described how McCall responded to Pataki campaign ads that emphasized the governor's role in 9/11: "Mr. McCall had wanted to attack Mr. Pataki, to accuse him of politicizing Sept. 11, of using Sept. 11 to avoid discussing real issues of state, but whenever he tried to, no matter how gently, it backfired. It either managed to highlight Mr. Pataki's role during the crisis—which helped boost the governor's standing—or it aroused the anger of sympathetic groups who then hailed Mr. Pataki's role during the crisis."

While the governor ran a savvy campaign in a number of other respects as well—notably forging a deal with Hospital Workers 1199 head Dennis Rivera on the eve of the election to provide funding for increased wages for Rivera's members in return for deploying the tremendous political clout of that union on the governor's behalf—his prominence in the rebuilding effort allowed voters to see him as a strong, effective leader. In November 2002, Governor Pataki scored a solid victory over McCall, even gaining 39 percent of the vote in New York City, setting a recent high-water mark for the share received by any Republican candidate.

THE IMPACT ON THE 2004 PRESIDENTIAL ELECTION

Although many reasons have been advanced to explain why the hotly contested race between President George Bush and Massachusetts senator John Kerry culminated in Bush's narrow but clear victory in November 2004, one principal cause was the president's effective projection of his image as a national "first responder" to the terrorist attacks. The national exit poll showed, for example, that of the one-fifth of the electorate who ranked the war on terrorism as the most important issue for their vote (closely following similar shares who cited "moral values" and "the economy and jobs"), seven out of eight voted for Bush (CNN 2004).[3] In such a close race, this was clearly a determining factor, just as it had been in the mayoral and gubernatorial elections in New York City.

The electorate's mixed feelings concerning the president's prosecution of the war in Iraq and overall management of the economy did not prevent a majority of voters from seeing him as tracking down the perpetrators of the September 11 attacks. President Bush worked hard to assert this symbolic position by choosing to hold the 2004 Republican National Convention in New York City, close to the third anniversary of the attack, and giving a prominent role at the convention to former Mayor Rudolph Giuliani and supporting roles for his police commissioner at the time of the attack, Bernard Kerik, and Governor George Pataki, all of whom campaigned vigorously for the president. (Bush later nominated Kerik to be the secretary of the Department of Homeland Security, a move that proved to be a debacle when many shortcomings in Kerik's record came to light.)

Because both campaigns considered New York a "safe state" for Kerry, neither nominee spent much time campaigning in the city or state, visiting mostly to raise money. As predicted, New York City voted overwhelmingly for Kerry, and the state was also in his column. It is worth noting, however, that President Bush improved his share of the city's vote by one-third, from 18 to 24 percent, from his performance in 2000. While lagging far behind the 39 percent that Governor Pataki won in the city in 2002 and Mayor Bloomberg's 50 percent in 2001, it is instructive to examine exactly where the Bush share of the vote increased between 2000 and 2004. The geography of this improvement followed the long-term fault lines within New York City's electorate. As might be expected, the president ran best in the white Catholic outer borough neighborhoods of Staten Island and Brooklyn and worst in African American neighborhoods like Bedford Stuyvesant. When the Bush vote is compared to the underlying distribution of party registration, it clearly shows that the president, like fellow Republicans Governor Pataki and Mayor Bloomberg, attracted Democratic defectors in Italian American, Hasidic Jewish, and Chinese neighborhoods, while Kerry attracted considerably more votes than there were Democratic registrants in areas characterized by many white, middle-class, professional independents. (This latter group had given Mayor Bloomberg a considerable share of its votes in 2001.) Moreover, the president drew more votes than might have been expected from the underlying party registration in Hispanic neighborhoods, as had Pataki and Bloomberg before him.[4]

These national and local patterns illustrate the power of patriotism and attachment to members of the uniformed forces that the September 11 attacks and their immediate aftermath highlighted so distinctively. The attacks elicited a national wave of sympathy for New York City, and citizens all across the country donated funds to help the families of those who had lost their lives, especially from the fire and police departments. The event accelerated a change in the national image of New York City—already under way as a result of the Giuliani administration's policies—from "welfare sinkhole" to "line of heroes." President Bush appeared at Ground Zero only days after the attack and several times thereafter. His support of the federal aid package for the city embodied his identification with its response to terrorism. (He made sure, of course, that this aid would be administered by close political allies, who in turn distributed it to a number of firms that had historically made significant political contributions to these allies.) The same trends in public opinion continued during the 2004 presidential election in New York City—attracting some constituencies, particularly white Catholics and orthodox Jews, while repelling others, mainly the swing group of white professionals concerned that the war in Iraq was harming, not improving, U.S. national security.

THE "THREE NEW YORKS" AND THE 2005 MAYORAL ELECTION

In retrospect, the impact of the attacks highlighted the importance of political constituencies that had not received much attention from those who have reported on New York City politics in recent years. One can distinguish three overlapping but conceptually distinct "New Yorks." All those living within the city's political boundary make up the first New York. This is the New York

City depicted in census statistics and the discussion of how immigration has transformed the city's resident population. In this New York, 47 percent of the residents live in a household headed by an immigrant, while a mere one-quarter of the total live in households headed by a native-born, non-Hispanic white person. The ethnic groups that once dominated the political landscape of this city, such as Italian Americans and East European Jews, have diminished to the point of being relatively small minorities. (The native-born African American and Puerto Rican populations have also been declining.) Meanwhile, immigrant minority ethnic groups, ranging from Dominicans to Chinese to West Indians to, more recently, the Muslim South Asians described by Lorraine Minnite (this volume), have been growing. Clearly, these groups will predominate in the city's future populations.

The second New York City is made up of those who are eligible to vote in New York City elections. The older groups that are waning in the population as a whole are much more prevalent in this second New York, although native-born non-Hispanic whites are a plurality, not an absolute majority. Over the last three decades, New York City politics has been strongly shaped by the evolution of whites from a large majority of the first two New Yorks into a small minority of the first and a large plurality of the second. This trajectory has modified the political competition between Jews and white Catholics, which marked the previous period, into a tendency of whites from all backgrounds to vote for candidates they see as responsive to their backgrounds over candidates they see as representing rising minority groups (Mollenkopf 1993, 2003). The discrepancies between the first two New Yorks are explained by the higher levels of adulthood, citizenship, education, and socioeconomic status among native-born whites compared to other parts of the city's population, together with the great diversity of these other groups. As a result, whites hold a substantially disproportionate share of elected offices compared to their presence in the resident population as a whole (Logan and Mollenkopf 2003).

In a manner loosely reminiscent of the shift of white southerners from the Democratic Party to the Republican Party, white voters have tended to respond to the risk of losing political power to minority groups by favoring a succession of relatively conservative and even Republican candidates since 1977. (The term "relative" is used because most of these candidates are far more liberal than the national Republican Party on issues such as abortion or immigrant rights.) Meanwhile, the great diversity of the potential members of a multiracial liberal coalition has made it difficult for all of them to coalesce behind one candidate, as the electoral difficulties of David Dinkins, Ruth Messinger, Mark Green, Fernando Ferrer, and Carl McCall demonstrate.

Although racial polarization has helped relatively conservative white candidates win office, they know that demographic trends are gradually reshaping the electorate in an adverse direction for them, and many have sought to increase their support among rising groups, most notably among culturally more conservative Hispanic voters. In this respect, the 2004 election in New York City, like its predecessors in 2002 and 2001, showed that Republican candidates can have at least modest success in attracting Hispanic voters on a platform of patriotism and opposition to abortion or gay marriage.

September 11, however, revealed a third New York City: those who are of the city, who are deeply connected to it, but who do not live in it. The most obvious connection is that of employment: firms based in Manhattan in general, and in the World Trade Center complex and its adjoining area in particular, employed a great many people who resided outside the political boundaries of the city. Of the 3.7 million people who worked in New York City according to the 2000 census, about 782,000, or one out of five, lived outside the city. (Some 528,000 of these worked in Manhattan.) Almost half lived in New Jersey and one-quarter in the Long Island suburbs. This group is predominantly non-Hispanic white (70 percent), with a good deal of education (62 percent with college degrees) and living in upper-income households (with a median of about $100,000 in 1999). Two quite distinct parts of this group were highlighted by the September 11 attacks: those working in the twin towers who lost their lives or were traumatized by evacuating the buildings and losing coworkers, and members of the uniformed services (fire, police, and emergency medical services) who lost their lives or who survived but were also traumatized by the experience of responding to the attacks.

In the months after the attack the *New York Times* led the media in doing an excellent job of identifying and profiling as many of those who lost their lives as possible, published as "Portraits of Grief" (*New York Times* 2002). While this coverage revealed the broad social cross-section who toiled in the twin towers, the number of professional workers from white ethnic immigrant backgrounds, especially Jewish, Italian, and Irish Americans, was striking. Maps published in the *Times* and other papers showed the direct personal and economic linkage between lower Manhattan and suburban clusters near to and far from the city. The profile of the stricken amply illustrated how lower Manhattan both served as a place of employment for new immigrants, who mostly lived in the city, and continued to provide upward mobility for the children, grandchildren, and great-grandchildren of the last great wave of migration, many of whom had by now moved to sometimes far distant suburbs.

For months after the attacks, funerals were also held for the 343 firefighters (the largest loss of life ever sustained by an emergency response agency in American history), the 37 members of the Port Authority Police Department (the largest loss ever suffered by a police force), and the 23 members of the New York City Police Department (the second-largest loss ever suffered). These were solemn and dignified affairs, drawing fellow uniformed officers from across the region and country. Mayors Giuliani and Bloomberg and Governor

Pataki attended many of these events, which constantly reminded those who witnessed them or reported them of the heroism, patriotism, and devotion of those who gave their lives and the bonds between the communities from which they came, the elected officials who represented them, and the symbols, especially the American flag, that represented their values.

Notwithstanding the great public doubt about the course of the war in Iraq, there can be no doubt that the public has a similar bond with the American troops stationed there, some of whom come from the New York region. Recently, one more funeral in this long procession took place. Chris Engeldrum, a New York City fireman who had responded on 9/11 to the World Trade Center and also served in the New York National Guard, shipped out to Baghdad on November 2, 2004, and was killed by a roadside bomb on November 29, becoming the first New York City employee to lose his life in this conflict. As at so many funerals before, thousands of fellow firefighters, this time joined by guardsmen, lined the blocks of Otis Avenue leading to St. Benedict's Church in the Throgs Neck neighborhood of the Bronx. The *Times* coverage provided the following description:

> Sergeant Engeldrum's funeral was a snapshot of New York, an old New York, which the pundits and the pollsters never seem to talk about. The American Legion was handing out American flags. Old men from the neighborhood lined up to take them. The fire hydrants were painted red, white and blue. . . . There was talk of patriotism, heroism and duty to one's country. "It's how you're raised," said Lt. Col. Neil Skow, a guardsman and a firefighter, who came to mourn Sergeant Engeldrum. "We live in the greatest country in the world and we owe it something. The Police Department, the Fire Department, the Army—they're all honorable professions." (Feuer 2004)

The surrounding neighborhood of Throgs Neck is a representative part of the older, gradually diminishing part of New York inhabited by white Catholic families; it has voted solidly for Mayors Giuliani and Bloomberg, Governor Pataki, and President Bush, although it also elects Democrats to represent it in the City Council and State Legislature.

It is too soon to say how this amalgam of issues, values, and symbols will play out in the November 2005 mayoral election scheduled to take place shortly after the fourth anniversary of the attacks, but it is sure to have an impact. As Sagalyn and Moss (this volume) have indicated, Mayor Bloomberg has played a somewhat ambivalent role with respect to 9/11 and its broader symbolic politics. On the one hand, he has attended the funerals, spoken quietly but eloquently at the anniversaries, praised the efforts of the governor and the president to help the city rebuild, and been supportive of the various planning efforts necessary for the rebuilding to succeed. The core of his electoral support in November 2005 will certainly come from areas of the city that have most heavily favored the governor and the president and from the constituencies that most strongly identify with firefighter Engeldrum and his brethren. To win reelection, Mayor Bloomberg must elicit an enthusiastic response from these quarters.

On the other hand, the mayor proposed, and the City Council adopted, a substantial property tax increase (18 percent) to cope with the budgetary gap that opened up in the wake of September 11; that increase was heavily felt by homeowners in neighborhoods like Throgs Neck. The mayor also enacted the most thoroughgoing ban on smoking inside structures frequented by the public of any city in the United States, including the many bars and saloons that are fixtures in these neighborhoods. When combined with his tough stance on negotiating contracts with city employees, including the uniformed services and teachers, these measures produced a sharp decrease in the mayor's approval rating in these areas in 2003. Moreover, their residents may suspect that he, as a wealthy resident of the Upper East Side who has contributed to many liberal causes in the past, may not fully share their enthusiasm for the Bush administration's foreign policy. Mayor Bloomberg worked hard in 2004 and 2005 to improve his standing in these areas, with some real success. Whether he feels completely comfortable with it or not, it is probably imperative that he wrap himself in the flag being waved by President Bush and the Republican Party and be seen as a strong supporter of the rebuilding.

At the same time, support from these quarters alone will not be sufficient to provide an electoral majority for the mayor. He also needs strong support from constituencies and areas that are less positive about President Bush or Governor Pataki, less identified with the uniformed services, and more doubtful about the war in Iraq. These constituencies are concentrated in areas that voted in greater numbers for John Kerry than the underlying party registration would have suggested, such as the Upper East Side and Brooklyn Heights. Moreover, as Moss (this volume) has pointed out, the mayor clearly thinks that the West Side, not Ground Zero, is the main place where new office space should be constructed, and therefore the crucial fulcrum for Manhattan's future economic development. His vision for lower Manhattan stresses residential construction and the creation of new amenities that would diversify the functions of that area. His plans include a controversial new stadium that would serve not only as a place for the New York Jets football team to play but as a key venue for the proposed 2012 Olympics and an expansion space for the Jacob K. Javits Convention Center. Some $600 million in public funds would be expended to build a platform over the Long Island Railroad storage yard that currently occupies the site. These plans not only have drawn opposition from stadium opponents but lay the mayor open to charges that he is not sufficiently committed to the vision articulated by Governor Pataki, the Port Authority, and the LMDC for Ground Zero. As Governor Pataki's plans for rebuilding Ground Zero encountered new difficulties in May 2005, Mayor Bloomberg was once again criticized for not paying enough attention to the rebuilding process.

On the Democratic side of the aisle, the potential candidates have yet to develop coherent positions that respond well to the symbolic and practical politics of September 11, fighting terrorism, and rebuilding the WTC site. Given the underlying political terrain, Democrats' challenge will be to find ways to support the troops (and by extension the uniformed services) while opposing President Bush's foreign policy and to oppose subsidies for corporate office buildings, market-rate residential housing, and a new stadium for the Jets and the 2012 Olympics in favor of outer-borough neighborhoods and jobs for New York City residents while still being seen as respectful of the terrible damage done on September 11, the need to rebuild the site, and the imperative of promoting the city's core economic functions. This challenge is much easier to state than it will be for them to master.

NOTES

1. Analysis by the author of election district results from the New York City Board of Elections.
2. The following paragraphs draws on Mollenkopf (2002).
3. Four out of five of those ranking "moral values" as the top issue also voted for Bush (CNN 2004).
4. Analysis by the author of election district results from the New York City Board of Elections.

REFERENCES

CNN 2004. National exit poll for president. Available at: www.cnn.com/ELECTION/2004/pages/results/states/US/P/00/epolls.0.html.

Cooper, Michael, and Randal C. Archibold. 2001. "Runoff Campaign Turns Confrontational as Candidates Trade Charges." New York Times, October 10.

Cooper, Michael, and Adam Nagourney. 2001. "Green Says He'd Top Giuliani in a Crisis." New York Times, October 2.

Feuer, Alan. 2004. "Two Proud Traditions Honor a Firefighter Killed in Iraq." New York Times, December 10.

Hernandez, Raymond. 2002. "Bush Offers Details of Aid to New York Topping $20 Billion." New York Times, March 8.

Logan, John, and John Mollenkopf. 2003. People and Politics in America's Big Cities: A Critical Conversation about the Implications of the Profound Demographic Transformation Now Under Way in Our City. New York: Drum Major Institute (May 15).

Mollenkopf, John. 1993. *A Phoenix in the Ashes: The Rise and Decline of the Koch Coalition in New York City Politics.* Princeton, N.J.: Princeton University Press.

———. "Who Decides and How? Government Decisionmaking After 9/11." *Properties* (9/11 issue) (April): 392–409.

———. 2003. "New York: Still the Great Anomaly." In *Racial Politics in American Cities,* edited by Rufus Browning, Dale Marshall, and David Tabb, 3rd ed. New York: Longman.

Nagourney, Adam. 2002. "Tenuous Grip on Rebuilding Could Hurt Bloomberg's Term." *New York Times,* January 30.

Nagourney, Adam, and Marjorie Connelly. 2001. "Poll in New York Finds Rosier Views on City's Future." *New York Times,* August 15.

New York Times. 2002. *Portraits 9/11/01,* foreword by Howell Raines, introduction by Janny Scott. New York: Times Books.

Slackman, Michael. 2004. "New York Offers a Lesson on Using 9/11: Tread Lightly." *New York Times,* March 15.

INDEX

Boldface numbers refer to figures and tables.